THE SIGN LANGUAGE OF THE MYSTERIES

The Sign Language of the Mysteries

By
J. S. M. Ward, M.A.
Late Scholar and Prizeman of Trinity Hall,
Cambridge.
P.M., P.Z., P.M.W.S.

New York
Land's End Press
1969

PREFACE

AMONG the various readers into whose hands this book will ultimately pass, the subject with which it deals will doubtless be of interest for various reasons. To my brother Freemasons I need say little. Previous works of mine have set forth my views as to the history and ancestry of what is now known as Freemasonry, and I believe that a full and complete vindication of my theories will be established to the satisfaction of every fair-minded student after he has completed a perusal of this book. For reasons which will be obvious to all the fraternity, it has been impossible to dot the I.s and cross the T.s without disclosing things which are the private affairs of our great Order, which explains why I have carefully avoided any definite reference to modern Freemasonry, knowing full well that all who have passed through the same ceremonies as I have will realise that the ancient Sign Language here set out is of more than passing interest to them. Moreover, Freemasonry is avowedly a peculiar system of morality, veiled in allegory and illustrated by symbols, and though no doubt the rituals have been heavily revised in the 18th and early 19th centuries, yet it must be obvious that just as the Church has her traditions, so has our Order, and a right interpretation of them is the first essential for any who would endeavour to make a daily advancement in Masonic knowledge. Thus rightly understood this book should serve two purposes. Firstly, to indicate the truth of the saying "Ancient no doubt it is, having existed from time immemorial," and how and why that is true, and secondly, to reveal to the serious student that everything that takes place in the Masonic ceremonies has a definite inner meaning and is not arbitrary or accidental. Which and what signs are of interest to Masons concerns them alone, and the higher a brother has gone in Masonry the more he will doubtless see in this book, but there are of course included in it signs which are in no way connected with the Western descendants of the Mysteries, and this has been done of set purpose. Partly, so as to render it the more difficult for an outsider to discover matters concerning Freemasonry which really do not concern him, and equally because

PREFACE.

these signs are part of the ancient Mystery Language and there are other descendants of the Mysteries besides Freemasonry to whose members they may possibly be of considerable importance.

To those interested in Ecclesiastical matters and Mediaeval Art, the evidence herein set out of the existence of an ancient Sign Language with a definite symbolical meaning will, I hope, prove of real value by enabling them to interpret more accurately the symbolical significance of many of the pictorial relics of the Middle Ages which have fortunately survived down to the present day.

Mediaeval art was avowedly symbolical and therein lies one of its chief fascinations. It was almost exclusively the product of the labours of the Clergy, assisted in no small measure by the Operative Masons, who were organised into elaborate Guilds and no doubt did the bulk of the actual sculpture work in the Churches, Abbeys and Cathedrals. How far the clergy were actually responsible for the general design and the choice of the subjects illustrated, it is difficult to say, but doubtless if they did not dictate the actual scenes they were continually consulted by the expert craftsmen. A considerable amount of this book, however, is illustrated by work of a definite ecclesiastical origin, and in the term, ecclesiastical, we of course include members of the Monastic Orders, who were responsible for most of the illuminated manuscripts, the embroidered vestments and the like.

Until nearly a hundred years ago, it was generally assumed in England that anything which appertained to the old Mediaeval Church was anathema and the mere fact that certain things were done before the Reformation was considered to be a sufficient reason for regarding them as most undesirable. But during the last Century a profound change has come about and, without allowing oneself to be dragged into matters of religious controversy, it is permissible to say that a far more broad-minded and tolerant attitude has developed, with the natural result that the services of the Church have tended to become more ornate and beautiful, and the buildings themselves to be decorated with an avowed revival of much which formerly made the Mediæval Churches galleries of art. To-day we get beautiful stained glass windows, frescoes and sculptures, embroidered vestments, and many other of the appurtenances of the Mediæval Church. Yet it seems to me as if these modern revivals fail to a large extent because they lack that essentially didactic note which is characteristic of the ecclesiastical art of the Middle Ages, and I would humbly suggest

PREFACE.

that when being consulted about the insertion of a new stained glass window or other adornment our clergy should use their influence with donor and artist alike to incorporate into the design the correct symbolic gestures, so that the picture may truly express certain definite sentiments and leave, as it were, a story in stone, glass or painting. Although to the adult didactic pictures may not be necessary, every teacher knows how valuable they are when instructing the young, and the knowledge contained in this book will not only enable those clergy who are in charge of churches which have relics of the past to interpret them correctly to the visitor, but if the same traditions are adopted in modern decorative art, they would often be of direct assistance to the clergy in their work.

To the still wider public who are interested in Mediæval Art for its own sake, this book will also prove of value. Many may prefer the more naturalistic art which came into vogue at the time of the Renaissance, but it must be remembered that previous to that date most ecclesiastical art was didactic and intended to teach an illiterate world much of the instruction which would now be given through printed books.

The Renaissance and the Reformation to a large extent shattered the old symbolic system, so that it is not surprising that to-day a very definite and important fragment of it such as this has become almost entirely lost. Nevertheless, with the coming of photography, which from the naturalistic point of view can probably more accurately hold up the mirror to nature than can the painter, modern art students may well wonder whether it would not be better to depart somewhat from the old naturalistic school of work and revert to the symbolical. It is, indeed, evident that if art is to survive some such change is becoming necessary, a fact recognised by many of the younger artists and typified by the cubist and similar schools which have come into existence during the last few years. I suggest, however, that by reviving the Mediæval system of symbolism, wherein the ancient Sign Language was an integral part, a most fruitful source of inspiration may be found.

In conclusion I must return thanks to the various individuals and institutions who have kindly given me permission to reproduce various illustrations in this book. By gracious permission of His Majesty the King, I am able to include reproductions of the three works of art which appear opposite pages 34, 116 and 202. I must likewise express my thanks to Sir A. Evans for permission to reproduce from

PREFACE.

his famous work "The Palace of Minos at Knossos," the figures on pages 98 and 99 and the plate opposite page 16, and likewise to Sir Wallis Budge for those on pages 6 and 114. To the Royal Anthropological Society I am indebted for the pictures shown opposite pages 82, 84, 232 and for the rock painting from Papua, while the picture opposite page 92 appears through the courtesy of the Bodleian Library. My thanks are also due to the National Gallery for permission to reproduce the picture opposite page 108, to "Country Life" for that which appears opposite page 150, and to the Supreme Royal Arch Chapter of Scotland for the painting shown opposite page 194.

In the case of the Capital B which comes from the Winchester Bible and is shown opposite page 76, I have to thank the Dean of Winchester for his kind permission to reproduce it, and also the authorities of the Victoria and Albert Museum for the actual photograph. It is indeed most pleasing to find that Winchester Cathedral still keeps this ancient treasure which has passed down unscathed through so many generations. Long may it continue to rest within the walls of the sacred edifice for which it was originally written nearly 750 years ago. On the other hand the fact that excellent photographs of it can be studied in the Victoria and Albert Museum is a great advantage to all students. To the Director of this Museum I must tender thanks for permission to reproduce quite a long list of illustrations, viz., those shown opposite pages 4, 12, 20, 22, 36, 40, 46, 50, 72, 76, 100, 112, 124, 128, 132, 172, 188, 198, and without the assistance of this museum and of the British Museum it would have been exceedingly difficult to obtain the necessary illustrations for this book. To the latter body I am indebted for the pictures shown opposite the following pages : 6, 8, 28, 48, 52, 68, 70, 92 (Dante), 114, 130, 142, 156, 168, 178, 208, 222, 234, likewise for the frontispieces of the two volumes and for the line blocks on pages 12, 27, 171,

There is still, however, one body to whom I owe a debt of gratitude, namely, The Smithsonian Institute of the U.S.A., for all the illustrations dealing with Ancient Mexico and the two stone carvings from Jamaica are shown through their kind permission.

In conclusion I have in the text given many references and quoted many authors to all of whom I must express my indebtedness, for without their help I could never have completed this work.

J. S. M. WARD.

July 21st, 1928.

CONTENTS.

ILLUSTRATIONS.

ILLUSTRATIONS.

ILLUSTRATIONS.

ILLLUSTRATIONS.

ILLUSTRATIONS

ILLUSTRATIONS.

ILLUSTRATIONS.

CHAPTER I. *Being Introductory to a Study of the Ancient Sign Language.*

OME TWENTY YEARS ago I came to the conclusion that there still existed remnants of an ancient Sign Language, probably dating back to a period in the evolution of man when he was hardly able to put any abstract ideas into words and depended largely on gestures and signs to communicate his feelings and passions. Just as the gorilla expresses anger not merely by roaring but by beating his breast at the same time, so, it seemed to me, primitive man was compelled to eke out his scanty vocabulary by signs and graphic gestures.

I therefore set out to collect, co-ordinate and study certain signs, and found that not only were such signs in use to-day among primitive races, but that they were well known and regularly employed among specific groups of people even in civilised Europe. I further discovered that many of them could be traced back through the ages to a date long preceding the Christian era, and that the same gestures always had the same basic ideas underlying their use.

It is possible to trace the historic descent of such signs because of their repeated use in sculpture, painting and the arts generally, and they are always found to be most easily traceable in art which is based on symbolism rather than on an attempt to reproduce nature.   Thus ancient Egyptian and Mediæval art have proved a more prolific source of information on the subject than has the art of Classical Greece or of the later Renaissance period.

For all that, symbolism is never entirely absent in any art, particularly when it is connected with religion, and thus it comes about that even in the periods mentioned we find a number of examples of these signs, showing that the ancient traditional knowledge did not die out.   To-day where tradition is strong, as in the Roman Catholic

*Quetzalcoatl, with corn in his hair, is
wounded in the foot.*
T.5.

Church, we still find these signs cropping up, often in the most unexpected places.   In like manner they exist among savage races, generally associated with certain incidents in the Initiation Rites of a boy into manhood, while races which have passed far beyond the condition of savages have preserved them, and depict their gods in characteristic, symbolic attitudes wherein these same signs play an important part. Thus we find similar gestures used by the Gods in Egypt, India and ancient Mexico, all of which are clearly the same as those depicted in

THE MARRIAGE FEAST AT CANA.

QUEEN MARY'S PSALTER.

14TH CENT. MS.

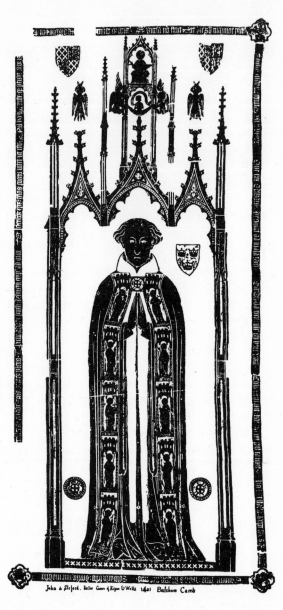

THE MONUMENTAL BRASS OF JOHN SLEFORD, BALSHAM, CAMBS.

L.84.

Mediæval Christian art and have the same fundamental significance, a good example being that shown opposite page 10, which should be carefully compared with the Egyptian picture on page 12 and with that of Hanuman, opposite page 220.

When, moreover, we compare the Rites of Initiation which are common among Savages with those worked by certain secret societies, such as the Hung Society of China, and even with certain quasi-secret societies found far nearer home, we discover that not only is the basic matter of these Rites similar, but that identical signs are used during the ceremonies.   These facts all go to support the theory I now venture to propound, namely, that far back in the dawn of time there was a basic Sign Language, common to all, or nearly all, the members of the human race, and that this has survived to a far greater extent than has been suspected by most students.

It has already been pointed out that one of the chief vehicles which has contributed to the survival of this traditional Sign Language is Religion, but this is not the only line of descent, for in addition to Secret Societies of Initiation, Mystery Cults and the like, which are partly religious, quite a number of signs have survived among the humblest strata of civilised men as magical signs, forms of vulgar abuse, and even as secret hints among members of the submerged tenth.   School children have their traditional signs, and the vulgar little boy who puts his fingers to his nose is only carrying on a very ancient tradition, just as the children who cross their fingers, and claim thereby that they are immune from the chastisement which some insult or piece of "cheek" justifies, have probably borrowed the sign from their elders in days when the making of the Sign of the Cross was the equivalent of a mantric prayer.   It may seem a long journey from the stately Church gesture of an ecclesiastic as he makes the Sign of the Cross at some important point in the service of the Mass, to the mere crossing of a couple of fingers by two children in the midst of their play, but there seems little doubt that this is the true origin of the childish symbol.

In like manner the sign of the horns, which is still used by superstitious people, particularly in Italy, to avert the evil eye, seems undoubtedly to be descended from Classical times and refers to the crescent moon of Diana.   Its use, however, is not restricted to countries whose history has been moulded by Classical Rome, for it is a very important sign in the Hung Society of China and even to-day is constantly used to indicate membership of that dreaded secret brotherhood. Although we have thus seen that this sign is used in Europe by superstitious people to avert evil and in China by a secret society to indicate membership, yet it also has a religious significance, as is proved by the fact that figures of Kwan Yin, the co-called Chinese Goddess of Mercy, are often depicted making it.[1] That even in Europe it was not always restricted to the ignorant peasantry is shown by the design on the back of the Martelli Mirror, which is Italian work, dating from between 1386 and 1466, and is reproduced on the opposite page. An elaborate and beautiful piece of work such as this could only have been made for someone of wealth and culture, and yet we see one of the figures clearly and emphatically making the "Horns."

Another sign with which we shall deal at considerable length also has its vulgar, modern equivalent. When a coster boy wishes to impress a person with the fact that he is speaking the truth, he first wets his index finger, then draws his right hand across his throat, saying at the same time, "See that wet, see it dry; God cut my throat if I tell a lie!" The full significance of this will be discussed later, for it undoubtedly has a great and sublime meaning, stretching back into a very early period of history, and is closely connected with religious beliefs and observances, yet in its present survival among the humbler sections of the community we have another typical example of the way in which the ancient Sign Language lingers on all around us.

Another kind of secret code is that used by the Hatton Garden Diamond merchants, who are able to carry on a long discussion, or a fierce argument over prices, by means of hand signs, known only to themselves, which may be regarded as a secret trade language restricted to members of the profession. Thieves, tramps and prostitutes likewise have their secret sign languages, of which very little is known, and finally, in the modern deaf and dumb alphabet we have a practical application under modern conditions of a system still

---

[1] See illustration opposite page 164.

THE MARTELLI MIRROR.

L.38.

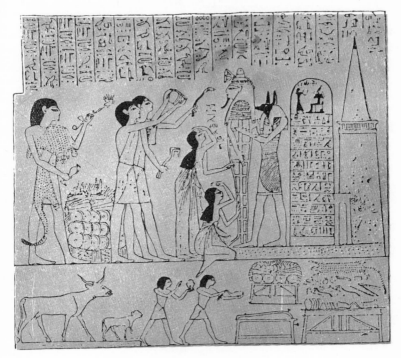

FUNERAL CEREMONIES AT THE TOMB.
From the Papyrus of Ani.

A22.

found among the Australian Bushmen, while a very similar system is part of the secret code conveyed to an initiate in the Hung Society of China.

Nor does this by any means limit the number of such secret languages, although as yet but little has been done to place them on permanent record.   Probably the most elaborate and complex of all is that which still survives among the Red Indians of North America. Most of these tribes speak dialects which are so distinct and different from each other that a man from one tribe cannot understand a member of another except through the medium of an interpreter, but they all have, or had, for it is beginning to die out, a common sign language, whereby two men who could not understand a word of each other's vocabulary could carry on a lengthy conversation purely by means of manual signs.   In this connection it is interesting to note that a very usual method of salutation of one Indian by another is to stretch out his hand and then draw it sharply across his throat. I have myself seen this done.

Before concluding this introductory chapter, it seems desirable to point out two well known ecclesiastical signs which are always taken for granted by everyone, because I maintain that these are only two out of numerous signs formerly used by the clergy, and indeed to some extent still used by them to-day, although it is probable that the majority of Englishmen may not have noticed the fact. Of all ecclesiastical signs the best known is the Sign of Prayer, which consists of placing the palms of the hands together, with the tips of the fingers upwards, as is shown in the monumental brass illustrated opposite page 2.   An alternative method is to fold the hands together, interlocking the fingers.   No one seeing this sign in a picture would have much doubt as to its symbolic meaning, namely, that the person was praying.   The other sign is the Sign of Blessing, made by a Priest or Saint.   When the Priest blesses the people ancient tradition prescribes that he should fold the third and fourth fingers on to the palm of the hand, hold upright the index and second finger, and either fold the thumb on the third finger or else hold it erect. There are a few minor variations of this sign, but these two are the most common forms.   There seems little doubt that in Mediæval Christian Art when it is made with thumb and two fingers erect, the significance conveyed is that the blessing is in the name of the Holy Trinity (See illustration L.6 opposite page 28).

The meaning of these two signs will be admitted by all readers, and the purpose of this work is to show that other signs also appear in connection with religious beliefs and stories, that they each have as definite a meaning as the Sign of Blessing, and further, that the tradition concerning them stretches far back into the dawn of time and has been preserved to us by the natural conservatism of Religious Teachers, of Trade Guilds, and sometimes of Secret Societies.

CHAPTER II. *Relating how Certain Sign Languages Survive even to-day.*

 T HAS ALREADY been pointed out that the modern deaf and dumb alphabet has its counterpart in other parts of the world, particularly among certain primitive races. Of these the best known are the Red Indians and the Australian Blacks, and how dependent some of the former were on this language is shown by the fact that there are certain tribes of Digger Indians who, when first discovered by white men, were unable to talk properly with each other in the dark, as their spoken language was so meagre in words that without the use of signs to help them out they could not understand each other properly.

Moreover, it is doubtful whether two Italians could satisfactorily talk together if they were prevented from making the numerous gestures and signs with which they punctuate their spoken language, and the Neopolitans actually have an elaborate sign language of their own, in which they can carry on a lengthy conversation, as is shown in the *First Annual Report of the Bureau of Ethnology*, published in Washington in 1881.

Let us therefore now turn to consider the sign language used by the Arunndta tribe of Australian Bushmen, of which a very full account is given by H. Basedow, to whom I am indebted for much of what follows. To a very large extent this language is intertribal, is very elaborate, and is one in which it is possible to carry on a long conversation even at a great distance, without the use of any words. If he wants to summon anyone to him, the Bushman stands erect, throws both his hands upwards to above the shoulder on one side, then swings them down in front of his body, and right round behind on the opposite side, at the same time bending his body forward from the hips. The man summoned answers by placing his hands on his chest and then throwing them outward towards the stranger. When the two are sufficiently near to enable each to see the fingers of the other's hands, a lively conversation becomes possible. If one man wishes to say, "Which way?" he holds up his index finger, closes the other three fingers and the thumb on to the palm of the hand, and moves the index finger several times in front of his face with a downward motion. If he wishes to inform his questioner that something is on the top of a hill, he extends his whole hand, fingers slightly apart, and then with it taps the top of his head. If he desires to indicate that someone is his son, he taps his chin with his index finger.

In short, by altering the position of the fingers, closing one or two and extending others, it is possible for these people to give all kinds of information and with great precision. Thus they can indicate the presence near by of particular animals, such as a carpet snake or a tiger snake, or of an evil spirit, for the latter the sign being as follows: point the hand downwards and make the sign of the horns, i.e., index and small finger extended, but with the thumb also extended.

In this last example we have a variant of the form of the "Sign of the Horns" which is found both in China and Europe. It will be remembered that in Europe the sign is intended to ward off the evil eye, and here we find the same basic principle underlying its use. In the Hung Society, however, it is said to mean "Man," who is half way between Heaven and earth. On closer investigation this apparent contradiction disappears. Man is a spirit and among most primitive races the spirits who are most feared are usually those of departed men, and it may be added that even in China the same fear actuates a large section of the community.

Now let us turn to consider the similar hand sign language of

THE SLAUGHTER OF THE INNOCENTS AND THE MARRIAGE FEAST AT CANA.

From The Arundel Manuscript.

K.2.

CHRIST DISPUTING WITH THE DOCTORS.
By Borgognone.

A Fresco in St. Ambrose Church, Milan.

L.7.

the Hung Society.   This, like the Australian language, appears to some extent to be arbitrary, as is our own deaf and dumb alphabet, but it undoubtedly incorporates some of the far more important mantric signs, which are the main theme of this book.   Two characteristic examples are reproduced in the diagram opposite page 228. The top one reads as follows :—

"(a)—Heaven ; (b)—Earth ; (c)—Man."

This means, first of all "descended from Heavenly ancestors," and hence, secondly, the Triad Society.   Its inner significance is that man is the offspring of Heaven and earth.   It will be noted that the sign for man is not in this case the sign of the horns, while the Chinese characters underneath the three hands show that the fingers are meant to simulate certain written characters.   The lower sentence reads :—

"(1)—The Country (is) (2) Prosperous ; (3) The people are satisfied or peaceful."

This is a typical Triad motto and once more if we compare the position of the fingers with the Chinese characters they represent, we shall perceive that to a considerable extent the hand sign language appears to be based on the written language.

At first sight it might seem as if this definitely established the fact that the Hung Hand Sign Language cannot be really old but must rather have been based on the written language, but it would be dangerous to dogmatise, for although this is a possible explanation we cannot ignore another alternative.   It is usually assumed that the Chinese characters have been evolved from hieroglyphics, which themselves evolved out of simple line drawings of certain objects, as was the case in ancient Egypt.   If this were absolutely established, then the Hung Sign Language must be later than the present script, but it is possible that in part at least the Chinese language is not evolved from hieroglyphics, but from an attempt to represent the hand sign language on paper in as simple a way as possible.

The hand sign language in fact may be earlier and may itself be a method of representing various objects about which men wished to talk to neighbours whose tongue was unfamiliar.   Even to this day, although Classical Chinese can be read by an educated man from any part of China, the man from the North usually cannot understand the spoken language of a man from the South.   Now, it is important to note that in a large number of cases the Australian Sign Language is clearly a crude attempt to depict an object by means of representing it by the fingers.   Thus, if the Australian Bushman wants to say "See the ears of a kangaroo", he closes the third and fourth fingers, holds upright the index and little fingers at an angle which makes a "V", and then waggles them, as the animal waggles his ears.

In view of facts like these we cannot hastily come to the conclusion that the Hung Sign Language was copied from the written one, and if the reverse is the case the subject is obviously of considerable importance to students of early alphabets.   It should be noted that such a sign language would doubtless need the addition of numerous characters which have never been formed by the hand, because the object was unimportant to savages but had become important by the time the Chinese had evolved sufficiently to require a written language. These additions might well be based on hieroglyphs or simple drawings of the objects themselves.

The two hand sign languages just described incorporate a few of the great mantric signs, of which the "sign of the horns" is one and the "sign of touching the crown of the head" is another, but our main interest is in what I will call the *Mantric Signs*, rather than in those which may be grouped as belonging to the same type as the modern deaf and dumb alphabet.   It has nevertheless been necessary to deal with this alphabetical sign language in order that we may distinguish it from the more important signs, and also because such sign languages are valuable as indicating the practicality of such methods of communication, thereby strengthening the case in favour of my theory that what I call the *Mantric Signs* are merely survivors of a vast group which constituted a sign language in the past, and which may have been used as the secret religious language long after fairly complex vocabularies had been evolved by the various nations.

Religion is always conservative and loves to retain the usages, customs, and even the language, of a long past epoch.   It is not only the Christian Church which retains dead languages in the public services, but the same tendency is noticeable among non-Christian races. Ancient magical spells are often spoken in a language which is unintelligible even to the Medicine Men.   Sanscrit is still used by the Hindus and the Koran must be read in Arabic by good Mahomedans of every race.

This insistence on retaining the ancient words is not only due to natural conservatism on the part of the priests, but also to the widespread belief that certain words and phrases have a mantric power. The chanting of such words in the proper key is supposed automatically to produce a power which will influence the supernatural forces and create thought-forms which will ascend, even into the presence of the Divine. Although many Western people may query this view, it is undoubtedly a widespread belief, and those who have heard such chanting are aware that the effect produced on the human beings present is peculiar, and that the chanting of the translations of such phrases seems to lack the power inherent in the original words. A Parsee gentleman once told me that there was a certain prayer in the ancient Zend language which he had been in the habit of saying all his life, although he could not understand a word of its meaning. A few years ago he got a scholar to translate it for him but found that when translated the prayer failed utterly to satisfy his soul and bring peace, which it had never failed to do when said in the Zend language. In the end he returned to the original language and found that when thus spoken the prayer once more regained its potency.

The mantric signs to which we shall presently devote our attention are clearly very similar to the prayers offered in dead languages, and I believe it is because they were very ancient and were already believed to be mantric that they were not discarded when the spoken, or the later written, languages became prevalent. If I am correct, these signs are not mere gestures intended to give emphasis to a certain religious prayer or action, but are themselves prayers, or one might even say spells, of the greatest mantric power conceivable. When therefore a man makes the sign which I shall describe later as the *Sign of Preservation*,[1] the very fact of making it implies a prayer for preservation, and the mantric force of the sign to a great extent ensures that the request will be granted.

It must not be forgotten that in primitive days the border line between magic and religion was very thin. To-day in the West we

---

[1] See illustration opposite page 24.

humbly petition God of His graciousness to grant our prayers, but many savage races still adopt a very different attitude and believe that if they utter the right word in the right tone of voice, at the same time performing certain necessary actions, they can coerce the Gods or Spirits and *compel* them to grant their requests.   Although this attitude has passed away among civilised people, the ancient signs still truly represent a mantric influence, but to-day it would merely manifest itself in a feeling that for some inexplicable reason the Divine Power prefers that the humble petitioner should use a certain formula and adopt a certain attitude when presenting his petition, probably because it was hallowed by long years of usage.

Indeed, it may well be that priests of all religions, realising the natural weakness of man and understanding his psychology, believed that by adopting these ancient signs, ancient words and attitudes, the man himself would be put into the right frame of mind to make his petitions effectively.   In conclusion it is well to point out that such signs are often associated with words of power, secret passwords and the like, a fact which itself supports the view that they are mantric.

PRAISING RA AT SUNSET.
From the Leyden Papyrus.

A I.

TWO ROUNDELS OF 17TH CENTURY PAINTED GLASS (GERMAN OR SWISS WORK).

a.   Moses and the Brazen Serpent.

b.   The Israelites Picking up Manna.

N.11.

PART OF A MOSAIC REPRESENTING THE LAST JUDGMENT.
From the Baptistery at Florence.

I.2.

CHAPTER III. Concerning the Existence of Mantric Signs throughout the World.

AVING ALREADY pointed out that these are by far the most important signs we shall consider, it is now necessary to prove that they have two most striking characteristics. Firstly, a very long history, stretching back into the dawn of civilisation, and secondly, a wide distribution throughout the whole world. In order to prove both these statements, it seems desirable to concentrate attention for the moment on one particular sign, leaving a detailed consideration of each of the various signs to be dealt with in separate chapters.

For this purpose let us select the *Sign of Preservation*, because in itself it is such a peculiar one and least open to the glib answer that it is a purely natural sign, such as anyone might accidentally make. This is a plea which has been put forward to account for the appearance of certain signs in different parts of the world, under circumstances which preclude the possibility of their having been copied by men in one country from men in another, in recent years.

The *Sign of Preservation*, as I will call it, consists in placing one hand over the heart and raising the other so as to form a right angle at the elbow, with the hand pointing to Heaven, as is shown in the illustration of *Praising Ra at Sunset* on page 12. There are many minor variations, and although often it is the left hand which is upraised, this does not seem to be an absolute rule, and where, as in the Egyptian example just shown, it seems desirable in order to balance the picture, artists and sculptors have not hesitated to reverse the hands. In some cases, either from carelessness or to indicate a slightly different shade of meaning, the hand is not placed over the breast, but so long as the other arm is raised so as to form a square it should be considered to be a *Sign of Preservation*, as is shown by the fact that wherever there is a scene in which this sign is depicted it is obvious that the person making it is praying that he, or someone on whose behalf he is petitioning, may be preserved. If the hand is laid on the breast and the other hand is not raised to form a square, this is a different sign, and implies *faith, trustworthiness* or *fidelity*, rather than a prayer for preservation. It seems probable that the full sign, with one hand on the breast and the other arm raised in the form of a square, should be translated into words somewhat as follows:

"*By my trust in Thee and fidelity to Thee, I pray Thee, O God, to preserve me.*"

The omission of the hand on the breast, of which we get many examples, may therefore indicate a slightly different idea. It should be noted that in many cases the sign is used to imply not only a prayer for preservation but also the fact that the prayer has been granted. In particular it appears as if when there was no doubt that the prayer had been granted it was customary to omit placing the hand on the breast, thus very often in Mediæval paintings of the Last Judgment we find that the souls who are rising from their graves to Salvation make only the sign of the squared elbow, omitting the hand over breast, indicating thereby that they have actually been preserved from Hell and acknowledge it, therefore they do not pray. A very good example is the 12th Century mosaic from the Cupola of the Baptistery at Florence, reproduced opposite this page, wherein the souls are seen rising from their tombs. Two representations of this sign are shown, and in neither is the other hand placed on the breast. There is also a third, which is a little doubtful. The man appears to be making the *Sign of Preservation*, but is so busy trying

to help another man out of his grave that he makes it somewhat carelessly. On the other hand, there are two souls who are emphatically
not making this sign; one of them, on the contrary, is making one of
a very different significance, to which we shall refer later. It is often
by the use of such signs that a mediæval artist indicates to those who
see his work that one particular soul is saved while another is lost.
Frequently, however, this piece of symbolism seems somewhat unnecessary, as usually he is careful so to arrange his picture that
the good souls all rise on the right hand of our Lord and the lost on the
left. Still, the artist of this period was anxious to push home his
allegory to the ignorant and not too well educated laity.

It will be necessary in the special chapter we shall devote to this
sign to go more fully into the matter, and therefore we will now turn
to another important variant of it which shows how, by combination
with another, a sign can acquire a fuller meaning. It is quite usual
to find our Lord depicted making this sign, as in the fresco of Him
preaching to the Doctors, painted at St. Ambrose, Milan, and reproduced opposite page 10, where it implies that the boy Christ is preaching the way of Salvation or Preservation. Often, however, He is depicted in this attitude but with the third and fourth fingers closed on
to the palm of the hand, to give the further implication of blessing.
(See illustration opposite page 28). The import of this attitude
would therefore be that our Lord assured those who turned to Him
that He *would* preserve them, for the combined sign signifies that
the Blessing implies the promise of Preservation.

Let us now show that this sign stretches back to a very early date
in the history of the world and is carried down to the present day by a
regular sequence, which done we must next prove that it is found all
over the world, and that examples of its use exist in Europe, Asia,
Africa and America. Having thus established its wide-spread nature
and ancient traditions, we can turn to consider others of equal
antiquity and world-wide use.

Although, as we shall see later, there is good reason to believe
that the primitive races who in point of archæology preceded the
ancient civilisation in Egypt used this sign, nevertheless, we must
be content with Egypt as our starting point, because its monuments
can be dated with considerable exactitude, whereas even when we

find relics of primitive races of this nature, it is difficult to say whether they are four, three, or only two, thousand years old.

The Sign of Preservation is found in numerous examples of Egyptian art, of which two must suffice. One is the Vignette from the Leyden papyrus in the British Museum, which is reproduced on page 12, and the other is on the fascade of an Egyptian Temple, now at Bath Museum, and is of the date, (circa) 1333 B.C. This is illustrated in *The Secret of Ancient Egypt*, and is a good specimen of an early representation of this sign.

Travelling to the mysterious kingdom of ancient Crete, we find numerous examples of its use on seals and in votive figures, who are avowedly standing in ritual attitudes. Thus on seals of the Minoan period, reproduced opposite page 16 (C6 and C12), we have some striking representations of its use, while in a ritual figure illustrated in Bossert's work[1] on the same subject, we have another example.

The civilisation of Mycenæ has strong affinities with that of ancient Crete, although it is probably later in date, and on a gold ring illustrated by Dussaud,[2] is a group of women, two of whom are making this sign. The scene is clearly a ritual one, connected with the Fertility Cult, and therefore the signs are of special importance as proof of their mantric significance. As we find numerous other examples of similar mantric signs in ancient Cretan art, it is clear that these *Signs of Preservation* are only part of a group well known to the men who built Knossos and Mycenæ.

If we next turn to that other great centre of civilisation, Babylon, we shall find similar examples, thus the representation of the descent of Damuzi, or of the Sun God, into the Underworld shows that Deity making this sign, with the left arm raised in the form of the square, while an attendant god is in a similar position, although the left arm is not quite so well squared as is the case with the principal character.

The scene appears on one of those cylindrical seals common in ancient Babylon, and the reproduction is from an impression of the seal made in plaster. (See page 168.) It should be compared with the impression of a second seal illustrated on the same page, wherein the same god is shown rising from the Underworld. Behind him are

---

[1] T. H Bossert, *Alt-Keta*.
[2] M René Dussaud, *La Civilisation Préhellénique dans la Bassin de la mar Egée*.

MINOAN SEALS SHOWING SIGNS.

1 (C. 7) and 3 (C. 11) from Hogea Triada.   Horror and Water.

2 and 4 (C.6) from Zakro.   Preservation.

5 (C12.)   Clay sealing from Zakro.   Preservation.

6 (C. 13)   A gold signet from Mycence, depicting the Great Goddess and the death of her young
lover.   Note the tree growing from the tomb and the use of "The Sign of Water."

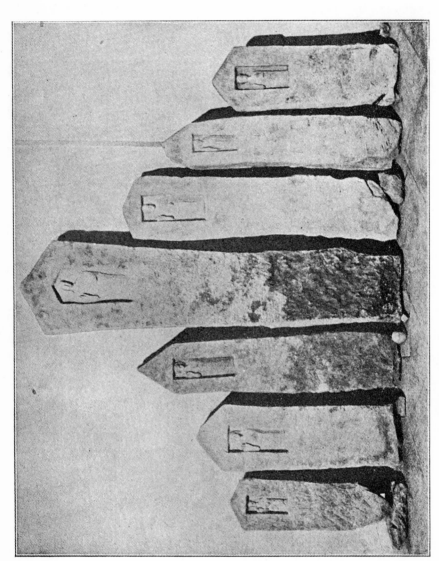

SEVEN STELES OF PUNIC PRIESTS FOUND AT CARTHAGE.

E.1.

the flames of the rising sun, while two attendant deities draw back the gateways of the Dawn.   Once more the god is making the Sign of Preservation, and thus the general import of both seals is that although the god apparently descends into the Underworld, he will be preserved therein and, by his act of rising next day, will preserve mankind on earth.

Let us now pass to ancient Carthage, where we find numerous

TWO PUNIC TOMBSTONES OF THE LAITY.
Now in the Constantine Museum, Algeria.

E.10.

representations of the same sign.   Thus in the Bardo Museum, Tunis, are a number of gravestones of Punic priests found at Carthage.   These are illustrated opposite page 18 and are peculiarly significant, for on Punic gravestones it is only the priests who are represented making this sign, whereas the tombstones of the ordinary laity, here depicted, have on them a crude figure of a man making a sign which indicates distress, or a desperate appeal for help.   As we shall have to consider this latter sign later, this passing allusion is all that is necessary here, but it is important to note that the Priests, who were Masters of the Mysteries of Tanit, the Carthaginian form of Astarte, the great Mother-Goddess, relying on her protection, felt certain that they would be preserved after death and enter Paradise, whereas the ordinary and uninitiated laity had no such sure and certain hope.   It should be noted that in most of the Carthaginian examples it is the right hand which is raised and the left which is placed across the breast, but there are a few representations of the reverse position, which again shows that too much importance must not be attached to which arm is raised.   These priestly tombstones date from between 600 and 400 B.C.

After the destruction of Carthage the spot was left desolate for many years, but the city was ultimately rebuilt by the Romans, and specimens of Roman pottery and sculpture show that this sign was regarded by them as having precisely the same meaning as it had among the Carthaginians.   Thus a statue of Ceres, who under the Romans to some extent replaced Astarte, was found on the site of Carthage, and is now exhibit number C. 1015 in the Bardo Museum, Tunis.   The arm is slightly damaged, but for all that it is perfectly clear that the Goddess is making the *Sign of Preservation*.

Of about the same date is a broken terracotta figure of Venus and cupids, found on the same site and illustrated on page 19.   The goddess clearly makes this sign, and it is interesting to note that in her left hand, of which the top is broken, and which is raised with the elbow forming a square, she probably held a basket or an apple.   The point is important because the Indian god Hanuman, depicted opposite page 220, similarly holds a fruit in his left hand and his arm in this position.   The legend relates that it was the fruit of the tree of life, with which Hanuman restored life to the warriors of Rama who had fallen in the battle against Ravena, the Demon King of Ceylon.   It appears therefore as if the Goddess Venus, who in Roman times took on some of the attributes of the Great Mother, by this sign promised preservation to her devotees, and probably eternal life through the apple.

Carthage remained a Roman colony for many years, and in the 3rd and 4th centuries the Christians developed a vigorous church there. We therefore find numerous examples of Christian art, dating from the third to the fifth century, and in several cases we have this sign, with the same inner meaning, appearing in unquestionably Christian scenes.   Thus in the Bardo Museum, Tunis, is a Roman sarcophagus showing incidents in the lives of Daniel and Jonah, and the latter

A Terracotta Statuette of Venus and Cupids from Carthage.
E.II.

is testifying to his preservation as he comes out of the belly of the whale by making the *Sign of Preservation*.

We have laid considerable stress on Carthage because there was more or less continuous occupation of the site for over a thousand years, and during that period three definite religious cultures held sway, namely, Punic, Heathen Roman and Christian, and, as the examples quoted show, each religion in turn has used precisely the same sign with exactly the same meaning. The reference in the case of Jonah is especially important because this sign is associated with him right through the Middle Ages, and so in this scene we have a definite link century after century.

Leaving behind us the shores of Africa, let us pass to the actual territory of the conqueror of Carthage. In a fresco at Pompeii, in the house of the "Tragic Poet", is the scene representing the preservation of Œdipus, reproduced opposite page 180. The legend relates how it was foretold that Œdipus would slay his father and commit incest with his mother, whereupon the former instructed one of his servants to take the child and kill it. The servant, however, apparently hesitated to carry out the ferocious command and, to avoid having to bear the blood guilt on his conscience, drove a nail through the two feet of the child so that it could not crawl and abandoned it, still alive, in a lonely spot. It was subsequently found by a shepherd who took compassion on it and brought it home to his farm. This is the scene actually depicted in the fresco. We see the shepherd handing the child to one of his women, while another woman is making the sign which implies the words, "Preserve the babe". As a result the child was saved and lived to carry out his terrible fate.

Let us now turn to Christian art of the Roman period. We have already seen that on a sarcophagus in Carthage there is a representation of Jonah making this sign, and on another stone coffin, this time in the Musée Lapidaire at Arles, is a scene of the Nativity, in which there are three shepherds, one of whom is pointing to the star, while another makes the *Sign of Preservation*. The date of the tomb is about the end of the 4th century, and on another sarcophagus of the same period and in the same museum St. Peter is shown raising Tabitha while a kneeling relation makes this Sign. (See illustration opposite page 96.)

Coming to the 9th century, we find in the Vatican library an illuminated manuscript wherein is an excellent picture of the Virgin making this gesture, showing that the tradition had not been forgotten, while in the Cathedral Library at Winchester is a beautiful old Bible, which was illuminated between 1154 and 1189, and the scene reproduced here of Christ harrowing hell shows the souls greeting

AN ALABASTER CARVING OF THE INCARNATION.
Circa 1475 A.D.

L.5.

PART OF A CHASUBLE EMBROIDERED WITH SCENES
FROM THE LIFE OF THE VIRGIN.

L.3.

their preserver in a similar attitude. (See illustration opposite page 76). Readers should note that our Lord is rescuing one of the souls by grasping his squared arm. Bearing in mind the Roman example of Jonah and the Whale, the reproduction opposite page 98 of a photograph of the famous Comacine pulpit at Ravello, near Sorrento, is of interest. Its date is about 1280.

Travelling on to the 14th century, the illustration of the Marriage Feast at Cana, from Queen Mary's Psalter, which forms the frontispiece of this volume, is an excellent example. The bride, seated on the right of our Lord, is asking that she may be preserved from the disgrace which will fall upon her and her husband if there is not enough wine for the feast. It has been suggested by competent critics that the reason there was a shortage of wine was that the young couple, although they had invited our Lord, had not anticipated His arriving with a number of His followers, whose presence threw out their calculations. The Virgin, on behalf of the petitioner, pleads her cause, and reverses the sign, while our Lord promises to grant the petition and so preserve the young couple from the disaster. As He is *granting* the favour, His right hand is not over His breast, and the import of His sign is, "They shall be preserved." The fourth person, on the extreme left, by placing his right hand on his breast, symbolically says, "I have faith in the Master that He will carry out His promise." We thus see that the signs convey a complete conversation, or at any rate the thoughts of the four characters who sit on the further side of the table.

Another illustration of about the same date comes from the Arundel manuscript, in the British Museum, and is reproduced opposite page 8. The two scenes are the Slaughter of the Innocents and the Marriage Feast at Cana. The latter is of special interest because the artist has depicted a slightly different set of emotions in the chief characters, and the principal sign therein, which is made by the Virgin, will therefore be discussed later. In the scene of the Slaughter of the Innocents the woman who is holding the child in her hand and kneeling before Herod is begging him to preserve her unfortunate infant, whereas the one kneeling at the back. whose child is in the process of being slain, has abandoned all hope of its preservation, and makes instead a sign symbolising her terrible distress. The combination of these two signs is worth noting, for thereby the artist subtly conveys the desperate hope of the one mother and the hopeless distress of the other.

In the fifteenth century we have such an abundance of examples that we must content ourselves with referring to but a few. Reproduced opposite is a photograph of an English Chasuble made in the early part of that century, of which the original is in the Victoria and Albert Museum. On it are three embroidered pictures of incidents in the life of the Virgin, and in the top one, which shows her presentation in the Temple, her mother, St. Anne, is making this gesture, but her other hand is not on the breast. The High Priest who is receiving the young vowess responds by making the complete sign, with the left arm squared. In the second scene, in which the Virgin is leaning over the sacred babe, an attendant is also making the sign.

Another example of the same period is from *Mandeville's Travels*, now in the British Museum, ref. Add. MS. 24089 F. 11. Therein a king is being shown some of the Hallows, including the Cross and the sponge which was soaked in vinegar and given to our Lord. At the sight of these instruments of the Preservation of man from damnation, he raises his right arm with his elbow squared and places his left on his breast. The illustration opposite page 28 is from the Psalter of Humphrey, Duke of Gloucester, which is early 15th century work, and contains an interesting variation. Therein our Lord is seen rising from the tomb in the presence of a King and a noble. He makes the sign, but in such a way as to indicate His wounds, implying that through His blood the kneeling devotees are preserved. Another devotee, who appears behind our Lord, makes the same sign with reversed hands, while in the top, right hand corner, God the Father looks down and makes the combined *Sign of Preservation* and *Blessing*, thereby, as it were, endorsing the action of our Lord. The fact that God the Father holds the globe in His hand, indicates the wider lesson that through Christ's mediatorial sacrifice the whole world has been preserved and blessed. This picture should be compared with the illustration of Christ in Glory, from A. Ballini's *Monte Sancto di Dio*, Florence 1477, reproduced opposite page 28, the original of which is in the British Museum.

That this combined sign was by no means rare, is shown by

another representation of the same date, also of the Florentine school, showing the Virgin and Child, with St. Helena and St. Michael standing one on either side, the original of which is likewise in the British Museum. Here the infant Christ is again making the combined *Sign of Preservation* and *Blessing*, while in an alabaster carving of St. Christopher bearing on his shoulders the child Christ, now in Victoria and Albert Museum, the child is making the *Sign of Preservation* only, and holding the globe in His hand against His breast.

In an alabaster carving of about 1475, reproduced opposite page 20, is depicted the Mystery of the Incarnation. The Second Person is descending in the Vesica Piscis towards the Virgin, who is apparently much distressed at the news that she, although a maid, is to become a mother, but she is being reassured by two female figures, both of whom are making this sign. That on the left of the picture, in the foreground, is easily recognisable, but the one on the right is apparently deliberately disguised by holding a scroll. Such attempts slightly to disguise the sign are by no means uncommon in Mediæval art, and seem to imply that the artist was giving hints to those entitled to know the meaning of these signs while not wishing to parade them too obviously to the outside world. We learn from Matthew Paris that there was a sign language known to members of the Monastic Orders, for he says:— "Let us all endeavour to learn the necessary signs."[1] There are other references to these signs in Matthew Paris, from which it appears that while all ecclesiastics ought to know them it was not necessarily the case that the laity should.

In a late fifteenth century fresco in St. James's Church, Southleigh, near Oxford, reproduced opposite page 30, we have an excellent example of English Mediæval art, representing St. Michael weighing a soul, while a Saint, almost certainly the Virgin Mary, pleads the cause of the deceased seated in the scale near her. In the opposite scale is a devil, beneath whom yawns the mouth of hell. Another devil is cheating by climbing on to the end of the beams of the scales, but St. Michael, brandishing his sword in his hand, makes the *Sign of Preservation*, thereby showing that despite the cheating tricks of the devils the soul is to be preserved from hell. The clever way in which this sign is worked in without disturbing the main features

[1] T. D. Fosbroke, British Monachism (1802), Vol. II, p.5 citing Matthew Paris, 403.

of the picture, namely, the weighing and the defending sword of St. Michael, deserves particular attention.

Another interesting example of English work appears on the monumental brass of B. Roucliffe, a judge, and his wife, which is shown opposite page 230.   The date of the work is 1494 and the figures are depicted holding between them a model of the church they built.   The Judge makes the sign with his right arm and his wife with her left, implying that they hope for Preservation because they have made this offering to God.   It is very rare for any sign other than that of prayer to appear on a brass, and for purposes of comparison that of John Sleford, Rector of Balsham, Cambs., 1401, is reproduced opposite page 2.   He is vested in a cope and makes the sign usually found on brasses, namely, that of Prayer.

Of a rather different type is the picture of the Baptism of Our Lord by St. John, painted by F. Francia, who was born in 1450 and died in 1518.   The original is in Hampton Court Palace and is reproduced opposite page 34, by the gracious permission of His Majesty.   It will be noticed that one of the onlookers in the left hand corner is clearly making this sign, while a figure in the background seems also to be doing it.   Seeing that Our Lord's ministry really commenced with His Baptism, the significance of this sign is obvious, but it should also be noted that it constantly appears in connection with baptism, even if the person being baptised is someone of comparative unimportance.   Doubtless the reason is to be found in the prevalent view that every child was born in sin and doomed to destruction, from which it was preserved by the saving grace of baptism.

Turning to the early part of the 16th century, four examples must suffice, although many more could be quoted.   The first, illustrated opposite this page, is a Spanish wood carving representing our Lord. It is an admirable example of this sign with the left hand raised, but on careful examination it will be noted that once again the Christ is drawing attention to His wounds, as in the Gloucester Psalter, for a nail is sticking through His left hand, while with His right he covers the wound over His heart.

An interesting variation is to be seen in a French manuscript of the 16th Century, now in the British Museum.   (See M.1 on list.)   It represents the Nativity, and a shepherd has removed his hat and makes

A **16TH** CENTURY SPANISH WOODCARVING OF CHRIST.

THE TOMB OF CARDINAL LAVIGERIE.
At the Cathedral, Carthage.

P.1.

the Sign of Preservation to imply that he recognises in the tiny infant
the promised Saviour Who shall preserve mankind. and prays to Him
for Preservation.   The infant Christ is answering the sign of the
shepherd by raising His left arm in a square, but does not place His
right hand on His breast.   Here we have a key to the inner significance
of the variant form of the sign.   By thus raising His left hand only,
the Christ replies to the suppliant, "Thou shalt be preserved."

A picture to which we shall have to refer again and again in this
book is "The Last Judgment", by Hans Dyg, in the Town Hall, Basle,
painted about 1519, for in it are represented no less than five of these
important mantric signs, and it is therefore reproduced opposite page
186.   For the moment, however, we need only refer to the man who
is seen rising from his grave making the Sign of Preservation,
while just in front of him a devil is dragging away one of his victims.
The man we are considering is praying to Christ, Who is coming in
glory, to preserve him from the terrible fate which has befallen the
other man.   In the reproduction the upper half of the picture, showing Our Lord seated on the clouds, has been omitted.

In the miniature from a Printed Book of Hours, circa 1527, illustrated opposite page 132, of which the original is in the Victoria and
Albert Museum, we have another example in which a series of signs
appear, for it will be noticed that the Virgin and one of the people at
the back, probably a shepherd, are clearly making signs, but it is the
Sign of Preservation made by the Christ Child which for the moment
rivets our attention.   By this gesture He promises His worshippers
Preservation.

And now we have come to the Reformation, which in Northern
Europe shattered respect for tradition and, although it did not entirely
root it out, to a great extent obliterated all traces of the sign language so
far as it was connected with exoteric religion.   Considering the bitter
opposition shown by most of the reformers to pictorial or sculp-
tural representations of scriptural themes, their absence is not surprising.   Even when the first outburst of iconoclasm had passed, we
find few representations of these signs in pictorial art or sculpture,
for the Post-Reformation artists, imbued with the spirit of realism
inherited from the Renaissance, eschewed symbolism and endeavoured
to depict even sacred subjects as "naturally" as possible.   Henceforth

this traditional language of signs tended to go underground and survived only in strange places.   On the Continent, however, although the influence of the Renaissance militated against the widespread use of these symbolic attitudes, they did not entirely vanish, particularly in areas where the Roman Catholic Church remained strong, that ·is to say, in districts where tradition was still respected.   Thus in the private chapel of the Bishop of Coire, within his palace, the ceiling was decorated in the 18th century with pictures of cherubs, and near by the altar is one making the *Sign of Preservation*.   Likewise, in the Museum at Zurich, is a fine four-poster bed of the early 18th century, which has a solid wooden roof whereon is painted a picture of Jacob's dream, showing the ladder, down which are descending angels, some of whom are making this sign.

We should not expect to find much regard paid to symbolic attitudes in the art of the 19th century, nevertheless there is an example, and a particularly significant one.   It is the tomb of Cardinal Lavigerie, in the Cathedral Church at Carthage, a photograph of which is reproduced opposite this page, and there is a peculiar suitability in the fact that here once more we should see this ancient sign.   The Phœnicians used it, the heathen Romans carried it forward on the same site, the fifth century Christians depicted it, and here we have the same sign in connection with a tomb set up to the great cardinal who did so much for the people of Tunis in the 19th century.   His greatest triumph was that he obtained the freeing of all slaves in Algeria and Tunis, and to commemorate that fact slaves are represented on either side of his tomb.   One, a man, holds up his broken fetters, while he makes this sign to demonstrate that the Cardinal preserved him and saved him from slavery, while on the other side stands a slave woman, whose little child also makes it to indicate that through the Cardinal he has been preserved from the fate which had been his father's.   It was within sight of this very cathedral that in August, 1926, I obtained striking proof that these signs were still a living force not only in Algiers but in the Roman Catholic Church.   Whilst seated in the Hotel St. Louis, I noticed a little Italian girl saying her grace after her meal.   She folded her hands in the well known *Sign of Prayer*, invoking as she did so the name of God the Father ; thence she passed to the *Sign of Preservation*, left hand raised with the arm forming a square, and right hand on the breast, as she prayed to Christ, the Preserver of the world, then, dropping her left hand she raised her right until it touched her left shoulder, as she invoked the Blessed Virgin Mary. Finally, keeping her right hand still in position, she crossed her left hand over it as she said "Amen". Now each of these signs, as we shall see later, are great and ancient mantric signs, and each was appropriately applied, but for our immediate purpose all we need do is to draw attention to the fact that the *Sign of Preservation* was associated with the name of the Second Person of the Trinity, Who by His death preserved mankind.

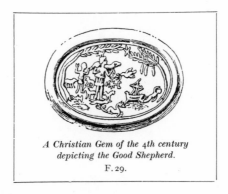

*A Christian Gem of the 4th century
depicting the Good Shepherd.*
F. 29.

A glance at the Roman Christian Gem of the 4th Century reproduced above shows that the Roman Church, who has carried forward this pre-Christian Sign throughout her whole career, here uses it in Association with Christ and Preservation. In it will be seen that Christ in His capacity of Good Shepherd is carrying on his shoulders a lamb and His arms are so arranged as subtly to indicate that He has preserved it.

We have thus shown a continual succession of this sign from the days of ancient Egypt down to the year of Grace 1926, and have proved that in every case it is used to convey the same basic idea. It would have been possible to give far more numerous examples, but some of these have been reserved for the special chapter on the *Sign of Preservation*, where they will take their place amid the whole series, but even that chapter must be limited in length, and not all the examples I have recorded can be contained therein. At the end of the book however, will be found a complete list of all the examples of this and every other sign I have so far recorded. Doubtless there are many more which could be added to the list, but all I wish to say here is that it seems to me impossible to pretend that each and every one of these signs is accidental and natural, and has no inner significance. The series is far too complete, and the inner meaning in each case so clear once we have the key, that even if we were not aware that mediæval ecclesiastical art was largely symbolical, it would be impossible to come to any other conclusion than that which I have suggested, namely, that these signs are deliberately depicted in order to convey a definite message.

Let us now turn to consider their widespread geographical distribution, which seems to show that the tradition enshrined in them goes back to an even earlier period than that of Egypt, and is bound up with the evolution of the human race, for if not, how comes it that we find the the same sign in Easter Island, in ancient Mexico, among primitive savages in Central Africa and among the gods in India?

"CHRIST IN GLORY."
A Wood Block of the Florentine School.
L.6.

"THE RESURRECTION OF CHRIST,"
FROM THE PSALTER OF HUMPHREY, DUKE OF GLOUCESTER.
Now in the British Museum (15th century work).
L.2.

A 15TH CENTURY FRESCO SHOWING ST. MICHAEL WEIGHING A SOUL,
In St. James's Church, Southleigh, Near Oxford.

L.4.

CHAPTER IV. Which Indicates the World-Wide Distribution of Mantric Signs.

S IN THE previous chapter we have shown that one particular mantric sign can be traced from the time of the Egyptians down to the present day, it is now necessary to prove that mantric signs are found distributed all over the world, and for the reason already given we will again concentrate on the *Sign of Preservation*. It must, however, be realised that the same facts, namely, great antiquity, regular descent and wide geographical distribution, appertain to all the chief signs we shall discuss later, and we have only chosen this particular sign and gone into it in such detail because it is such a markedly arbitrary one, and cannot be lightly thrust aside as a natural gesture.

AFRICA.

Such a large section of the last chapter dealt with Europe that it is not necessary to recapitulate in detail the vast number of examples to which we have drawn attention in that area. We have shown that Rome, Italy generally, France, Spain and England all supply examples of the use of this sign and therefore, without delay, we will turn to Africa.

In addition to the Punic examples in the Museum at Tunis

it should be noted that the Museum at Algiers also has a number of Steles which formerly marked the graves of Punic Priests, whereon the figures are represented making the *Sign of Preservation*, and there is also a Berber tombstone of about the 7th century whereon a crude human figure is drawn in this position.   As we have quoted examples of Roman figures making the same sign, it is only necessary now to show that the tradition is by no means extinct among the native inhabitants of Algeria even to-day.   A fine old Kabyle carpet in the Hotel De France, Setif, seen by me in August, 1926, had crude human figures making the *Sign of Preservation* woven into it.   In each case, one hand was raised with the elbow squared, but the other hand was not across the breast.   That this was a deliberate sign was further proved by the fact that in another part of the carpet a figure was depicted making the *Sign of Distress.*

Coming next to the West coast of this continent attention is drawn to the carved Yoruba gates from Oyo, a photograph of which is reproduced opposite page 21 .   Thereon are carved in bas-relief numerous figures, several of which are clearly making mantric signs, and among them is a man making the *Sign of Preservation*, who stands beside a woman.   The composition suggests that he has preserved the woman from some dire fate, a fact that is supported by the appearance of two figures further down on the same board of the door, who are making the *Sign of Distress.*

In the Congo this sign made by a human figure appears on the ceremonial coffin in which local chiefs are buried, while Major Meredith Sanderson informs me that in Nyasaland it is used at a very important point in the ceremonies when initiating a boy into manhood. At the beginning of these ceremonies, which last for many weeks, it is customary to erect a tall pole, which action is performed with numerous magical rites, and while these are taking place the Medicine Men make this sign.   If the pole should fall down before the ceremonies are finished, it is the general belief that all the boys then undergoing initiation will die.   It is therefore perfectly natural that the Medicine Men should make this sign in connection with the erection of the pole.   The Yaos employ quite a number of these mantric signs during their ceremonies of initiation, a fact which makes the use of the *Sign of Preservation* the more important.

In East Africa I have so far been unable to obtain conclusive proof of the use of this sign, but as the natives in that area use that of *Distress* and also another important mantric sign, I hope that some of my readers who know the district will have had an opportunity of seeing the *Sign of Preservation* used there and will communicate with me.   In Egypt, of course, as previously mentioned, it appears on the ancient monuments and papyri.

ASIA.

In Asia quite a number of examples can be quoted.   The illustration reproduced opposite page 80, is from an early 17th century Turkish manuscript and shows the Dancing Dervishes performing their famous ritual dances.   It will be noted that practically all the men are making mantric signs and in particular the *Sign of Distress*, in three distinct positions, concerning which we shall speak later. But it is to the man who is making the *Sign of Preservation* that special attention is now directed.   In the course of their dancing these Dervishes invoke Allah under his variant names or attributes, and alter their signs to correspond with the name of God invoked.

Passing to Persia we also find examples, of which one must suffice. In a Persian painting representing the legend of Mohammed's flight into Paradise, now in the British Museum, at least two of the angels who surround him are making this sign.   The date of the illumination is 1539 A.D.

Turning to India the following are worthy of special notice.   In the Berlin Museum is a Painting of about 1600, entitled "The Visit of a Prince" (see illustration opposite page 32), in which is shown a man petitioning the Prince, who is riding on an elephant.   A servitor is trying to drive away the petitioner with a stick, while the latter casts up his hands to heaven in the *Sign of Distress*.   The prince replies by raising his left arm with his elbow squared, thereby promising to preserve the man from whatever is distressing him.   In the same Museum there is also another example of an Indian painting of the same date.   This is a fantastic picture of a devil leading a camel across country and on the back of the animal is seated an angelic being.   But it is the camel itself which rivets our attention, for it seems to symbolise the created universe, being made up of hundreds of beautifully drawn figures of beasts and men, among whom one man in a prominent position is shown making this sign.

Perhaps, however, the most important example of all is the illustration reproduced opposite page 220, of Hanuman, the Monkey God, bearing in his left hand the fruit of the Tree of Life. His left arm is correctly squared and although his right arm does not properly cover his breast this is merely because had the artist so depicted him, his battle club would have covered his face. I have seen other examples of Hanuman, however, not bearing the club, and in such cases his right arm covers his left breast and his left arm is properly squared. The significance of the attitude can be seen from the legend, to which allusion has already been made in the last chapter. Hanuman was the faithful attendant of Rama, who was the 7th incarnation of Vishnu, the Preserver. Rama's wife having been carried off by Ravena, a Demon King who reigned in Ceylon, Rama pursued him thither and attacked him with a large host. After several days, however, the bulk of Rama's army lay dead and dying on the field. Then Hanuman sped over sea and land to the far distant Himalayas and brought back with him the fruit of the Tree of Life, which he placed to the nostrils of the dead and dying, who immediately arose and renewed the battle until Ravena was defeated and Rama's wife rescued. It is for this reason that he is depicted making this sign when carrying the fruit of the Tree of Life.

Two other examples from India must suffice. In the Victoria and Albert Museum, reference number I.S. 15, is a bas-relief of the 13th century A.D., in black stone. It represents an Indian Garu, or teacher, and his disciples, and the former is making this sign. Down below it is a smaller bas-relief, wherein two soldiers are apparently addressing two comrades and while so doing are also making the sign. The Second, representing the Death of Bhishma, is reproduced opposite this page and speaks for itself.

Although I have found numerous other mantric signs in China I have not been able definitely to establish the use of the *Sign of Preservation*, but one of the Hung signs appears to be taken from it. It is probable therefore that it does exist, but beyond that it is impossible to say anything for certain. Before leaving Asia, however, we must not forget that already I have pointed out in the previous chapter two

THE LAST HOURS OF BHISHMA.
A Miniature of the Mogul School. Late 16th Century.

U.62.

ST. JOHN BAPTISING CHRIST, BY F. FRANCIA.
At Hampton Court.   Late 15th Century.

By Gracious Permission of His Majesty the King.

L.8.

examples of the use of this sign in ancient Babylon, while it is also known to the Bektashi Dervishes in Arabia.[1]

OCEANIA.

One of the most isolated spots in the world is Easter Island, which belongs to Chili and is believed to have been the sacred island of an early civilisation that has vanished.   Scattered all over the island are hundreds of figures crudely, yet vigorously, carved in the human shape. Two specimens are in the portico of the British Museum in London, and if one is examined on the back the so-called Egyptian ankh cross will be found carved in bas-relief.   The fact that it is in bas-relief is important, for had it been incised it might have been thought that this emblem had been carved by some modern European conversant with ancient Egyptian symbols.   The weather-worn state of the back of the statue, however, quite precludes the possibility of this symbol having been added subsequent to the carving of the rest of the statue. Whether its existence indicates a direct cultural connection between ancient Egypt and Easter Island it is impossible to say, but it proves that the men who carved these statues had a good knowledge of symbolism, using this very ancient symbol to adorn the backs of their statues, probably to indicate that they represented Divine beings, blest with eternal life.

It is therefore the less surprising to find that they had a hieroglyphic script, of which a few examples survive, carved on pieces of wood.   These are illustrated opposite page 232.   The figures consist mainly of human and animal forms, although there are others of a more evolved type which cannot be definitely fixed as representing any known object.   It is believed that this script is a summary of Initiation Rites, but so far attempts to decipher it have failed.   One of its peculiarities is that whereas the top line has the figures the right way up, apparently the writing is reversed on the second line, for here the figures are standing on their heads.   The third line again has them correctly placed and the fourth line reversed.   Now among the human figures which appear are several who are clearly making the *Sign of Preservation*, whereas in the same line are some making that of *Distress* which we so often find set in opposition to the former sign.

---

[1] H. L. Leon. Masonic Secretaries Journal.   Sept. 1918.

Among the Australian Bushmen numerous mantric signs occur and on page 90 of the *National Geographic Magazine of U.S.A.*, Volume 51, No. 1, i.e., January, 1927, appears an interesting photograph of a number of these men standing on a rock, against which they have filed their spears and other weapons. The actual place is Sunday Island, and because the display is somewhat war-like the men are reassuring the onlookers by making the *Sign of Preservation*, which here may be interpreted as meaning, "Despite our warlike weapons, you are safe," i.e., "We guarantee your preservation".

Among the Maoris of New Zealand this sign is also used, my informants being several New Zealand friends, one of whom showed me a photograph of a boy making it perfectly with both hands, that is to say, with left elbow squared and right hand on the breast.

In Samoa this sign is one of the most important made during the famous Sitting Dance, which is enacted by the Taupou, or official hostees of the village.   One lady is appointed to this position and is supported by a number of female attendants.   Important guests are welcomed by a dance, which consists of graceful movements of the arms and body, but the dancers remain seated the whole time.   The arm movements constitute a pantomimic language, whereby the guest is welcomed to the village and promised protection and preservation from all hostility.   An excellent photograph showing the use of this sign appears opposite page 122 of "Customs of the World" Vol. I.[1]

These examples must suffice for Oceania, but in considering them it is important to bear in mind that this is only one of the important mantric signs found there, for the strength of my argument is naturally increased by the fact that other mantric signs are used by the same races in the same neighbourhood.

AMERICA.

We have already pointed out that in America the Red Indians have an elaborate sign language and use the definite mantric sign of drawing the hand across the throat, hence it is not surprising to find among the glyphs left behind by the ancient Aztecs and Mayas numerous examples of mantric signs. For our purpose the most important is the picture reproduced on page 2 which shows the Mexican

---

[1] Pub. by Hutchinson & Co. London.

Preserver, Quetzalcoatl, who is making this sign at the moment that he is being wounded in the foot by a spear, wielded by the giant

T.II.

Quetzalcoatl

Dancing

Before some

Higher

God.

against whom he is supposed to have fought. In addition to this example another appears in *The Bulletin of the Smithsonian Institute of U.S.A.* in which he is being wounded in his knee and at the same time makes this sign.

An interesting variation of it, which is reproduced on the last page, represents Quetzalcoatl in his jaguar cloak dancing before some higher god, who bends down from Heaven towards him. This god has his right hand on his breast and his left elbow squared, but the hand, instead of pointing up, is pointing down towards Quetzal- coatl himself. This is the only example I have come across of this variation, which no doubt had a special significance to the Priests; now unfortunately lost to us.

We have thus shown the use of this sign in every one of the five Continents and have indicated that it is known and venerated by modern savage races as well as by civilised peoples of ancient days. Even if they stood alone, these facts would be sufficient to indicate its great importance in any attempt to rediscover the significance of the ancient sign language, but subsequent chapters will prove that equally numerous examples of other signs, which clearly form part of the same symbolic language, can be found in all parts of the world. In order therefore that we may study this sign language in its en- tirety we shall proceed in the following chapters to tabulate and consider all those signs which I have reason to consider belong to the group which I have designated Mantric Signs.

A MINIATURE SHOWING THE CRUCIFIXION AND OUR LORD IN GLORY.
From an Illustrated M.S. now in the Victoria and Albert Museum.

I.13.

THE LOWER RIGHT HAND SECTION OF THE MOSAIC OF THE LAST JUDGMENT.

In Torcello Cathedral, near Venice.

I.10.

Chapter V.   Describing Signs Connected with certain Occult Centres, and firstly, the Throat.

OR THE PURPOSE of clarity it is necessary to adopt some system under which we can schedule the principal signs to be discussed. Among the greater mantric signs it will be noticed that several seem to be connected with what, in India, are regarded as certain important occult centres, such as the throat, the breast, the solar plexus and the reins, while others are clearly connected with some outstanding feature of the human frame, such as the shoulders, the hands themselves, the head, eyes, lips, etc. We will therefore deal first of all with the chief occult centres, for, seeing that I have already indicated that these signs are to a large extent mantric, it is natural to expect them to be grouped around these particular centres of the human body.

The first that we will consider is the throat and connected therewith we find an important sign, which consists of drawing the hand across the throat as if to cut it. In a picture, where the action must be arrested, the sign is generally depicted by folding the arm across the throat beneath the chin, so that the thumb points to the throat itself. Usually it is made with the right hand, but occasionally it is made with the left. Whether this variation implies a slightly different shade of meaning or is dictated solely by the position in which the characters stand, which renders it difficult for the artist to raise the right hand, is not quite clear. An excellent example showing both forms of the sign appears in the 12th century fresco at the Cathedral on the Island of Torcello, near Venice, which is reproduced opposite. The scene shown in the picture represents souls in Hell, and the significance of the position is increased by the fact that most of the people are making signs, to which we shall refer later.

The earliest reference we get to this sign is in ancient Egypt, in Chapter 90 of *The Book of the Dead*, where it is also associated with Hell and the destruction of the foes of Osiris. Here the deceased prays that his head may not be cut off because of his sins. In two Greek steles from Athens a suggestion of the sign appears. One, number D.4, now in the National Museum of that country, is reproduced opposite page 176. In this the sign might be taken as a purely natural gesture on the part of an onlooker, if it were not that it is associated with what appears to be a ritualistic grip. A seated woman, the deceased, is being gripped by the hand by a standing woman, whose thumb is pressed into the first knuckle joint, while a man who is looking on places his hand to his throat. As this stele is undoubtedly a funeral one, we obtain a definite association with death, which we shall see later is the characteristic of this sign. The other example from Greece, D.5, is the sepulchral stele of Archagora, now in the British Museum. Here again we have the dead woman seated on a chair while her hand is gripped, in this case by a man. The third figure, a woman, who is looking on, apparently carelessly places her hand up against her throat.

Having pointed out the 12th century example at Torcello, attention is now directed to another of the same period, listed as I.13., and reproduced opposite page 36. It is from a mediaeval manuscript now in the Victoria and Albert Museum and consists of two panels, in the lower of which is depicted the Crucifixion. On the left side of the Cross stands the Virgin, making a sign which indicates regret, as we shall prove later, while on the right, St. John makes the sign we are discussing. In the panel above, our Lord in Glory makes the

Sign of Blessing.   Thus it will be seen that all three persons are making signs, and once more it will be noted that the gesture of cutting the throat is associated with death.

It has previously been pointed out that when the 20th century street arab wants to emphasise that he is telling the truth he utters an imprecation, "God cut my throat if I tell a lie," and draws his hand across that organ, and the Soudanese Negroes along the Nile also confirm an oath in exactly the same way, namely, by drawing their hands across their throats.   In Nyasaland, Major Sanderson, the Chief Sanitation Officer of that country, informs me that the usual manner of taking an oath among the Yao tribes is for a man to place his left hand on the grave of his father and draw the right across the throat. Here again we have the association of death with this sign, and are able finally to interpret it.   It implies either that you are faithful unto death, or that if you are not faithful and true, may you be cut off from the land of the living.   In the case of St. John at the Crucifixion, it will be remembered that he was the only one of the disciples who ventured to appear near the Cross, and so we can interpret it here as implying that St. John was faithful to His Master unto His death.

The peculiar association of this sign is borne out by another example, this time of the 14th century.   A stained glass medallion in the top of the tracery of the East window of the Church at Whichford, near Shipton-on-Stour, represents Christ on the cross.   On the one side stands St. John making this sign of *Fidelity to Death* with his right hand, but there is an important variation, for his left arm is squared, implying preservation.   On the opposite side stands the Virgin, with her right hand on her left shoulder, a sign which we shall discuss later, but which implies acquiescence, or submission to fate.   In this case the interpretation would be that our Lord has just said to the Virgin, "Woman, behold thy son." (St. John 19. 26). The Virgin by her sign implies acquiescence, while St. John, by means of the two signs, implies that he will watch over her and preserve her until her death, a promise, it should be noted, he faithfully kept.   It is by thus combining the meanings of the various signs depicted in these ancient pictures that the artist was able to convey a number of subtle shades of meaning, which are entirely lost to the modern observer unless he can recognise their ancient significance.

Bearing in mind that the basic idea underlying this sign is faith-fulness unto death, we are now able to understand the significance of the Redskin gesture to which we previously alluded, namely, drawing his hand across his throat when saluting a friend.

In the Arundel Psalter, which is in the British Museum, on the page whereon we find a large capital B containing the tree of Jessie, there appear in the border figures of a number of saints and prophets, making signs. Among them is Amos, who is making an excellent example of the sign, "True (or faithful) unto death," while Jacob is making a combined sign, the left hand as if cutting the throat and the right elbow squared, to imply preservation. The date of the work is 14th century, the reference "K20", and parts of it are reproduced opposite page 156.

A very significant example is shown in the Woodcut of the end of the 15th Century reproduced opposite this page. The scene is the Temptation in the Garden of Eden, and as Eve offers Adam the Apple the latter draws his *left* hand across his throat. We might interpret the whole picture as follows:—It depicts the fall of Adam, and the dreadful penalty entailed thereby on his sinful posterity, no less than death. By his very act Adam implies that the stiff-necked and disobedient shall be cut off from the land of the living by the judgment of God, even as the head is severed from the body. The same picture also shows the Expulsion from the Garden, and here occur two other signs. Adam is making one to which I refer later as the *Sign of Reverence*, although here it is not very accurately drawn, while Eve makes the *Sign of Preservation*, in allusion to the promise that God would send His Son to save and preserve those who bend with humility and resignation beneath the chastening hand of the Most High. This woodcut and the Torcello fresco give us a further sub-meaning of the sign, for both Adam and the lost souls in Hell imply that they are cut off from the land of the living because of their sins.

Having already given examples of the use of this sign in America and Africa, as well as in Europe, it is interesting to find a good example of it depicted on the left arm of the gilt cross from Abyssinia, S.6, reproduced opposite page 178. We shall have to deal with this cross later as it contains examples of several other signs, but this scene depicts the Nativity, and implies that the infant Christ will prove faithful to His mission, even unto death.

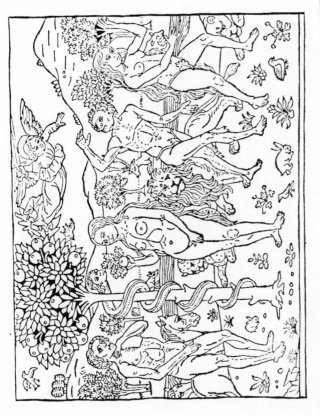

"EVE GIVING ADAM THE APPLE" AND "THE EXPULSION FROM THE GARDEN."

A woodblock from "Supplimentum Chronicarum," by J. P. Foresti.
C. 1490. Original in the V. & A. Museum.

L.66.

THREE SARCOPHAGI of the 5th CENTURY.
In the Museum at Arles.

a. *Jonah and the Whale.*
b. *Daniel in the Lion's Den.*
c. *Daniel in the Lion's Den.*

F.12.

CHAPTER VI. *Concerning Signs connected with other Occult Centres, such as the Heart.*

ONNECTED WITH THE heart are a whole series of signs of which three are definitely associated with that organ, whereas others cover the whole of the chest. It is with the first three that we shall deal in this chapter, as it will be found that very often two or three of them are combined to form a more complex sign.

Unfortunately, in sculptured or painted representations of these signs the artist has been compelled to fix one position, and it is therefore only when one has seen the whole series given together that one is able to say definitely that the three movements all work up towards one definite meaning.

The first sign is made by placing the hand over the heart, and survived as a polite gesture from a man when approaching a lady, at any rate as late as the 19th century. It was in this way that a courteous gentleman bowed to a lady before asking her for a dance in the mid-Victorian period. It was also customary in the 17th and 18th centuries for a gentleman to remove his hat, sweep it gracefully in front of his body, and bring hand and hat to rest over the heart, as a salutation to one of the opposite sex.

The right hand placed on the heart constantly occurs in ancient sculptures, an early example being a figure found in Crete, belonging to the Minoan period, illustrated in "Alt-Kreta" by H. T. Bossert. It apparently represents a priestess of the Minoan cult and the date would be not later than 2,000 B.C. In ancient Egyptian sculptures and frescoes numerous examples occur but one illustration must suffice. In the Vignette which heads the papyrus of Nu, now in the British Museum, the goddess Hathor appears, and behind her stands the deceased, who is making this sign with his left hand. Also in that which heads chapter 104 of the papyrus of Nebseni, the deceased is again depicted making the same sign.

Turning to Roman times, three excellent examples occur on a tomb now in the Arles Museum. Thereon are sculptured various Christian scenes, including Jonah and the Whale. The most significant figures, however, are those representing the man and woman who were buried in the tomb, evidently husband and wife, who are both depicted making this sign with the right hand. See F.12, reproduced opposite this page.

Coming to the tenth century, a Byzantine ivory triptych, now in the Louvre, shows several figures making signs, including two apostles who are making the one we are considering. This is illustrated opposite page 44.

In the atrium of St. Mark's Cathedral, Venice, a 12th Century mosaic representing the Creation adorns the dome, wherein most of the figures are making signs of a symbolic nature, and among them are three examples of the one we are considering. Thus Adam, on being reproved by God for having taken the apple, makes this sign, while Eve makes the Sign of Preservation.

In a 13th century mosaic in the Church of St. John Lateran our Lord is seen in glory, seated on a throne and supported on either side by the Saints and Apostles, several of whom are making signs, one being that under consideration.

It would be possible to go on quoting examples from century after century, but as to a large extent this is but a minor sign we will now turn to consider its meaning when it thus appears by itself. It seems to imply fidelity, either that the man so depicted has proved his faith, hence its use by the saints in glory, who have proved their fidelity to their Master both in life and death, or else it signifies faith in some person or, more usually, in some God.   Thus the Egyptian deceased, by his gesture, implies his faith in Hathor, who at this point in *The Book of the Dead* acts as his spokesman.   In the Roman example the two dead persons signify their faith in Christ and the fact that they died in the sure and certain hope of the resurrection because of the Christian faith to which they were faithful.

It is not difficult to see how this sign has evolved.   Among many nations the heart has been regarded not only as the centre of physical life but also of the principal attributes of the soul, such as love, fidelity and courage.   We constantly speak of true, or stout-hearted, and as early as the time of *The Book of the Dead* the phrase, "True of heart" had become a recognised formula.   It seems probable, indeed, that it is to ancient Egypt that we owe the outstanding symbolic importance in Europe of the heart as the centre of the emotions and as epitomising the soul of man.   In *The Book of the Dead* it is the heart of the deceased which is weighed by Anubis, and according to whether that organ proves to be true and faithful, or the reverse, the decision of the Egyptian gods is registered.   It should be noted, however, that not everywhere in the world is the heart so regarded.   Some races consider the stomach to be the centre of such emotions as love and courage, and the Chinese do not speak of a "stout-hearted man" but of an "iron-livered" and "copper-galled" individual.   In this connection it is as well to remember that though we do not speak of a stout-livered man, we designate a coward as a "white-livered cur."   So far I have been unable to trace the Sign of Fidelity among the Chinese, probably for this very reason.

This sign takes on a more important aspect in combination with that of Preservation, of which indeed it really constitutes a very considerable section, but before dealing with it in this form we will consider a curious variation which is so distinct that it must be regarded as constituting a separate sign, although this sign itself is sometimes combined with that of Preservation in order to give a slightly different meaning to that gesture.   If, instead of laying the hand flat on the heart it is clenched in such a way as to appear as if the man were gripping a piece of flesh which lies above that organ, this constitutes what may be regarded as a sign indicating *Tearing out the Heart*.   It is found in great numbers in the monuments of ancient Egypt, both alone and in combination with that of Preservation. A good example of it in the simple form is now in the British Museum. It depicts a scene painted on the wall of a tomb at Thebes, circa, B.C. 1500, wherein are seen a number of men and women seated on chairs and being waited on by two female attendants, who are giving them food and drink. It represents either an initiation ceremony or a supposed incident of the journey of the soul, through the Underworld, to Paradise, of which the ancient Egyptian Mysteries were a dramatic representation.

In order to prove that this sign is widely distributed, let us turn to ancient Mexico. In the illustration reproduced on page 35 Quetzalcoatl is depicted performing a ceremonial dance in front of a divine being, who looks out from Heaven and makes the sign of Preservation, but with the left hand pointing downwards instead of upwards. Quetzalcoatl is looking up towards him and with his left hand is plucking at his heart. In this example the hand is made to look like the head of an animal, no doubt to emphasise the point that the action symbolises tearing out the heart. This representation is important because Mexico gives us the key which unlocks the symbolism of the gesture. In that country it was customary to offer human sacrifices, and the most usual method adopted was to cut open the breast of the victim, tear out the heart and present it to the God. The meaning of this gruesome action was that the worshippers offered the life and, as it were, the soul of the victim to the gods. The man thus sacrificed was supposed to be received by the gods and henceforth to dwell among them in a happy paradise, there to plead the cause of men on earth. Therefore, the meaning of this sign is that the person making it offers to the god worshipped his whole life and soul. It is not merely a question of being faithful to the god, but rather that the worshipper voluntarily places his whole life at his disposal.

One or other of these two signs is often found in combination with a third movement, made with the other arm. If the right hand is placed on the heart, then the left arm is raised so as to form a square at the elbow, or the hands may be reversed, the right up and the left on the heart. In either case the action implies a prayer for preservation, as has been shown in Chapter III. If, however, only one hand is

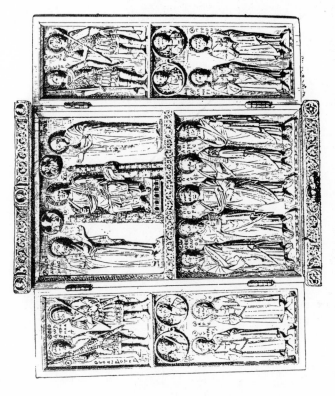

A BYZANTINE IVORY TRIPTYCH, NOW IN THE LOUVRE,
SHOWING CHRIST SURROUNDED BY SAINTS.

G. 5.

A 14TH CENTURY WOODEN CHEST CARVED WITH THE LEGEND OF ST. GEORGE AND THE DRAGON.

In the V. & A. Museum

K.25.

used, namely, the one raised with the elbow in the form of a square, this seems to imply, not a prayer for preservation, but an acknowledgment that the person making the sign has been, or is being, preserved. But it is dangerous to be dogmatic, for in certain examples it seems probable that the artist, being anxious to use the second hand for some other purpose, simply dropped the less important part of the sign, namely, the hand on the breast. There is, moreover, a third implication when the squared arm by itself is employed. The 14th century chest front illustrated opposite page 46, gives us two excellent examples of the use of this sign minus the hand on the breast. In the top, left hand corner St. George offers to preserve Sabra from the dragon. Now he is not praying to be preserved, and so the artist makes him merely square his left arm, leaving his right free to hold his horse by the bridle. In the scene beneath this one St. George is shown fighting the dragon, while Sabra is praying for his victory and is making the well known Sign of Prayer, that is to say, hands folded together. In the bottom, right hand corner of the carving Sabra is leading away the wounded dragon and is making the Sign of Preservation, with her left hand only, to show her father and mother, who are looking out from windows in their palace towards her, that she has been preserved.

On the other hand, on a similar carved chest front which, like the former, is in the Victoria and Albert Museum, is also 14th century, Flemish work, and is probably from the same school of carvers, we have scenes in the life of the Virgin, wherein there are no less than four examples of the sign of prayer for preservation. Thus, two shepherds, on seeing the angel appear in the sky, are not unnaturally perturbed thereat, and one of them is making this sign as a prayer for preservation. In like manner the Virgin makes the same sign to the angel at the Annuniciation.

Another picture which admirably shows the subtle difference between the meanings of the different forms of this sign is the Miniature from Queen Mary's Psalter, now in the British Museum which depicts the Marriage Feast at Cana and is reproduced as the frontispiece of this volume. It, like the chest fronts, is 14th century work, and the four principal characters are all making signs. The woman on the left is undoubtedly the bride herself, who is praying that she and her husband may be preserved from the disgrace which would be their lot if the supply of wine gave out.   The third figure from the left is the Virgin, as is shown by her crown; she has taken up the appeal of the bride and is asking our Lord to preserve the young couple from this disgrace.   Whether or not there is any special significance in the fact that the Virgin has reversed the position of her hands, that is to say has the right arm squared and the left across her breast, it is difficult to say.   It may be that thereby the artist meant to imply that she was praying, not on her own behalf, but on behalf of someone else, but it is also possible that he thought the figures would balance· better if thus arranged, for certainly they do.   Our Lord, Who is the second figure from the left, answers, "They shall be preserved," that is to say, He squares His left arm but His right lies negligently on the table.   Being Divine, He can guarantee Preservation, and does not pray for it.   The fourth figure is either St. John or the husband, but probably the former.   He is making the Sign of Fidelity with the right hand, to show his faith in our Lord's promise that the prayer of the young couple will be granted.   Thus by reading the signs we are able to obtain a clear insight into the emotions of the four principal characters as clearly as if the written text gave their words.

In connection with this subject, which was a very popular one in the Middle ages, readers should compare the Miniature from the Arundel Manuscript dealing with the same theme illustrated opposite page 8.   There they will see the Sign of Fidelity made with the left hand, but instead of making the sign which indicates a prayer for preservation the Virgin graphically depicts the distress of the young couple.

Having in Chapter III. dealt with this sign at considerable length and shown how it can be traced from the days of ancient Egypt up to the 20th century, it seems unnecessary to deal with it again in similar detail, but as there are one or two periods which were passed over somewhat lightly, in order to compress that chapter into a reasonable length, attention is now particularly directed to them.

We have already given Egyptian examples of the use of this sign, but it is interesting to note that Sir Wallis Budge in *The Egyptian Language*, pages 43 and 44, gives a selection of hieroglyphic characters with their phonetic values and meanings, which include at least four examples of it, and in three cases he translates them as having the phonetic value of *hen*, meaning "To Praise." In the fourth example, as the man is kneeling, he gives the phonetic value as *sa*, or *remt*, but does not attempt to translate it. Their numbers in his book are 7, 12, 93 and 89. From what has been written above, it will be seen that I should interpret this hieroglyph as meaning not so much praise, as prayer for preservation, and I regard the sign of the hands raised up in front of the face, phonetic value, *tua*, which he interprets "To praise or to pray," as more correctly representing *Praise*, than does the hieroglyph, *hen*.

It will be noticed that in the previous chapter we gave no examples of the use of the Sign of Preservation during the following epochs. The Greek period, i.e., 600—400 B.C. ; the Dark Ages, i.e., 6—10th centuries inclusive; the 11th century, and the 17th, 18th and 20th centuries, although I quoted a personal experience at Carthage proving that a 20th century Italian child used this sign during her prayers.

On a gold ring from Mycenæ illustrated in M. R. Dussaud's "La Civilisation Préhellenique dans la Bassin de la mer Egée" several women are shown performing a religious rite and one of them is making an excellent example of the Sign of Preservation. The date of this ring cannot be later than about 1000 B.C.

Nearly 500 years later we find the sign still in use, as will be seen by turning to page 48, opposite which is reproduced a picture of an Athenian black-figure hydria or water jar, circa, B.C. 550. A number of women are drawing water from a fountain and as the life-giving fluid falls into their jars they make the Sign of Preservation. Now assuredly it is correct to say that it is water, above everything else, which preserves not only human life but all life on earth, and that this sign should be depicted on a jar to carry water is not surprising. Numerous Roman examples have already been given, but the 4th Century Red Porphry Sarcophagus of the Empress Helena, shown opposite page 60, deserves a brief reference. Therein the kneeling Roman Soldier makes this sign lest by mistake his comrades should slay him for an enemy.

During the Dark Ages the continual ravages of predatory bands of warriors, such as the Danes, not only destroyed countless precious relics of the past, but interrupted the normal life of the times to such an extent that it is surprising that any examples of the art of the period have survived.   For the most part they are few and scanty, and are found mainly in certain favoured spots, where for some reason a strong defensive position, or other circumstances, rendered life more tolerable and gave opportunity for something other than self-defence. Byzantium was one such spot, and hence it is that many of the finest art relics of this period came originally from that city, where the ancient Roman tradition merged with that of Greece to form a new style.   In carvings in ivory and in early illuminated manuscripts especially, the Byzantine tradition played an important part, and from the 6th century onwards we have numerous examples of ivory carvings which emanated from· that school,   wherein   the   ancient traditional signs appear.

We shall have occasion in the next chapter to describe an ivory box of the 6th century, which is now in the British Museum, wherein the Sign of Distress appears, but we mention it now in order to prove that the ivory triptych now in the Louvre and illustrated opposite page 44, although of the 10th century, is the direct descendant of earlier work, which links it with ancient Rome.   In this particular example we not only have the Sign of Fidelity depicted in two places, as previously mentioned, but the two saints who stand on either side of our Lord in Glory are both making the Sign of Preservation.   In this example we find a good representation of a peculiarity often associated with this sign, namely, a deliberate squaring of the thumb on the hand of the arm which is squared.   This peculiarity is most frequently seen in cases where the artist has found it difficult to extend the arm straight out from the shoulder and was perhaps adopted to direct attention to the arm, whose squared position might have been missed by the observer, owing to the fact that the upper part of the arm is pressed rather close to the body.   A somewhat similar example, "G4," can be seen in the British Museum where, in an ivory panel of the same date, the angel is shown appearing to the shepherds, of whom one in the foreground is undoubtedly making this sign, and one behind him is probably so doing.

A third example, in an entirely different medium and at least 100 years earlier, is a Christian medallion engraved with the story of Susannah, made for Lothair, King of the Franks, probably about

AN ATHENIAN BLACK FIGURE WATER JAR
(B.C. 550).

D.2.

THE BAYEUX TAPESTRY.   EDWARD SENDS HAROLD AND A FRIEND TO
NORMANDY.

(C. 1080 A.D.)

H. 1.

860 A.D. (Reference "G3"). It is reproduced opposite page 72, and it will be noticed that while Susannah, the figure in the middle, is making the Sign of Distress, two onlookers are making that of Preservation, evidently praying that the poor lady may be preserved from the lying machinations of her accusers. It will be remembered that Susannah was falsely accused of misconduct by the two elders because she refused to misconduct herself with them.

Passing next to the 11th century, we find that the Bayeaux tapestry gives us ample proof of the importance of this sign at that date, as the illustration reproduced opposite page 50 shows. It must be remembered that this tapestry sets out to vindicate the character of William and to show that Harold behaved with great treachery and disloyalty, a view naturally not held by the Anglo-Saxon chronicler. The scene reproduced depicts Harold and another messenger being despatched by Edward to William with a message that the King has nominated him to be his successor to the English throne. Hence it is appropriate that both Harold and his companion on receiving their instructions should signify their assent by a gesture which may be interpreted as implying, "God preserve the King," the age-old formula of acquiesence by a subordinate to the orders of his superior. Readers should note the carefully squared thumbs of both messengers.

In like manner in the scene depicting Harold taking the oath of fidelity to William some of the on-lookers are making this sign as a prayer to Heaven that Harold would keep his obligation, for probably in their heart of hearts they suspected that he would not, while to break an oath sworn on the holy relics was considered mortal sin and in the case of Harold brought down on him a decree of excommunication from the Pope. In a third scene, we are shown the Coronation of Harold as King of England, and a crowd of onlookers is represented as saluting him with this sign, corresponding with the well known formula, "God preserve the King."

The Mediæval period has already been adequately covered, but there is one example of especial interest, namely, the front of a coffer in Ivory, now in the Louvre Museum, and illustrated opposite page 58. This is North Italian work of the 15th century and represents the Triumph of Renown, a theme very popular in the art of this period. Commencing at the left we have a series of heroes, beginning

with Hercules, who is easily recognisable because of the club he carries:
next comes Sampson with the jaw-bone of an ass, and after him Caesar:
next Judith bearing a head and making a variation of the sign we
shall discuss in the next chapter.   Semiramis, Helen and Cyrus follow
in that order, then comes Homer making a variation of the same sign
as that made by Judith, and finally Joshua, the character who
at the moment interests us.   There is a very old tradition that when
Joshua made the sun and the moon stand still he prayed to the
Almighty to continue the light of day, at the same time making the
Sign of Preservation, and we can see that this tradition was well
known to the 15th century sculptor who carved the front of this ivory
coffer, for not only is Joshua making the sign, but above his head is the
sun, standing still.

The association of this sign with this particular prayer is no
doubt because through the miracle the Jews were able to continue the
fight until they gained the victory, and so were preserved from defeat
at the hands of their enemies, but if the tradition has any basis in fact,
it would be because Joshua, who came from Egypt, had inherited the
sign from the Egyptian priests, for if we glance at the illustration
on page 12, entitled "Praising Ra at Sunset," we shall perceive that
this sign was already associated with the setting sun, and the prayer
was doubtless that it might be preserved during its dangerous journey
through the Underworld at night.

It is not necessary to refer again to other examples until we
come to the 17th century.   Despite the fact that the lamp of tradition
burnt low, owing to the Reformation in Northern Europe and the
predominance of Renaissance Art in South Europe, where a realistic
rather than a symbolic representation of sacred pictures was in vogue,
we have sufficient evidence to prove that the old symbolic ideas were
not entirely forgotten.   The English embroidered panel reproduced
opposite page 124, which is now in the Victoria and Albert Museum,
depicts Abraham feeding the Angels and the Sacrifice of Isaac.   One of
the angels is making the Sign of Preservation in answer to Abraham,
who on his knees is praying to the angels, of whom he appears to be
somewhat frightened.   It is important to note that Abraham makes
the full Sign of Prayer for Preservation, whereas the angel answers by
squaring one arm, but deliberately places the other on the table, show-

ing that he has answered the supplaint's prayer by a promise of preservation. In the background, the baby Ishmael, seated on his Mother, Hagar's knee, makes the full sign. It will be remembered that as a result of the visit of the angels and their promise Sarah gave birth to Isaac, and soon after demanded that Hagar and her son should be driven out into the desert, hence the fact that the child is making the Sign of Prayer for Preservation is significant.

Another example, of which the original is also in the Victoria and Albert Museum, is reproduced opposite page 12. It shows two roundels of Swiss or German painted glass, and in the second, depicting the Jews picking up manna under Moses' direction, we see God the Father, by the use of this sign indicating that He has thus preserved His chosen people. The other roundel depicts the Brazen Serpent and is discussed in the chapter dealing with the Sign of Distress. There is yet a third roundel of the same series which is not reproduced. This depicts Jacob's Dream of the ladder, at the top of which sits God, making the Sign of Preservation.

A mosaic, dated 1660, at St. Mark's, Venice, is illustrated opposite page 120. It shows the arrival of St. Mark's body at that city and several of the onlookers are making signs, including the one we are considering. This is made by a sailor in the boat, who thereby announces to the people on shore that they have brought the body safe and sound from Alexandria and owing to its presence on board the crew have been preserved.

Towards the end of the century, i.e., about 1695, we have another example of the use of this sign in the painted ceiling of the bedroom of William III. at Hampton Court. The painting represents Momus, the God of Sleep, surrounded by numerous allegorical figures, two of whom are making the Sign of Preservation, i.e., one arm squared only, denoting that by sleep men are preserved in health.

In the 18th century I have so far only traced three examples, one at Coire and another at Zurich, to which reference has already been made in Chapter III., and a third in a drawing by John Flaxman to illustrate Dante's *Paradiso*, iii. and xxxi., the original of which is in the British Museum. I also mentioned a 19th century example in the Cathedral at Carthage. Two more occur in the illustration reproduced opposite page 134: it shows the mosaic over the West door of

St. Mark's, Venice, made in 1830, wherein we have several examples of this sign language, including at least two of the signs we are now considering.   The picture represents our Lord in Glory coming to judge the world, and one of the angels, who is blowing his trumpet to summon the dead to rise, is making the sign, with one arm squared, thereby promising preservation to the good, but he does not *pray* for preservation because the hour for repentance is past.   One of the souls, who is apparently rising from his grave, also makes the same sign, although his may be a prayer for preservation, for although the squared arm is visible the other is hidden by another soul, who on rising is making a different, but very significant, sign.

Of 20th century examples quite a number are to be found and, significantly enough, they are all connected with monastic work.   It is just in such societies as those of monks and nuns that we should expect to find the old traditions strongest.   Thus, in the British Museum is an illumination of a Pastoral letter from Cardinal Mercier, by the nuns of Maredret, in Belgium, presented to the British Museum by the Abbess in June 1921.   The letter was despatched in 1914 to hearten the Belgian people, whose country was then occupied by the Germans.   One page is reproduced opposite, wherein the top picture represents Daniel in the Lion's Den, being fed by the prophet Habakkuk.   The latter makes the combined Sign of Preservation and Blessing, which is answered by Daniel with the left arm squared, to indicate that he recognises that he is being preserved.   Daniel is intended to symbolise Belgium and Habakkuk, U.S.A., who sent food to the Belgians during the German occupation.   Below, British and French troops come to the assistance of Belgium and attack the Germans, and one of the latter is making the Sign of Distress.   It should be noted that throughout the nuns have adopted the traditional style of illumination; even the soldiers are habited in mediæval armour and the ships belong to the same period, and there is no doubt that the signs thus employed are not accidental, but are deliberately chosen to convey to the initiated the inner feelings of the principal characters.

Coming nearer home, in the Abbey of Buckfast, which has been rebuilt during the 19th and 20th centuries by an Order of Benedictine monks who came hither from France, several of the altars, actually

AN ILLUMINATION OF A PASTORAL LETTER
OF CARDINAL MERCIER.
C.1915.

R.1.

THE REREDOS OF THE ALTAR IN THE CHAPEL OF ST. BENEDICT.
Buckfast Abbey.

R.5.

sculptured in the 20th century, contain panels, wherein various ancient signs occur, appropriately applied. Thus the altar of St. Benedict, reproduced opposite page 54, shows examples of three different signs, but it is to St. John, who stands beside our Lord on the Cross and prays for preservation, that I wish now to draw attention.

In the altar of Holy Souls, a photograph of which is opposite page 90, we see the dead rising from the sea at the call of the angels, and two are making the same sign, while in the altar to St. Joseph, in the panel depicting the marriage of St. Joseph to the Virgin, the Priest who is performing the ceremony makes it to show that he is praying for the preservation of the pair. It will thus be seen that the use of this sign can be traced from the days of the ancient Egyptians down to the present time, always with the same basic meaning, and in like manner it is to be found all round the world.

It has been necessary to devote considerable attention to this and to the Sign of Distress, which we shall consider in a later chapter, because they are by far the most important of all the mantric signs. No doubt by now my readers are beginning to ask how it is that this sign is so world-wide in its distribution, but as the same question will arise with regard to some of the others it seems best to leave this problem until we have tabulated and considered them all, when I shall endeavour to show that there is a perfectly reasonable theory to explain not only the ancient lineage but the wide distribution of these great signs of mantric power.

For the benefit of students there is printed at the end of the book a complete list of all the examples of the use of Mantric Signs which I have been able to collect. So as not to weary my readers I have only mentioned in the text a few Signs from each century or country, but, as will be seen on consulting the list, in many cases far more examples exist than have been quoted, and doubtless still more could be added.

Having in Chapter IV. given numerous examples of its use, it seems hardly necessary to produce further evidence, and a reference to the geographical areas in the lists at the end of this book should suffice. Nevertheless, for the purpose of regularity we will take a glance at the illustration opposite page 200, which represents a magnificent Hindu bas-relief.   Therein Vishnu is seen asleep under the Sacred Cobra, but he is about to arouse himself and descend to earth to help mankind against a giant.   Many of the figures are making mantric signs, but it is to that of Preservation made by one of the Gods who, seated on the clouds, are gazing down at Vishnu, that attention is directed.   The gesture tells the student that mankind will be preserved from the giant by Vishnu's descent to earth.

CHAPTER VII. Deals with Signs connected with the Occult Centre known as the Solar Plexus.

 F ALL THE OCCULT centres of the human body the solar plexus is regarded as the most important, and among mystics it has become associated with the emblem of "the point within the circle," which latter is a symbol of the Supreme Being. While in part this association is probably due to the obvious similarity between the navel and the geometrical figure, the connection is also largely owing to the fact that among mystics one of the recognised methods of obtaining the beatific vision is by gazing upon this point in the body. In particular this is the method adopted by the monks of Mount Athos, and it is probable that it is one of the most general methods used whenever the mystic attempts to obtain that highly advanced stage in his evolution.

For all that, however, among occultists it is considered that this is one of the most dangerous centres to arouse until the novice has advanced a considerable way along the path, and Masters warn their pupils that if the occult powers which are dormant there are aroused at too early a period the result may be physically disastrous. It is probably because of this fact that signs connected with the solar plexus seem always to bear as their fundamental idea the word "Destruction." Unfortunately we do not find many examples of these signs, but in almost every case identified they clearly have this significance.

In India, where the occult sciences are still followed, figures of Shiva, the Destroyer, are often depicted making a sign connected with this centre, and in the example illustrated opposite this page the God is not only placing his right hand over his solar plexus, but has folded his fingers so as to form the sign of the horns, thereby combining the sign which drives away the evil eye with that of Destruction, of which he himself is the embodiment. As if further to emphasise the fact that the sign does mean destruction, the sculptor has placed in that hand the lariat of death, for as such it is always described, although to the Western eye it looks almost more like a necklace. Shiva, of course, is the third person of the Hindu trinity, embodying the destructive side of the Deity, and so his use of this sign is perfectly appropriate. The fact that the horns are made further implies that in reality it is only the powers of evil who need fear the destructive side of Shiva, for although he is the Lord of Death and Destruction, he is also the Lord of Birth, through whose hands the dead man's soul passes once more into reincarnation. But the powers of evil can expect no such transmutation, and against them he is always represented as waging a ruthless war.

Although Shiva is pre-eminently the Lord of Destruction, while Vishnu symbolises the Preservative side of the Deity, there is one incarnation of the latter god, the so-called "Lion Incarnation," wherein he takes on many of the characteristics of Shiva. According to the legends, Vishnu descended in the form of a lion in order that he might overthrow a great ogre, who was oppressing the earth. Leaping upon him, he disembowelled him, and therefore representations of Vishnu in this incarnation are usually depicted with both hands placed over the solar plexus, thumbs pointing to the centre. In the illustration reproduced opposite page 144, the lion incarnation is depicted and Vishnu is shown coming out of a pillar which in splitting open forms the vesica piscis. The god himself, with both hands, makes the sign just described. It seems probable that the legend is an allegory of the dire results which may befall an occult student who, not

AN ALABASTER STATUE OF SHIVA.

U.9.

THE TRIUMPH OF RENOWN.

An Italian Ivory Coffer of the 15th Century.

L.35.

having achieved sufficient purity of life and evolution, endeavours through unworthy motives to arouse the latent powers of the solar plexus.

A third example, which is also Indian work and shows the more usual form of this sign, occurs in one of the sculptures at Borobudur. It depicts incidents in the life of an Indian prince who had just crossed to Java by ship and had nearly been wrecked. In the scene he is describing to his court his adventures and near escape from destruction, and while so doing makes a very perfect example of this sign with his right hand.

In China we find the sign in its double form, i.e., both hands pointing to·the solar plexus. Here it constitutes one of the Signs of the

Three of the Signs of the Five Elements used by the Hung Society, viz., of Earth; of Fire; of Water.

U.32, (a).

Five Elements in the Hung Society, a great and mysterious secret society which has a most wonderful ritual, symbolically representing the journey of the soul through the Underworld. In the course of the ceremony a large number of signs are employed, as is usual in ceremonies of initiation.[1] One group of these is called "The Signs of the Five Elements," for the Chinese recognise five, instead of four elements, as in the West, the fifth being gold, or metal. Now all these five signs represent examples of the great mantric signs we are

---

[1] See, *The Hung Society*, by J. S. M. Ward, M.A.

considering, and will be dealt with in their proper place, but the one we are now interested in is called "The Sign of Earth." Its association with earth is probably due to the fact that the Chinese consider this world to be the centre of the universe, as did the mediæval astronomers. By pointing to the centre of man this sign reminds the onlookers that the earth is the centre of the universe. Further, this element has always been regarded in symbolism as representing gross matter, and the thing which is peculiarly perishable, in opposition to the spiritual forces. In man the element of earth symbolises his physical body, which perishes, being liable to destruction by death and decay, in opposition to the immortal spirit, and so on closer investigation we see that in this example also the basic significance of destruction is still present. [1]

It is possible that this sign is also associated to some extent with an early form of sacrifice, which consisted of cutting the victim in half at the centre, just as the *Sign of Tearing at the Heart* refers to the method of sacrificing a victim by tearing out the heart and offering it to the gods. This method of sacrifice survived in the Philippine Islands until stopped by the Americans at the end of the 19th century. The Bagobos of Mindanao, one of the Philippine Islands, each December used to sacrifice a slave as a preliminary to sowing. The unfortunate victim was hung with his back to a tree, his heart was pierced with a spear and the body severed in twain at the waist line. The upper half was left hanging on the tree so that the fertilising blood might drain down into the soil. [2]

That either form of the above sign would bring to mind this method of sacrifice is obvious, and in view of the fact that both the *Sign of the Cutting of the Throat* and that of *Plucking out the Heart* clearly hint at a connection with methods of sacrifice, we cannot entirely ignore this aspect of the case, which may have helped to give additional sanction and emphasis to a sign of mantric power which perhaps was adopted for entirely different reasons.

I have not found many examples of this sign in Europe, but two striking representations which are illustrated in this book show that it is by no means unknown there. The first occurs in the frontispiece,

---

[1] See Illustration on the previous page.

[2] Fay-Cooper Cole, *The Wild Tribes of Davao District, Mindanao*. (Chicago, 1913), pp. 114 sq.

to our second volume which contains six pictures from the life of Christ, being a page out of the famous Arundel Manuscript, which was painted early in the 14th century.   The two bottom pictures depict, on the left hand, the Presentation of Christ in the Temple, and on the right, the Flight into Egypt.   In the former Joseph, who is holding a basket of doves in his hand, makes this sign, nor is the reason far to seek.   Every first-born male child among the Jews was dedicated to the Lord, but could be redeemed by offering in his place another life, the usual sacrifice being two or three turtle doves. Joseph, who is holding these birds in a basket, by this sign indicates their pending destruction.

Although the Canonical Books do not mention the fact, the apocryphal gospels state that during the Flight into Egypt as Christ passed the statues of the heathen gods they fell down, broken in pieces, and this incident was a very popular theme for the mediæval painter. In the example before us Joseph is making the Sign of Destruction with his right hand, while a male attendant behind is making it with his left.   In the extreme right of the picture we see one of the heathen statues on a pedestal, bending forward, as if about to fall down.

Another good example of the use of this sign occurs in the illustration shown opposite page 58 of a late 15th century Ivory coffer in the Louvre, which is described in some detail in the previous chapter. To the left of Joshua, who is making the Sign of Preservation, we see Homer, making the Sign of Destruction with his right hand, and still further to the left Judith, bearing the severed head of the general she had slain.   With her left hand she is making the Sign of Destruction, referring to the destruction of the hostile commander, whose death led to the dispersal of his army whereby she *saved* Jerusalem, but of course *destroyed* this enemy.   The reason she makes this sign is thus obvious and on careful consideration we shall see that it is likewise appropriate to Homer, whose great poem, *The Illiad*, deals with the destruction of Troy, not to mention the various heroes slain on both sides during the conquest.

It will thus be seen that this sign symbolises death and destruction, and we have shown that in every case quoted the artist has used it appropriately. The exact difference between the meaning of the sign according to whether one hand or both are placed on the solar plexus I have been unable to decide, but in addition to the examples already quoted this latter form of the sign appears on the illustration reproduced opposite page 80, which represents the Dancing Dervishes at Constantinople, and also in the Totem pole of a chief of the Haida Indians in Charlotte Island.   This pole, now in the British Museum, is illustrated on page 269 of *The Handbook of Ethnology*, published by that institution.   The fact that it has been found in such far distant parts shows that it must be a widespread sign, and I am yet hopeful of finding examples in Europe which will enable us more precisely to decipher its meaning.

THE RED PORPHRY TOMB OF THE EMPRESS HELENA.
Now in the Vatican Museum.

F.28.

THE SACRIFICE OF IPHIGENIA.
A Fresco from Pompeii. Circa A.D. 70.

Now in the Museum at Naples.

F.4.

CHAPTER VIII. *Wherein Signs connected with the Head are considered and more especially the Sign of Distress.*

MONG THE MOST important signs is that made by throwing up the hands with the palms turned towards the front, and slightly upwards, and then dropping them with three distinct motions to the sides. Thus it falls into three stages: the first, with the arms fully extended above the head; the second, with the arms bent and the hands in a line with the head; the third, with the hands in a line with the chin, after which they are dropped to the sides. In painting and sculpture all three stages are to be found, and in a few cases the artist has given an intermediate stage to indicate that the arms are in the process of dropping.

This is one of the widest and best known signs throughout the world, and even to-day among savage races it is regarded as having peculiar sanction, and if made will often save a traveller from an untimely fate. The 13th century "A" here shown contains a good example of it and it is as well to stress the fact that it is always regarded as a Sign of Distress, a last, desperate appeal for help. Nor is it difficult to see how in the very earliest times it took on this aspect. With the hands flung up above the head a man is absolutely helpless, for he cannot lower them to pick up a weapon without being immediately detected.   Thus   the   first   thing   that   an   American   horse thief is supposed to do is to call on his victim to raise his hands above his head, and when soldiers surrender they usually signify that fact by holding their arms upright above their heads.

In sculpture and painting care must be exercised not to mix this sign with another which may at first sight appear to be somewhat similar, but which on closer investigation can be perceived to be entirely different.   On Egyptian tombs and frescoes it is usual to see priests and priestesses worshipping or praising some Deity with uplifted hands, but the hands, instead of being held straight upright are sloped slightly forward, and the position clearly marks the first movement in bowing down to the ground, the Eastern salaam.   (See A1. on page 12). There is no excuse for mixing up the two signs.   The salaam implies reverence and praise, the Sign of Distress is an appeal for help.

In ancient Egypt we find several examples of this sign, thus painted reliefs in the Temple built at Bêt al Walî, in Nubia, by order of Rameses II, circa 1330 B.C., to commemorate his victories, contain examples of its use.   Copies of these are painted on the walls of the Egyptian Gallery of the British Museum.   The first represents a Libyan war, and depicts Rameses slaying Libyan prisoners, several of whom, not unnaturally, are making this sign.   Again, on a bas-relief in the Louvre, a man is shown being initiated into the Egyptian Mysteries and he also makes it.   Apparently it is a Pharoah who makes it to someone who may be regarded as the Hierophant, for he is seated at a sort of pedestal and above his head is a canopy.   Meanwhile two attendants, at a sign from the hierophant, are placing a collar round the suppliant's neck.   Passing next to ancient Crete, a curious votive figure illustrated in Bossert's *Alt-Kreta* proves that this sign was well known in Knossos.

Among the Phœnecians it appears to have been the regular symbol employed to mark the graves of those who were not priests or priestesses of Tanit, or, in other words, the common people.   In Chapter III, we have already drawn attention to the fact that the Priests, being fully initiated into the Mysteries of Tanit, or Astarte, signified by this sign that they lay down in a sure and certain hope of being preserved beyond the grave, but the ordinary laity had no such assurance and therefore their graves are marked by a crude figure of a man in a skirt, with his hands cast up to heaven. Very often this figure is accompanied by the caduceus of Mercury, the Messenger of the Gods, who was supposed to lead the dead through the Underworld, and by the open hand, which has survived to this day among the Mahomedans as the hand of Fatima. The drawing reproduced on page 17 gives an example of such tombstones, while a lamp found at Carthage and probably used in the temple ceremonies also bears this symbol. A reproduction of this is given below.

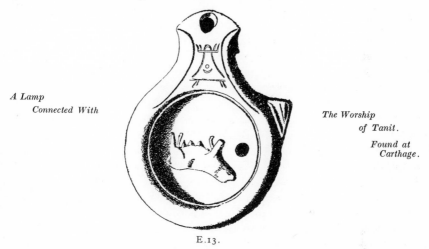

A Lamp
Connected With

The Worship
of Tanit.

Found at
Carthage.

E.13.

In this connection it should be remembered that the later Carthaginian art in many ways shows clear evidence that the original Punic culture had become considerably blended with Greek ideas, which probably accounts for the appearance of the caduceus, which is typical of the Greek Hermes and his Roman equivalent, Mercury. The conqueror of Carthage supplies a tremendous number of examples of the use of this sign. Two which pre-date the Christian era are deserving of special mention. The first is a fresco from Pompeii now in the National Museum, Naples, depicting the Sacrifice of Iphigenia. The unfortunate girl is being carried by Ulysses and another man towards the altar and artistic commentators lay stress on the fact that the way in which they are carrying her is extraordinarily unbusinesslike and awkward.   There is, however, a good reason.   The artist was anxious to depict the girl making this Sign of Distress, and only by representing her body in this somewhat awkward position was this possible.   To prove that this sign is no accident, I would also refer to a mosaic found in the ruined city of Djemila, Algeria, and now in the Museum on the spot.   It depicts the triumph of Amphitriton and all around him mermaids and other strange marine monsters are rising from the waters.   In the border a ship is shown in which a man, evidently frightened at the appearance of the god and his court, is frantically making this Sign.   For purpose of comparison with later examples, the fresco of the Sacrifice of Iphigenia is reproduced opposite page 62, and we will now pass to consider the relics of the Roman Christians, a period wherein we find a large number of examples.

In the Catacombs the soul is constantly depicted in this dramatic attitude, but one of the most interesting frescoes therein is the Sacrifice of Isaac, reproduced opposite this page, wherein both Abraham and Isaac are making this sign.   The work is late 3rd or early 4th century A.D..   It will be remembered that there is a good deal of similarity between the Biblical story and the Greek legend of Iphigenia ; in the latter case Artemis sent as a substitute a deer, and in the former Jehovah sent a ram.   The fact that Isaac and Abraham are depicted making the same sign as Iphigenia, in a work three centuries later, is a valuable link in the chain of evidence showing how these Mantric signs passed down from generation to generation with their inner meaning unchanged.   Another fresco showing the use of this sign is also given on the same page.   Both of these are from the Catacombs of Calixtus, as is likewise the fresco of St. Cecilia, wherein the saint is depicted making this sign, which in view of her martyrdom is quite appropriate.   It is reproduced opposite page 66, and is of the 5th or 6th century, while below her is a 9th century fresco of our Lord making the Sign of Preservation.

One scene wherein again and again we find the principal character making this sign, is that of Daniel in the Lions' Den.   Thus on a fourth century, stone sarcophagus in the Catacombs of St. Calixtus, Daniel, with a lion on either side of him, is shown making it, and a

THE SACRIFICE OF ISAAC.

F.20.

A SYMBOL OF THE EUCHARISTIC CONSECRATION.

Two 3rd—4th Century Frescoes in the Catacombs of St. Calixtus.

F.21.

A 4TH CENTURY SARCOPHAGUS IN THE CATACOMBS OF ST. CALIXTUS, ROME.
Depicting Daniel in the Lion's Den.
F.10.

A 6TH CENTURY FRESCO OF ST. CECILIA WITH A 9TH CENTURY FRESCO OF
⌊CHRIST BENEATH IT.
In the Catacombs of St. Calixtus.
F.23.

little farther on the soul of the deceased is also depicted in the same attitude.[1]

Two rather more elaborate sarcophagi in the Museum at Arles, which are also of the 4th century, again depict Daniel making precisely the same sign, once more accompanied by his two lions, the position of the hands, low down and in the third stage, being the same in both cases. These are reproduced opposite page 42.

Another interesting example, in an entirely different material and from a third district, is the Glass Disc with scriptural subjects found at Cologne, likewise of the 4th century. The original is in the British Museum and is reproduced opposite page 68 Here we have three representations of the use of this sign. The first is made by Daniel, who can be recognised by two lions on his right ; the second by the Widow of Nain, whose distress over the dead child makes its use most appropriate, and the third, unfortunately somewhat damaged, represents the distress of the three children in the fiery furnace, who are in a compartment immediately to the right of Daniel. Its use in this connection is of importance because, as we shall see later, the Copts in Egypt depicted the same theme and showed the same sign being made, but another interesting point is the fact that members of the Hung Society use this sign and call it *The Sign of Fire*.[2]

Numerous other examples of the use of this sign among the Romans are given in the list at the end of the book, but we have only time to draw attention to two. One is a 4th century Roman tomb, now in St. Mark's, Venice, the front of which is sculptured with two rows of figures. Those in the lower row represent the deceased, presumably at the moment of death, and are all making this sign of Distress, whilst in the upper row is depicted the risen man in Paradise, making a different sign and one to which we shall allude in a later chapter. The last example is a 4th century engraved gem, representing the Good Shepherd, bearing on His back the lost sheep, and with his hands in such a position as to suggest the Sign of Preservation. Behind him a soul makes the sign we are discussing, apparently pleading with the Good Shepherd to save him also. At the extreme right of the Gem,

---

[1] See illustration opposite page 66.

[2] See illustration on page 57.

Jonah is depicted falling into the sea.   This gem is reproduced on page 27.

We will now turn to the part of the Roman Empire which, under the protection of Byzantium, was able for a time to retain some traces of its old Roman Civilisation, though much altered.   The Coptic fresco from Wadi Sarga, in Egypt, which is now in the British Museum, belongs to the 6th century and depicts the three children in the fiery furnace, and certain Saints.   The part showing the children is reproduced opposite page 208, and is of particular interest because it shows the sign in two positions.   The two children on either side have their arms practically fully extended, but the one in the middle has reached the second position, with the hands on a line with the forehead.   In addition the scene is flanked by two large figures of Saints, namely, St. Cosmos and St. Damian, between whom stand three smaller figures, representing their brethren, all five of whom make the sign. One peculiarity of the figures is the fact that all three of the children wear the famous Phrygian hat which is associated with the Cult of Attis.   Probably, however, this implies nothing more than that the artist wished to intimate they were not Egyptians but people from Syria.

From Byzantium itself comes striking corroboration of the persistence of this Sign of Distress, in the form of a carved Ivory Box of the 6th—8th Century, now in the British Museum.   This is also reproduced, opposite page 70, and the observer cannot fail to be impressed not only by the survival of the sign, but by the presence of the two lions which appear on the Roman sarcophagi.

Coming next to the 9th century, it is interesting to find that despite the apparent chaos created by the barbaric invasions the traditions had not died out.   Another ivory carving, which depicts the Judgment of Solomon, is now in the Louvre.[1]   It should be noted that it is German work and therefore proves that the German invaders quickly absorbed the traditions of late Roman art.   This was probably due to the fact that at the re-establishment of the Holy Roman Empire the Germanic conquerors came into touch with Papal Rome and also with the Lombardic King, who in the middle of the 7th century granted a charter to a Roman Guild of Masons which had survived on the island of Comacina in the middle of Lake

---

[1] See reproduction opposite page 204.

Como. It is generally believed that these Comacine masons, as they became called, spread through Gaul and Germany to Britain in the 9th and 10th centuries, bringing with them that style of architecture which in North Italy is called Lombardic, in France and Germany, Romanesque, and in England, Saxon and, later, Norman.   If so it is probable that the appearance of this sign is directly due to the influence of these Comacine Masons.

In the scene depicted a soldier is about to divide the child in half, and the false claimant has extended her hands at an angle of about 39°, a sign, which, as we shall see later, seems to be associated with the phrases, "It is all over," "That finishes it," or, "It is finished."   But the true mother raises her hands to Solomon in deep distress, pleading for the life of the child.   In the upper part of the panel two of Solomon's attendants are making the Sign of Fidelity.

A second example is a crystal medallion made for Lothair, King of the Franks, which is now in the British Museum.   On it is engraved the story of Susannah, who, in the centre, is represented standing before the judge and making the Sign of Distress as her accusers relate their lying tale.   In another part of the medallion the two villains are receiving the just reward of their sins and one is making this sign. In Chapter VI we have already pointed out that the Sign of Preservation also appears on this medallion, which is reproduced   opposite page 72.   Although it seems most probable that the German carver who made the ivory carving and the engraver who engraved this crystal medallion inherited the tradition from ancient Rome, we have independent literary evidence that the Norsemen knew and venerated this sign, for it is referred to in fairly clear language at least twice in the Eddas.[1]

In the first instance it is associated with fire, as in the Hung Society of China, for we are told that Frey climbed to the high throne of Odin, from which it was possible to see all that took place in the whole world.   He chanced to turn his eyes towards Yotunheim, i.e., Giantland, and saw a most beautiful giantess raise her white arms above her head.   Her arms flamed like streaks of lightning in the darkness, whereupon he fell in love with her and subsequently married her.   It is generally agreed by scholars that her arms symbolised the lightning.   If this incident stood alone we should be justified in

---

[1] See Ward, *The Hung Society*. Vol, II., p. 144-5.

disregarding it, as a reasonable explanation exists which might make it appear to be an accident, but the second incident, which associates this sign with distress, cannot be brushed aside.   When Odin sent the Valkeries throughout the whole earth bidding them call on all things to weep for the slain Baldur, on their return to Odin they announced with streaming eyes and this appropriate gesture "all the world weeps, and we weep with it."   We thus see that the Norse of the 9th and 10th centuries regarded this as a Sign of Distress.

In the Bayeux tapestry, made about A.D. 1080, in the section depicting the Normans crossing to Pevensey, the man at the bow of one of the boats, who is on the lookout, makes this sign.   A reproduction appears in Vol. III of *The Encyclopedia Britannica*, opposite page 557, 11th edition.   Of the same century is a bas-relief of the stoning of St. Stephen in the cloisters of St. Trophime, Arles, which is shown opposite page 214.

Two particularly interesting examples of the use of this sign in the 12th century occur in illuminated letters from the Winchester Bible.   One, a capital B, is illustrated opposite page 76.   In the upper half thereof Christ is shown casting out a devil from a sick man which as it issues from the patient's mouth makes this sign.   On the other hand, the onlookers are making the Sign of Preservation. The other is a capital U, and also depicts the expulsion of a devil, who is flying away making this sign, while a crowd of onlookers make the Sign of Preservation.   We can quite understand the mediæval artist feeling a certain malicious glee as he drew the devil thus exhibiting his distress at having to depart from the abode in which he had taken up his residence.

The next example to which attention must be directed consists of scenes engraved in the interior of a bronze bowl of the 12th century, which is now in the British Museum and is reproduced opposite page 222.   The scenes represent incidents in the legend of St. Thomas the Apostle, and in two places he is shown making this sign, while in a third case another man is making it, although his left hand has all the fingers save the forefinger closed on the ball of the hand.   The exact, subtle difference here intended is not easy to unravel.   In addition, the Sign of Preservation appears twice, as further proof that the use of the Sign of Distress is intentional.

A 4TH CENTURY GILDED GLASS DISC FROM COLOGNE.

F.22.

A BYZANTINE IVORY CARVED BOX,
Now in the Brit. Mus.
Showing Daniel in the Lion's Den.
6-8th Century.

G.7.

FOUR SCENES FROM A ROMANCE.
A Carved Ivory Coffer of the 14th Century.

K.14.

In the Mosaic at Torcello Cathedral, a part of which has already been reproduced, it appears although, unfortunately, in a portion of the fresco not shown in our picture. One scene is of the beast of the Apocalypse and some of the people on beholding it make this sign. On the other hand, in the tympanum of the door, near the section already reproduced, the Virgin appears making this gesture, symbolising her distress at the sight of the lost souls on her left hand.

It is unnecessary to go on multiplying examples and one more must suffice. In the fresco from Chaldon Church, Surrey, reproduced opposite page 224, one of the souls falling from the ladder of salvation into hell is thus testifying to his distress. The particular figure has one foot resting on the first, or lowest, rung of the ladder.

In the 13th century a representation of Hell, in mosaic, in the Baptistery at Florence shows a soul being attacked by a hideous frog-like monster, and the unfortunate victim is making this sign, while in another part of the same mosaic, depicting the Descent from the Cross, one of those assisting is also making it. But perhaps the best example, from the same vast mass of mosaics, occurs in the scene in which the Sons of Jacob are bringing to their father the many coloured coat of Joseph, stained with blood. The old man sinks his hand on his head and makes that sign which later we shall prove indicates regret, while the mother throws up her hands to heaven in the manner we have been describing. This part of the mosaic is reproduced opposite page 74.

In a previous chapter we drew attention to the 14th Century illustration opposite page 8, which represents the Slaughter of the Innocents and the Marriage Feast at Cana. The Virgin's distress, as she appeals to our Lord to preserve the young couple from disgrace, is admirably shown, while in the scene of the Slaughter of the Innocents, the woman who is kneeling at the extreme left of the picture has good cause thus to express her feelings. It will be noted that while the Virgin is making the second position of the sign, the bereaved mother is making the third, or last, position.

We have now come to a period wherein any number of examples of this sign are to be found. In frescoes and in paintings, in illuminated manuscripts, stained glass and sculpture work, this and other mantric signs continually appear. An excellent example occurs on

a carved ivory coffer which is now in the Louvre Museum and a reproduction of which appears opposite this page.   This panel is of
particular interest because, unlike most of the others, it has on it a
secular theme, evidently from one of the Romances of the period,
and the whole story at once becomes far more intelligible if we are able
to interpret the signs.   The left hand compartment shows the maid's
discovery of her mistress dead or dying, probably the former.   At
any rate, she is praying that her soul may be preserved.   In the next
compartment, the dead woman's lover is seen committing suicide and
the maid throws up her hands in distress at the terrible sight.   In the
3rd compartment a man is drawing the sword out of the body of the
lover, but the lady's maid points with one hand to heaven and the
other to earth, a very widespread sign, which in the West is usually
associated with our Lord and indicates that He descended to earth
and subsequently reascended.   Here apparently, however, the maid
is telling the new-comer that it is too late to save the lover, for his soul
has ascended to heaven and his body must descend to earth.   Thus
in this example we have a very happy combination of the use of
three signs, whose correct interpretation greatly enhances the interest
of the whole scheme of decoration.

In like manner several signs appear in the illustration from
Dante's Paradise which is reproduced opposite page 92.   Dante
appears four times in this one miniature, but it is his first appearance,
at the left hand side of the picture, which now attracts our attention.
This is not the only case in which he is shown in this manuscript
making this sign, for in a miniature depicting the appearance of Fraud
in Hades, Dante throws up his hands in distress, but it does not seem
necessary to reproduce this as well, particularly as the original is in
the British Museum and can be consulted by any student.

We cannot spare time for a detailed consideration of most of the
examples quoted at the end of the book, but before passing to the
15th century feel we must draw attention to a fine 14th century fresco
at St. James's Church, Southleigh, which is well worth a visit.   It
represents the Last Judgment and the souls coming up from their
tombs include four who are praying to be preserved, while three seem
to have very grave doubts concerning their safety and prove it by
making the Sign of Distress.   Two certainly are on the side of the

fresco which indicates damnation, while another seems to be saying, "Alas, alas, my life has been in vain! "

The 15th century alabaster sculpture shown opposite page 20 is now in the Victoria and Albert Museum.   It represents the Incarnation, and the Second Person of the Trinity is descending towards the Virgin in the Vesica Piscis, while above the First and Third Persons are seen seated.   God the Father makes the Sign of Fidelity combined with that of Blessing, whereas God the Holy Ghost makes the Sign of Blessing, but the thumb is turned down on to the third and fourth fingers, leaving only two fingers erect.   This is a somewhat unusual sign and generally only made by the Second Person of the Trinity. Below Him one of the attendant virtues is holding her scroll in such a way as to suggest the Sign of Preservation, which is more clearly made by another virtue who, instead of the usual angel, is here announcing the message to the Virgin.   The latter, contrary to the general practice, is making the Sign of Distress, which evidently refers to her protest, how could she have a son as she had not known a man?   Although unusual, this position on the part of the Virgin is not unique, for there is a very good example at Wells Cathedral, where the work is probably a century earlier.   The combined interpretation of these signs would be as follows:—

God the Father, by the Sign of Fidelity, testifies to the fact that He has been faithful to the promise which He made to Adam, that He would send His Son to redeem man from the effect of Adam's fall. God the Holy Ghost blesses the Virgin with the Sign of the Second Person, to indicate that it is through Him she will conceive God the Son.   The Virtue holding the scroll declares to the Virgin that she will be preserved despite the unusual event which is about to take place, a reference of course to Joseph's dream, while the Virtue who is announcing the news to Our Lady is telling her that she will be Mother of the Preserver of the World.

The next two examples both represent scenes of the Last Judgment.   In the foreground of the picture shown opposite page 234 we see the damned falling into Hell, while the good souls are on the further side of the river.   One, on this side of the river, has made the Sign of Distress, which appears to have been answered, for he is floating away from the damned towards the saved.   The other example is from a Flemish Book of Hours, now in the Bodlein Library, and is reproduced opposite page 92. To the right of the picture we see St. John the Baptist making the Sign of Preservation, while several of the souls rising from their graves are making different signs, among them a man in the foreground, who is making the first position of the Sign of Distress.

Stained glass is no exception to the general rule, and although owing to the difficulty of the light reproductions thereof are not easy to obtain, I am fortunately able to show opposite page 78 a section from the West window of Fairford Church, Gloucester. There are several examples of the use of this sign in this window, but the portion reproduced here, and which represents a lost soul being carried off by one of the devils, gives a particularly excellent one. Readers should compare this with the Roman fresco of the unfortunate Iphigenia. Another representation of the Last Judgment, this time a fresco at the Church of St. Thomas, Salisbury, appears opposite page 216. Here the good souls are making the Sign of Preservation and a lost soul, the second position of the Sign of Distress.

Before leaving this century, however, there is one more picture which deserves particular attention. It is the fresco by Fra Angelico at St. Mark's Monastery, Florence, shown opposite page 184, and depicts the Circumcision. It is particularly important because it is seldom that our Lord is shown making this sign during this incident, although other examples exist. Its chief interest however lies in the fact that when a boy in East Africa is about to be circumcised he makes this sign as an intimation to the operator to begin. We shall refer to this in the next chapter, but it seems desirable to draw attention at this point to the fact that the Sign of Distress is thus associated with this operation in two such different parts of the world.

The examples chosen to illustrate the use of this sign in the 16th century have been so selected as to give specimens of five types of illustrative work. The tapestry panel from Hampton Court, which, by gracious permission of His Majesty, the King, is reproduced opposite page 202, was probably purchased by Cardinal Wolsey, and apart from the use of the sign is of interest because the Trinity is represented by three crowned figures, instead of in the more usual form—God the Father above, with the Son on the Cross and the Holy Ghost in the semblance of

A CRYSTAL MEDALLION ENGRAVED WITH THE STORY OF SUSANNAH
Made for Lothair, King of the Franks.

G.3.

A SECTION OF THE MOSAIC IN CUPOLA OF THE BAPTSTERY AT FLORENCE.
Depicting Joseph's Coat being shown to Jacob and other Scenes.

J.12.

a dove.   The tapestry tells the story of the Seven Deadly Sins and in the forefront we see Justice, represented as a woman brandishing a drawn sword, attacking a man, who symbolises Everyman, but Mercy intervenes to save man from the just reward of his sins, while an onlooker in terror makes the Sign of Distress.   In another scene, at the right hand top corner, a man is being stabbed in the heart with a javelin and by this sign calls for aid.   This is one of a series of four tapestries, and in the fourth piece appear several signs, including the one we are considering, which is made by various people who are being threatened by Justice.

Hampton Court Palace is indeed a happy hunting ground, for among the pictures and on the tapestries appear many representations of this and numerous other signs, but one more example must suffice.   A picture representing Death and the Last Judgment, No. 525, hangs in the public dining room and is the work of Marten Heemskerk, and here, as might be expected, we find a man showing his terror at the fate awaiting him, in the usual dramatic manner.

This is not the only place near London which well repays careful study, for in the National Gallery examples occur, as is shown by the picture reproduced opposite page 108.   It is by Piombo, an artist of the Venetian School, and was painted between 1517 and 1519.   The subject is the Raising of Lazarus and behind our Lord an old man is throwing up his hands in distress, apparently appalled by the sight of the rising corpse, while near by a woman, possibly Martha, makes another important sign, signifying horror at some terrible sight, a sign we shall discuss in detail later.   In the foreground, on her knees, is Mary, the sister of Lazarus, who makes the Sign of Fidelity, thus signifying her wonderful faith in the Lord and her trust that He could triumph even over death itself.   By the use of these two signs the artist has most skilfully depicted the different attitudes of the two sisters; Mary, faithful and trusting; Martha, essentially practical and rather materialistic, for we must remember that it was she who said that he had been dead three days and buried, and by now he stank.

As further proof that it is not necessary for my readers to go far afield in order to test the reliability of my theory that mediæval artists used a traditional language of signs to depict emotions and sentiments, the next picture, reproduced opposite page 132, is chosen from the Victoria and Albert Museum.   It is an illustration from a Printed Book of Hours, of about 1527, and the subject is the Birth of Christ. Herein almost every character is making some sign.   Thus, the shepherd in the background, with his hands folded together, makes the usual Sign of Prayer, whilst a baby angel raises his hands in distress at seeing his King, Whom he knew in the Courts of Heaven, in such humble surroundings as the delapidated stable, which He has to share with the ox and the ass.   But the Chirst Child makes the Sign of Preservation, while the Virgin is shown with yet a fourth sign, concerning which we shall speak later.

Our next illustration, shown opposite page 186, is from a fresco in the Town Hall of Basle.   It is a particularly fine example of the Judgment Day and unusually rich in Mantric Signs, of which there are at least five.   As we propose towards the end of the book to translate all of these, we will not now discuss it in detail, but will merely indicate that the sign we are at the moment interested in is made by the man in the foreground, whose back is towards us.   The section representing our Lord descending has been left out of the picture, but it is towards Him that the grief-stricken man is looking.

When we come to the 17th century we find that the influence of the Reformation in Northern Europe largely put an end to Ecclesiastical work.   Although not all the Protestant bodies took up the drastic attitude adopted by Calvin, yet it was rather an age of destruction than one during which men lavished wealth on beautifying churches. For the main part art tended to devote itself to satisfying the increased demand for luxury among the wealthy laity, who had often become rich through the plunder of the Church.   This fact is sufficient to account for the apparent pausity of examples which I have been able to discover, but it is not the only cause.   Even in countries such as Italy, where the demand for religious subjects continued and the old traditions in ecclesiastical matters held uninterrupted sway, the culminating effect of the Renaissance resulted to a great extent in art abandoning the shackles of symbolism and aiming rather at a naturalistic representation of all subjects, including even scriptural and ecclesiastical things, which till then had been peculiarly associated with the traditional sign language.

Nevertheless, the tradition was not entirely lost and certain mediums, such as mosaics, continued faithfully to carry it forward, even into the 19th century.   At the same time individual artists seemed deliberately to have adhered to the old traditions, although obviously influenced by the naturalistic school.   Of these Guercino, a Venetian artist who died in 1656, is an outstanding example, and he utilised his obvious knowledge of these signs not only in strictly scriptural scenes, such as the painting of Christ driving out the money changers from the Temple, which is now in the Palazzo Rosso at Genoa and is reproduced opposite page 196, but also in what appears to be a non-religious subject, which is now in the possession of the Supreme Royal Arch Chapter of Scotland.   This latter picture is also reproduced, opposite page 194, and is usually entitled, *The Raising of the Master*.   Four men, apparently building operatives, have discovered the dead body of a man, and one of them is removing a rod which seems to have lain on his body ; another is dangling a pair of compasses in his hand, evidently to show his profession, while the man in the corner is testifying to the distress which all of them feel at finding their friend thus dead.

It is interesting to compare the two pictures and to note that exactly the same sign is made by one of the money changers as he rushes away from our Lord in the Temple.   But this is not the only sign shown in the latter picture, for if we turn to page 196, where it is reproduced, we shall perceive that a man in the extreme left, who has fallen down, is apparently drawing his hand across his forehead, with the palm outward.   This is a rare, but not unique, example of another sign, which apparently also indicates acute distress, and we shall discuss it later.   Attention, however, is drawn to it now to prove that Guercino by thus introducing into one picture two signs meaning distress shows that he was well acquainted with the ancient Sign Language, and it is probable that a careful investigation of all his pictures would reveal the use of other signs.

We have already mentioned that in the more restricted field of mosaics the use of symbolic signs continued almost unabated, due, no doubt, to the very fact that the nature of the art rendered it less practical to adopt the naturalistic style.   The example shown opposite page 120 was made in 1660, and appears over one of the West doors of St. Mark's Cathedral, Venice. It contains representations of no less than three signs, each used appropriately. The sailor in the ship, who is making the Sign of Preservation, thus testifies to the fact that the ship which bears the body of St. Mark has been preserved during its perilous voyage, for the scene represents the arrival of this body at Venice, but the man in the foreground is clearly dramatically relating the difficulties and dangers through which they have passed, and the distress in which they have been. Concerning the third man who is in the ship, with his hands crossed on his breast, we will speak in a subsequent chapter. It is hardly necessary to draw attention to the two clergy who are making the Sign of Prayer or to the third, who is making that of Fidelity.

Despite the iconoclastic tendencies of the more extreme reformers on the Continent, the use of stained and painted glass wherein were depicted scriptural scenes by no means vanished entirely, and the two roundels reproduced opposite page 12 give us a couple of interesting examples of German, or possibly Swiss, treatment of this subject. The first represents Moses and the Brazen Serpent, and in the background a woman, on seeing the corpses, casts up her hands in the Sign of Distress, while in the foreground a man is kneeling and looking towards the emblem. The other miniature, which shows the Israelites picking up manna in the desert, has already been described in the chapter dealing with the Sign of Preservation, as has also the third roundel which accompanies it, but which is not reproduced.

During the 18th century the lamp of symbolism burnt dim, but I have no doubt that other examples than the one I am now quoting exist. In a drawing of Dante listening to the tale of Ugolino, by Henry Fuseli, R.A., that poet is depicted making this Sign of Distress as he listens to one of the most tragic tales recorded in *The Inferno*. The original is in the British Museum and it is important to note that Fuseli drew it in 1777 while he was staying at Rome, the very place where one would naturally expect to find the old traditional mantric signs still known and used.

Moreover, we have proof that this science is still known to-day, and so a mosaic made in the 19th century containing this Sign may very well indicate that the men who made it knew perfectly well what they were doing. It is over a side altar in St. Peter's, Rome, and depicts

AN ILLUMINATED "B" FROM THE WINCHESTER BIBLE.
Showing (a) Christ Casting out a Devil. (b) The Harrowing of Hell.

I.i.

A STAINED GLASS WINDOW,
DEPICTING A SCENE FROM THE LAST JUDGMENT.

In Fairford Church, Glos.

L.30.

St. Peter raising a beggar.   The incident is, of course, the healing of the lame man at the Gate Beautiful, and we are told in the Bible that St. Peter raised him by taking his right hand.   Now the man who made this mosaic has most carefully depicted a certain grip, which, as we shall have cause to see later, clearly has some special significance, as it occurs in other examples of an earlier date.   Meanwhile St. John makes the Sign of Fidelity, while a woman makes the third position of the Sign of Distress.   Thus we have three significant gestures in a 19th century mosaic, and although it is possible to say that the work-men have merely copied an old picture, the fact that in another 19th century mosaic, which is at Venice, two mantric signs are clearly made, and that there is no reason to think that this was copied from a Mediæval picture, shows that the old knowledge had not died out. As these mosaics at St. Peter's were all made by artists of a special school attached to the Cathedral, it is less surprising to find an artistic and symbolic tradition surviving among them than in independent work done elsewhere.   We shall have occasion to refer to the mosaic at Venice, which is reproduced opposite page 134, in a subsequent chapter, but as proof of the survival of the tradition it had to be mentioned here.

Two examples of work done in the 20th century are reproduced, and it is significant that each is the work of a Monastic community, exactly the place where we should expect reverence to be paid to old traditions and a knowledge of the meaning of such signs to be pre-served.   The illumination of a Pastoral letter, sent by Cardinal Mercier and shown opposite page 52, has already been described in Chapter VI., therefore all that now seems necessary is to point out that at the bottom of the picture British and French troops are shown com-ing to the assistance of Belgium and attacking the Germans. one of whom is making the Sign of Distress.   Now the important fact to note here is that no original for such a design could exist, and further-more, the whole design is avowedly intended to be symbolical.

The other example is a carved stone reredos in the Chapel of the Holy Souls at Buckfast Abbey Church, shown opposite page 90, and if we examine the bas-reliefs we shall find more than one example of mantric signs.   Thus, in the top left panel the souls are shown rising from the sea, one of whom is making the Sign of Preservation, and careful examination of the picture will reveal a second example. On the other hand, in the right hand upper panel one of the souls rising from the sea is making the 3rd position of the Sign of Distress. If any body might be expected to retain the old traditions assuredly that body is the Order of Benedictines, the most ancient monastic order in the Western world, a few of whose members have themselves been building this church.

Other examples of the use of mantric signs occur in the sculpture work of this Abbey and thus we have been able to show that this Sign of Distress comes down in an ordered sequence from the dim, red dawn of time and is still understood in the 20th century by those who have not lightly cast aside the old traditional wisdom. It now behoves us to show that this sign is not only ancient but widespread, and so abundant is the evidence that it must form the subject of the next chapter.

Before doing this, however, we will refer back to the other form of this sign mentioned on page 75. It appears to imply that the one making it is wiping from his brow the sweat which his grief and distress have engendered, and an early example, of the 11th century, is reproduced opposite page 198. It is an ivory carving of the Crucifixion, from Cologne. At the lower, left hand corner, an onlooker casts up his hands to Heaven, while on the right, St. John indicates his distress by wiping his temple. Several other mantric signs occur, in this piece of work, including that of Regret, a sign to which we shall refer later. It is significant that, as in the picture by Guercino, both the alternative forms of this sign are shown in the same work.

CHAPTER IX. *Which indicates the Widespread use of the Sign of Distress.*

ECAUSE WE HAVE already shown that the Sign of Distress can be traced from the 3rd millenium B.C. down to the present day in various parts of Europe, and further that its use can be demonstrated in most of the countries of that Continent, we need spend no further time thereon, but will immediately pass to Asia. Starting with the Near East, there is clear evidence that this sign is well known to the present generation of Arabs, for when passing through the Red Sea on a steamer in 1917 a friend of mine noticed an Arab boat which was obviously sinking, and a man ran to the bow of it, threw up his hands to heaven, and dropped them with three distinct motions. He repeated this action several times, evidently in the hope of arousing the pity of the captain of the passing steamer. It is pleasing to be able to say that the Captain, on seeing the sign, changed the course of his ship, and rescued the crew of the Arab vessel, which latter sank within half an hour.

That this sign is well known to the various Orders of Dervishes is perhaps not altogether surprising. There are quite a number of distinct Orders, who all seem to have elaborate rituals of initiation, which include passwords and the use of signs, such as those we are discussing.   Among these is the Sign of Preservation and the Sign of Destruction, i. e., the hand across the Solar Plexus, previously described.   The illustration reproduced opposite this page is by a 17th century Turkish artist and represents the Dancing Dervishes at Constantinople.   In it we can recognise one example of the Sign of Preservation and three of the Sign of Distress, the hands in each case being in a slightly different position.

Now it must be remembered that the Dancing Dervishes are not like an ordinary group of dancers, who perform for the delectation of an audience.   Their dancing is a religious rite, with a very definite object in view.   As a result of their repeated whirlings they work themselves up into a state of ecstacy, in which condition they see visions, and in some cases claim they obtain the highest mystical state possible, namely, the Beatific Vision.   This, indeed, is the object of most of the Dervish Orders, who, however, obtain their end in different ways.   Another well known Order are the Howling Dervishes, who likewise dance and whirl but, unlike the ordinary Dancing Dervishes, continually give out a series of cries, most of which consist of varying names of Allah; they, like the Dancing Dervishes, also use mantric signs, including the Sign of Reverence, which we shall describe later.   Hence it is that the use of the Signs of Distress and Preservation by the Dancing Dervishes under such circumstances is both appropriate and significant, for they indicate appeals to Allah for strength to persevere in the exhausting ceremonies, and for help in the form of visions.

Passing to Persia, a specially interesting example is the 17th century painting reproduced opposite page 136.   The scene is the Descent from the Cross and although the subject is Christian the whole treatment is purely Persian.   It must be remembered that Islam recognises Jesus Ben Miriam as a great prophet and a Moslem saint, although repudiating His divine birth.   Hence we are not entitled to assume that this painting was either copied from a European picture or even necessarily done for Christians in Persia, of whom there have never been many.   Indeed, had it been copied we should have expected to find traces of European costumes, and in particular that our Lord would have been represented with nothing more than a loin cloth, as is usual in Western art.   It is the crowned

THE DANCING DERVISHES AT CONSTANTINOPLE.
A Turkish Miniature of the 17th Century.

U.1.

A TIPPERU OR BULL-ROARER.
Used in the Initiation Rites, New Guinea.

THE DANCING BELT OF A FULLY
INITIATED MAN.

From New Guinea.

W.5.

W.4.

figure in the centre background who is making this sign, which is not the only sign shown, for a figure in the left, towards the back of the picture, is making another mantric gesture.

The picture illustrated opposite page 154 entitled, "The Visit of a Prince" is by Mihr Tchand, an Indian artist of about 1600, and we have already shown how significant is the fact that the petitioner is thus appealing to the Prince, who by a sign intimates that he will preserve and protect the unfortunate stranger. Of the other examples quoted at the end of this book perhaps that of *The Deposition of Dubun* is the most important. Several of the friends of Dubun, and also some of his women, are thus testifying to their distress at his deposition.

Passing to China, the line illustration shown on page 57 contains signs actually used by members of the Hung Society during their ceremony of initiation. Among them this is called *The Sign of the Element of Fire*, and we have previously pointed out its association with this element among the Norse, also its appearance in the Coptic illustration of the Three Children in the Fiery Furnace. It seems probable that the association with fire is a derived and secondary connection, due originally to the fact that fire is one of the most terrible elements of destruction in the world, against which a man might well appeal to Heaven for protection.

The illustration opposite page 84 is of a drum which is Malay work but was found in New Guinea. How it came there nobody knows, but it was probably originally used in connection with religious rites in Malaya. On it will be seen a figure making this sign. Indeed, there are four such figures, all in exactly the same position, and the fact that the knees are bent outwards should be carefully noticed, for somewhat the same position is adopted by the Chinese when making the Sign of Fire. This drum serves as a convenient link between Asia and Australia, for not only was it made in the former continent and found in New Guinea, but the natives of the latter island use this sign in connection with their Rites of Initiation of a boy into manhood, and in their representations of it usually have the knees bent outward. They also recognise it as an appeal for help when in distress, and honour it as such. Thus in the Introduction to *The Hung Society*, Vol. I., Dr. Haddon writes, "The Sign of Fire in the

Hung Ritual, elsewhere known as the Sign of Distress, is of peculiar interest. A great many years ago James Chalmers, the well known missionary, said . . . . that he was in great danger of death owing to native hostility and as a last resource he made the sign, which he firmly believed saved his life.''

The two examples reproduced opposite this page are a tipperu, or bull-roarer, and a dancing belt from New Guinea. The former

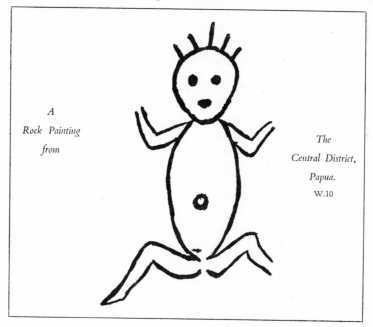

A

Rock Painting

from

The

Central District,

Papua.

W.10

instrument is used during the Ceremonies of Initiation to make weird noises in the Jungle, which latter are explained to the boys as being the voices of the ghosts. But when the boy has completed his course of initiation and is admitted as a fully-fledged member of the tribe, he is given the Dancing Belt as the insignia of his exalted rank. There is also a tradition that the figure represented is that of the God of Initiation. A third example, from Papua, is shown above. It is from a rock painting in the Central District of Papua and the original appears on plate N of "Man," No. 119, Dec. 1923. The fact that the

knees are drawn up in these last three cases shows that the god is associated with the Circumcision Rite, for reasons which we shall discover
when we turn to East Africa.

This sign also occurs among the Australian Bushmen, more
especially in connection with Biame, who is a kind of hero god. An
Australian friend of mine came across a rock carving of this Deity
which was very similar to the quaint little figure from Papua. Like
that figure, Biame had five rays coming from his head, and his hands
and legs were similarly drawn up. Furthermore, on one occasion my
friend saw a party of bushmen at sunset appealing to the setting sun in
this position, and came to the conclusion that among the older men
Biame was identified with the sun, although this fact was not known
even to the younger men of the tribe, much less to the women. According to legends, Biame was a man of ancient times who travelled
to the West, to the land of the Setting Sun, and after a series of
trials and adventures reached Paradise. In the case of the rock
carving of him, it was associated with other carvings in a secluded
spot, which was known to be used by the Bushmen for Initiation Rites
of a very special order, restricted to the older men and particularly to
the Medicine Men of the tribe.

Let us now pass to Africa, where we shall find the explanation of
the peculiar, drawn up position of the knees. The illustration reproduced opposite page 84 originally appeared in article No. 39, Plate F.,
"Man," 1915, and represents a boy about to pass through the Initiation
Rites of the Chuke tribe of Kenya. The operation is deliberately
made exceedingly painful, in order to test the boy's pluck. When
the old men are about to begin, the boy is instructed to place his knees
in the position shown and cast up his hands so as to make this sign.
Moreover, he must keep his hands in that position during the whole
time that the operation absorbs, and lest he should drop them an
attendant holds them up. As has been said, the operation is painful
and if he were not thus supported he might drop his arms, which
action they believe would be unlucky and possibly result in his dying
from his wound.

The holding of the hands thus, reminds us of an incident in the
Bible wherein Moses in this position prayed all day for victory, while
the Israelites fought in the valley, and because he was old two men

had to hold up his hands, for when he dropped them the Israelites began to lose the battle.

The position of the knees of the Kenya boy is obviously for a practical purpose, and therefore the fact that so many of the drawings representing this sign show the knees in the same position suggests that its use originated in circumcision rites. In this connection we must not forget the painting by Fra Angelico of the Circumcision of Christ, wherein He also is making this sign, although His knees are straight, not bent.

The two examples from Nyasaland, shown opposite pages 86 and 88, are of designs made on the ground in white flour for the initiation of a boy into manhood among the Yaos. The first represents the Great Mother, depicted as a fabulous semi-animal monster, and it will be noticed that on either side of her are two small human figures making this sign. Major Sanderson, the Chief Sanitation Officer for Nyasaland, who has so far won the confidence of the natives as to be made Master of Ceremonies in these Rites, informs me that when he first saw these little figures he asked whether they represented men or women. To this the Yaos replied, "Why, of course they are men, for they have their hands above their heads; if they were women their hands would be by their sides." The meaning of this somewhat cryptic remark is made intelligible by the Kenya custom, for whereas a boy on being circumcised makes this sign, when girls pass through a somewhat similar rite they do not make it, but lie flat on their backs with their hands by their sides.

The other design is of the grave used in the latter part of the Yao Rites. It is cut out in the form of a man in this position and then outlined in white flour. Previous to the ceremony a man gets into this grave and is covered by a blanket, then past it the boys are led and their conductor asks the grave certain questions, to which the occupant suitably replies. The name given to this grave and to its occupant is a word meaning "God," and the implication of the ceremony is that God speaks to man from the grave. Therefore the association of this sign with the grave and, indeed, with the whole ceremony, is peculiarly appropriate.

That this gesture is constantly associated with death, has been already demonstrated in the chapter dealing with its use in Europe.

A MALAY BRASS DRUM,
Purchased in Borneo.

U.37.

INITIATION RITES OF THE CHUKE TRIBE, KENYA.

S.5.

THE GREAT MOTHER.
A Sand Drawing Used During the Yao Initiation Rites, Nyasaland.

S.2.

This was especially the case in the Catacombs, and therefore an illustration on page 238, Vol. II. of "George Grenfell and the Congo," by Sir H. Johnston, is of particular interest. It represents a roadside fetish shrine on the Zombo Plateau whereon there are six figures, four of them making mantric signs, of which three are Signs of Distress. These fetishes were, of course, closely associated with death and other unpleasant things. Passing across to West Africa, the carved Yoruba gates from Oyo show a number of figures making signs, among them a Sign of Preservation and, lower down, two figures making the Sign of Distress. (See illustration opposite page 218).

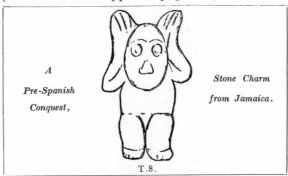

A
Pre-Spanish
Conquest,

Stone Charm
from Jamaica.

T.8.

We have now spanned Africa but there is still North Africa, which is too important to be ignored entirely, even if we omit ancient Egypt, which has been discussed in the last chapter. On the gilt, bronze cross from Abyssinia[1] appear two examples of the use of this sign, one on either side of the central shaft, while the modern Senussi of the Libyan Desert also use it. Several English soldiers who fought in that area during the war have told me that on more than one occasion a wounded Senussi made this sign to them and they honoured it. Furthermore, on a wooden bead in my collection, which formed part of the regalia of a Sudanese Chief, are carved two figures making it. Finally, the Kabyle people of Algeria evidently know its use for in a hanging made by them, and now at the chief hotel at Setif, appear figures making it and also the Sign of Preservation.

Crossing the Atlantic we are again greeted with the Sign of Distress, and an early example of its use is illustrated above. It is a

[1] See Illustration opposite page 178.

stone charm from Jamaica and predates the Spanish Conquest, while the other is a carving on stone from the same island and of the same period.[1]   In the case of the latter it should be noted that as in New Guinea the knees are bent out, and the same peculiarity is exhibited in the curious little Mexican figure shown below.   This represents the God Quetzalcoatl as Regent of the Star Venus.   The legend runs that after Quetzalcoatl had fought the great giant who wounded him in the foot, he continued his journey Westward until he reached the shores of a great sea, presumably the Pacific.   Here, finding that he was dying from his wound, he immolated himself on a funeral pyre and his soul descended into the Underworld, through which he continued to journey for several days, till at length he came out once more into the daylight, when he ascended to that Bright

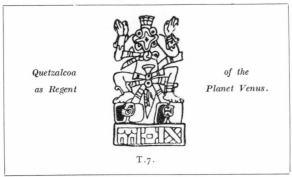

Quetzalcoa   of the
as Regent   Planet Venus.

T.7.

Morning Star whose coming heralds the Dawn, that is to say, to Venus, as a Day Star, where he now reigns and intercedes for men.   In the figure itself the face is covered by the emblem for the Star Venus.

Another excellent example from ancient Mexico is of the upper half of a skeleton which is sculptured on a broken stone yoke or vesica piscis.[2]   A great number of these stone yokes have been found among the ruins of Mexican temples and their exact purpose is still a matter of dispute among archæologists, the most widespread belief being that they were placed under the back of a human sacrifice to facilitate the operation of tearing out the heart.   Even, however, if this surmise is correct, it does not explain their peculiar shape, which is that of the

[1] See illustration on page 91.
[2] See illustration opposite page 88.

Vesica Piscis, and if they were only made for practical reasons a rounded block of stone would have been just as suitable.   I would suggest therefore that they are made in this peculiar shape in order, by symbolism, to convey an important lesson, namely, that the victim on passing through the Gates of Death found that they were really the Gates of rebirth into Paradise.   In support of this view I would point out that the ancient Mexicans declared that those who were sacrificed to the gods passed immediately into the realm of the blessed.   If this be so, the skeleton carved thereon represents death, and the sign made is most appropriate.   But it will be noted that the skeleton is on the outside of the yoke, and thus symbolically represents the Guardian of the Gates, and when the victim's soul passes through the Gates he sees no more the shadow of death, who is on the outer side of the lintel.

That the Sign of Distress was associated with death is also proved by the existence of a funerary vase found in a tomb of the Incas of Peru, which is now in the Museum of the Quatuor Coronati, in Great Queen Street.   Hereon is stamped a figure making this sign.   Nor is its use restricted to ancient days, for in *The Handbook of Ethnology* published by the British Museum, on page 287, is a picture of a basket with a woven pattern, made by the Unqua Indians of California, the original of which is in the British Museum.   On the basket appear figures making this sign, and it must be remembered in connection therewith that it was the custom among the Red Indians to send messages by means of signs woven into their baskets.   These designs were many and varied, usually of a somewhat arbitrary nature, but the man who made this particular basket evidently intended to convey thereby a message that either he or his tribe was in distress and needed help.

On our way from Amercia to Australia we come to Easter Island, in which place, as was previously mentioned, relics of a bygone race have been discovered, and among them pieces of wood, whereon are engraved pictographic writing, akin to hieroglyphics and believed to contain a summary of religious rituals.   The writing is curious, for each alternate line is upside down, and among the figures will be seen men making the Sign of Preservation and others that of Distress. Politically, Easter Island is a possession of Chili, but geographically it more properly belongs to Australasia, a continent with which we have already dealt.   One example of these inscriptions is illustrated opposite page 232, but those who wish to study the matter further will find a second example, as well as the one reproduced here, in the *Journal of the Anthropological Society*.

We have thus completely girdled the earth, showing again and again in each of the Continents conclusive proof of the use of this widespread sign, just as in the previous chapter we showed its descent century after century, from the days of Egypt and ancient Rome down to the present time.   Still more important, however, is the establishment of two facts; firstly, that it has a practical utility being still used by people in distress, as by the Arabs when their boat was sinking, and secondly, that even to-day it is closely associated with initiation rites, as in Africa and Australasia.

AN ANCIENT MEXICAN STONE VESICA PISCIS WITH A SKELETON CARVED
THEREON.

T.4.

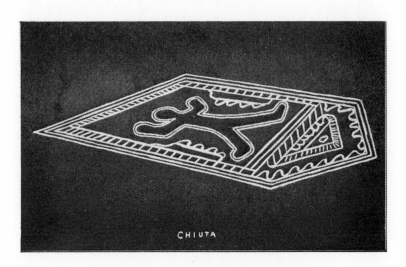

A GRAVE CUT IN THE FORM OF A MAN.
Used in the Yao Rites, Nyasaland.

S.3.

THE REREDOS OF THE ALTAR OF THE HOLY SOULS,
Buckfast Abbey.

R.3.

CHAPTER X. *Wherein is considered another Sign connected with the Head, denominated The Sign of Exultation.*

HIS SIGN IS EASILY distinguished from the last by the fact that the hands are raised above the head and the tips of the fingers made to touch, as will be seen from example illustrated opposite page 134, which is a mosaic standing over the principal West door of St. Mark's, Venice. The scene represents our Lord in Glory, and therefore the man in the extreme left is making what I will call the Sign of Exultation. The date of the work is 1830 and this is not the only sign contained therein, thus showing the survival among the mosaic workers of a knowledge of these signs.

That the sign is old is proved by the illustration on page 92, which is a miniature from a Flemish Book of Hours of the 15th Century, now in the Bodlein Library, Oxford, the scene being the Resurrection of the Dead. Quite a number of signs are made by the numerous figures who are rising from their tombs. Thus the man in the foreground makes the Sign of Distress and the soul immediately in front of him, in the centre of the picture, on seeing the face of our Lord, makes the Sign of Exultation. Still further in, beyond this figure, is a woman touching her head with both her hands, a sign we shall consider later in the chapter, while at the right side of the picture stands St. John the Baptist, making the Sign of Preservation.

Although I have not been able to discover very many examples of the use of the Sign of Exultation, the fact that it also occurs among the members of the Hung Society proves that knowledge of it is not restricted to Europe. There it is called the *Sign of Gold*, or sometimes of *Metals*, and is included among the group known as "The Signs of the Five Elements." It is reproduced below. Gold is a sign of royalty and also in itself is a desirable object. Moreover, in China, the use of the colour yellow is restricted to the Imperial house, so much so that it is called the imperial colour, just as in Europe gold is

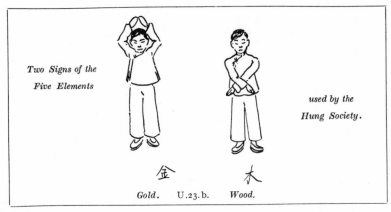

Two Signs of the
Five Elements

used by the
Hung Society.

金

木

Gold.   U.23.b.   Wood.

called the royal metal, being considered an attribute and symbol of kingship. It is easy therefore to see how a sign which generally seems to be used as a joyful salutation to some divine, or at any rate royal, person, should in China become associated with gold.

One other example deserves special mention, namely, a picture from a Book of Hours, painted towards the end of the 15th century and reproduced opposite page 234. Herein again we see a Last Judgment, the evil souls falling into the pit and the good souls passing to the right hand of our Lord, Who is seated on a rainbow. We have already pointed out that a figure in the background making the Sign of Distress has had his prayer answered, and is being wafted towards the saved, but attention is now directed to another figure, who is making the Sign of Exultation and is rising out of the general crowd toward the sky. Thus whereas all the figures around him are being drawn down and show only their heads, his body can be seen to below the waist. The illustration below will enable readers to see at a glance the difference between this sign and that of Distress, although, of course, in the latter sign the hands are often raised higher than in the example given, which depicts the second position, yet they are always

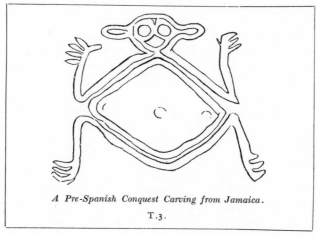

A Pre-Spanish Conquest Carving from Jamaica.

T.3.

well apart. On the other hand, the Sign of Exultation must be carefully distinguished from that which we shall discuss next, for unlike it, the hands do not touch the top of the head.

TOUCHING THE TOP OF THE HEAD.

The sign we will now consider is that of touching the top of the head. This has two forms; the first, with both hands touching the top of the head, and the second, with one only. Its exact significance is difficult to determine and it will be seen in the 15th century Flemish Book of Hours (*L.* 36) to which we have just alluded, where, as already pointed out, it is being made by a woman in the background. There is a tradition that this sign is intended to bring to mind the rainbow and in the particular example just quoted the fact that our Lord is seated on the rainbow, the symbol of Hope, would suggest that there is some foundation for the tradition, but I cannot say definitely that it indicates hope as it sometimes occurs in scenes where this interpretation does not seem appropriate. Nevertheless, in a 16th century painting of the damned being hurled into hell, attributed to Bosch and now in the Louvre, we see one soul making this sign and, curiously enough, he seems not to be falling, but rather rising upwards towards the angels.

When we pass outside Europe we find numerous examples of this sign in Asia and in Africa. Thus in the Indian illumination representing the Deposition of Dubun-i-Nayan wherein some of the figures are making Signs of Distress, others are placing their hands on their heads. In one case both hands are on the top of the head, in three others the left hand alone is placed thereon. In addition to these two sets of signs there is a splendid example of a man tearing at his heart with both hands, probably about to rend his garments.

Another Indian example is 18th century work and represents Krishna driving in cattle, accompanied by the female cattle drivers, two of whom are making this sign.

An interesting specimen from Persia is shown on a lacquered book cover of the 18th century, representing a battle, wherein the leader, while holding his sword in his right hand, touches the top of his head with his left, apparently as a signal to his followers, who are all mounted on horseback and towards whom he is turning.

Passing to Africa we have examples of both forms of this sign in connection with native dances in Nyasaland. Having previously pointed out that dancing was originally a ritual with a religious or magical significance, the fact that such a sign is associated with it is important. I have two illustrations of this dance, one showing the use of both hands and the other of one only. Having previously shown a 15th century Flemish example wherein both hands are used, I have this time selected for reproduction the photograph opposite page 94 where one hand only is employed which, as in the Persian and the Indian examples quoted, is the left.

In view of the fact that this sign is still found in ritual dances in Africa, its use among the Greeks becomes the more significant. On a Greek amphora, of circa 550 B.C., which is now in the British Museum,

"THE LAST JUDGMENT."
A Miniature from a Flemish Book of Hours.
Bodlein Library, Oxford.
L.36.

DANTE IN PARADISE.
From an Illuminated MS. of the 14th Century, now in the Brit. Mus.
K.21.

A NATIVE DANCE IN NYASALAND.

S.8.

the decoration consists of a frieze of dancing figures, alternatively women and satyrs, and one of the latter is touching the top of his head with his right hand. This form of the sign must be clearly distinguished from that which we shall next consider, namely,

THE SIGN OF SORROW OR SYMPATHY.

This is made by striking the front of the forehead with the fingers or palms of the hand, and must not be confounded with another sign, which means distress and consists of passing the hand across the top of the forehead with the palm outward, to which we have already alluded in the chapter on the Sign of Distress, pointing out that, in his picture of our Lord Cleansing the Temple, Guercino represents one man casting up his hands to heaven, while another makes this variant form.

The sign of sorrow or sympathy can undoubtedly be traced back to ancient Egypt, where we find numerous examples of its use, nearly always associated with funerals and mourning. Thus in the picture representing the funeral procession of Ani, which heads the chapter of "Coming Forth by Day" in the papyrus which belonged to that scribe, we see the mourners behind the hearse thus testifying to their grief at his death. This scene is reproduced opposite page 39 in Budge's Book of the Dead. The example illustrated opposite page 6 shows Ani's wife and daughter thus testifying to their grief in front of his mummy, which is supported by Anubis. Numerous other examples could be quoted from the old papyri, but one more must suffice, namely, a papyrus of the Ptolemaic period, made for Kemsher. The original is in the British Museum and it is reproduced on page 664, Vol. III. of *The Book of the Dead*, by Wallis Budge. In this we see Isis and Nepthys wailing over the body of Osiris, which Anubis is about to raise, and it is in this manner that they express their sorrow. Indeed, this method has survived in actual use up to the present day in the countries of nearer Asia, and numerous Biblical examples could be quoted to show that it prevailed among the Jews, but it is very doubtful whether as an actual practice it survived in Mediæval Europe, although its use as a Sign of Sorrow was well known. Thus in a 13th century mosaic in the Baptistery at Florence, representing Hell, one soul who is being carried into that region by a demon makes this gesture, while another lower down, as previously mentioned, makes the traditional Sign of Distress.

On the West front of St. Trophime's, Arles, is a 12th century sculpture of the last Judgment. Our Lord is seated in the centre surrounded by Saints, Apostles and Angels. In the illustration reproduced opposite page 182 it will be seen that the Saints on the extreme right of the picture are making this Sign of Sorrow while the angels above are making that of Distress.

Again, in the 15th century Flemish painting of the Last Judgment, reproduced opposite page 150, a soul in the foreground, towards the right hand corner, who has just got out of his grave, makes this gesture, and good reason he has to make it for he is clearly on the left hand side of our Lord, at the very edge of the pit of hell, and the soul next to him is actually being carried off by the demons. Close by a woman, who is falling into Hell, makes the Sign of Distress.

The next sign connected with the forehead is what I will designate *The Sign of Reverence*, and being a very important sign is dealt with at greater length in the next chapter. We will therefore pass to one which consists of plucking at the beard, as if one would pull it out.

TEARING THE BEARD.

There is a tradition that this sign is associated with the Templars and there seems to be good reason for thinking that this tradition rests on a solid foundation so far as Europe is concerned, although an example of its use exists on a Roman, stone sarcophagus of the 4th century, now in the Museum at Arles and reproduced opposite page 96. With this exception, however, I have found no representations of its use in Europe until the 12th century, and there seems to have been a very practical reason for its absence for such a considerable period. In the East it is, and always has been, customary for men to wear beards, and to this day a common sign of mourning is to tear the hair of the beard, just as the women tear the hair of the head. But in Europe, at any rate after the 10th century, the custom grew up for people to be clean shaven, and a study of the Bayeaux tapestry shows that although Edward the Confessor wore a beard, most of his Saxon subjects did not. Furthermore, William the Conqueror and his followers are likewise represented as beardless. This custom continued at least until the 12th century, during which period, however, we find that sepulchral monuments representing the Templars often show the dead knight as wearing a beard, whereas other knights are still clean shaven. It would seem, therefore, as if many Templars adopted the Eastern habit of wearing a beard, just as about the same date many ladies adopted the wimple, a form of the veil worn by Eastern women. In like manner it is during the same century that the pointed arch appears in Europe, and many architects contend that it was an attempt to reproduce the pointed arch of Saracen architecture.

In view of the above facts it is significant to find two clear examples of plucking out the beard in the sculpture work of the West front of the Cathedral of St. Laurence, Genoa, for it was in this cathedral that the Knights Crusader, including particularly the Knights Templar, signed an agreement with the Genoese to divert the fourth Crusade from Palestine to Byzantium, which incident is commemorated by a painting inside the Church.

The two examples to which I am referring occur as follows:— Firstly, a bearded figure, possibly God the Father, on the right hand jamb of the West door, reproduced opposite page 226, and secondly, to the scene in the tympanum above the West door, depicting the martyrdom of St. Laurence. Here, among the crowd who are watching the saint being slowly broiled on a gridiron, is a man thus testifying to his perplexity and grief. This work was probably executed towards the end of the 12th century, and it should be remembered that the date of the 4th Crusade was 1204, while the Templars themselves fell under the ban of the Pope in 1307.

Another good example of the use of this sign is shown in a 12th century carving of the Last Supper, in the cloisters of the church of St. Trophime, Arles. The fact that three of the apostles are thus plucking at their beards shows that the artist meant to convey to the onlooker the impression that he has depicted the scene at the moment when our Lord had said that one of those present should betray Him.[1]

I have only been able to find one example of the use of this sign after the 13th century. Among the "weepers" who stand on the upper part of the canopy over the tomb of Pope Innocent VI. is a man

---

[1] See also illustration I.18, reproduced opposite page 98.

making it.   This tomb is in the Chapel of the Hospice at Villeneuve-les-Avignon.   It may be worth mentioning that "weepers" are very often represented making various mantric signs of an appropriate nature, and deserve more careful study from this standpoint than they have previously received.   Unfortunately many of those on this tomb have been seriously mutilated, probably at the time of the revolution.   The date of the tomb is 1362, i.e., some 50 years after the suppression of the Templar Order, and, as I have said, it is the only example I can trace of the use of this Sign after the 13th century.   The disappearance of such a very expressive sign as this certainly tends to support the view that in the popular mind it was closely associated with the Templars.   Naturally, after the downfall of that Order, sculptors and ecclesiastics alike would be anxious to avoid using anything which had been peculiarly associated with the now discredited Knights, and therefore even if we cannot definitely say that its brief appearance and sudden disappearance were due to its close association with this great military Order, the above facts show that the theory is by no means unreasonable.

Doubtless the existence of other signs, such as that of striking the forehead, which likewise symbolised grief, rendered it less essential to sculptors and painters, who could depict this emotion by these other means and perplexity by the expression on the face.

A 4TH CENTURY ROMAN SARCOPHAGI AT ARLES.
St. Peter Raising the Daughter of Tabitha.

F.15.

THE ANGEL APPEARING TO THE SHEPHERDS.
A 12th century stone carving now in the Louvre.

I.18.

THE PULPIT AT RAVELLO CATHEDRAL, SORRENTO.
Comacine Work.   Circa A.D. 1280.

J.19

CHAPTER XI. Wherein the Sign of Reverence is considered and its world-wide distribution demonstrated.

EVERENCE IS indicated by shading the eyes with the hand. This sign is often made with the left hand, but the rule does not seem to be absolute, for although sometimes the right hand is placed on the heart and the left over the eyes, in cases where the right hand is not thus employed the artist often uses it to make the principal part of the sign. A third variation of it is to cover the eyes completely with the hand, but merely to shield them is by far the more usual form.

Its origin seems to be that you shield your eyes from the brightness of a superior's visage. In Italy this is the form of salute used by a soldier to his officer and the explanation of its use is as given above. In this form it was also employed in the British army in the 18th century, but has now degenerated to the flick in common use amongst us. It seems possible that when a gentleman removed his hat on meeting a lady originally the same idea was implied, for in the 17th century it was customary to cover the eyes, or rather to shade them with the hat, and then to place the latter on the heart. These two motions thus represent placing the right hand on the heart and the left over the eyes.

In Tibet it is a common form of salutation used by the peasantry to a Llama or a government official, and is there avowedly intended to symbolise shading the eyes from the brightness of the official's visage.

Two early examples of the use of this sign occur on two statuettes of the Minoan period found in Crete. The first, illustrated below, is of a man and the other is a woman, or possibly a goddess.[1] Numerous other figures making mantric signs have been found in

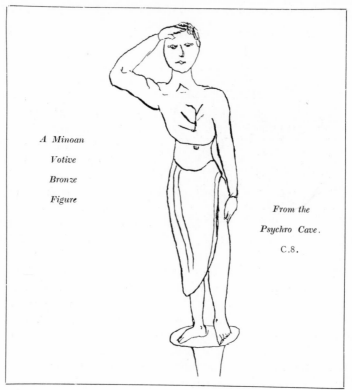

A Minoan

Votive

Bronze

Figure

From the

Psychro Cave.

C.8.

Crete and the bulk of them seem to have been either votive offerings or figures connected with religious rites, but it is not until the 12th century that I have been able to trace further examples, from which date, however, a regular sequence develops.

[1] See illustration on page 99.

Just as certain signs are specially found in scenes representing the Day of Judgment, as for example, the Sign of Distress, so the appearance of the angels to the shepherds, or the visit of the shepherds to the cradle of our Lord, form subjects wherein we most often find the use of the Sign of Reverence.   One of the earliest examples is a 12th

A Minoan

Bronze Figure

of a Priestess.

Now in the

Berlin Museum.

C. 9.

century sculpture, now in the Louvre, representing the angels appearing to the shepherds, reproduced opposite page 98.

An entirely different subject, however is an illumination from a copy of the Gospels in Greek, (I. 21) now in the British Museum.   It is probably Byzantine work, and in the upper part of the picture our Lord appears in the Vesica Piscis, supported by angels.   Below stands the Virgin, flanked by two other saints and surrounded by a number of men, two of whom are looking up towards our Lord and making this sign.   It should be noted that the two Saints flanking our Lady make the Sign of Preservation, while she herself seems to be making that of Distress. As the rest of the crowd have no haloes it seems probable that the scene represents a Last Judgment and Our Lady's distress is due to the sight of the lost, for she is constantly depicted pleading for humanity on such occasions.

A third example is from a 13th century fresco painted on the splay of a Norman window at Cocking Church, Sussex, wherein an angel appears to a Shepherd and his youthful assistant. This is reproduced opposite page 100 and we see the shepherds making this sign while the boy makes the Sign of Preservation.

But it is in the 15th century that we suddenly find an outbreak of it in subjects dealing with a variety of themes. The stained glass panel of the Angel appearing to the Shepherds, painted at this time and now in the Victoria and Albert Museum, shown opposite, gives us a good example, wherein one of the shepherds is shading his eyes with his left hand. The example chosen for illustration opposite page 140, by Fra Angelico, is of a somewhat less usual theme and represents the Resurrection. The original is a fresco in the Old Monastery of St. Mark's, Florence, and the scene contains at least three examples of mantric signs. In this case the artist has subtly given a picture of the Risen Lord above the women, but it is clear that none of them see it, for all are looking at the empty coffin. It is to the woman in the background, who is making this sign, that we draw attention; her attitude indicates the reverential awe with which she gazes into the empty tomb.

On the other hand, in "The Transfiguration," by the same artist and in the same monastery, which is reproduced opposite page 126, we again find him using the Sign of Reverence appropriately. It will be noted also that another of the apostles is making the Sign of Distress, evidently terrified at the amazing transfiguration, which he cannot understand.

Several other examples of the use of this Sign in connection with the Resurrection appear in the list given at the end of the book, and in most cases it is the Roman soldiers who make it, as they see the Lord rise from the tomb.

In the picture of the "Last Judgment" reproduced opposite page 150, to which we have previously alluded, the apostle in the

THE ANGEL APPEARING TO THE SHEPHERDS.
A 13th Century Fresco from Cocking Church, Sussex.

J.26.

THE EMBARKATION OF THE BODY OF ST. MARK.

A Mosaic from the West Front of St. Mark's Venice.

N.4.

middle background is making this sign as he looks towards our Lord, Who is seated on the rainbow. The fact that in so many cases this sign occurs alongside other mantric signs, increases the significance of its appearance.

In the *Sforza Book of Hours*, now in the British Museum, despite the clear evidence of Renaissance influence, we find in almost every miniature examples of the use of the old traditional signs. Thus in the scene of the Shepherds at Bethlehem, which is 16th century work, two of them are making the Sign of Reverence with the right hand, and one with the left. It also occurs in the miniature of St. Henry, the Bishop, wherein we have a woman shading her eyes with her right hand.

A third miniature from this book is reproduced opposite page 130. It represents St. Albert of Trapani and is of especial interest, as in this case we have one of the rare examples of that variation of the sign which is made by covering the eyes with the flat of the hand, instead of merely shading them. It is probable that this is really a distinct sub-sign from the ordinary form of reverence, and it will be noticed that the man's left hand is outstretched in rather a peculiar manner. Another figure in this picture is making a sign to which we shall have to allude in a subsequent chapter. I do not refer to the signs of Prayer, which are too well known to be worth special mention. Curiously enough, although the man is not making the Sign of Fidelity, a woman who is immediately behind him *is* making it.

Having thus seen that the sign is old, let us consider its widespread distribution. In Africa it is used by the Zulus as a mark of respect to a superior, and I have a photograph of a Zulu chief in the act of making it. Passing to the Near East I am informed by the Rev. W. A. Wigram, D.D., that in Turkey he has seen the Howling Dervishes use it under particularly significant circumstances. They opened their invocation with the cry of Allah, and after repeating it some hundreds of times and working themselves up to a state of great excitement, suddenly changed their cry to "Ya-huah" (i.e., Jehovah) and as they did so made the Sign of Reverence. In the Persian Painting of the Deposition from the Cross, to which we have already alluded,[1] one of the onlookers is making that form of the sign which consists in completely covering the eyes with the hand.

1 See illustration opposite page 136.

In Ceylon this sign is made by the Veddas, a primitive jungle race of non-Ayran descent, during the progress of certain ceremonies which take place after the birth of a child.   The father goes into the jungle and erects a kind of bundle of leaves, into which the spirits of his ancestors are supposed to enter.   To these ancestors he announces the birth of his child, at the same time making this sign.

In China, it is a highly valued sign among the members of the Hung Society.   If one of them is attacked by a footpad he places his right hand on his heart and shades his eyes with his left, and if his assailant is a fellow member of the Society he immediately lets him go.   See illustration printed below.

In Australia this sign is made by a Medicine Man as he leaves the circle of initiation after having passed through certain advanced initiatory rites, apparently to intimate that he has completed the ceremony, and a photo thereof can be seen in *Northern Tribes of Australia*, by L. Spencer and Gillan.   The actual ceremony is called the *Engura Ceremony*, and is associated with a great bonfire and a bush from which men speak, pretending to be spirits.   It thus has a striking similarity with the Vedda Ceremony, where this sign is also used.

From the above examples it will be seen that the Sign of Reverence is widely distributed and can be traced back to a very early date in the history of the world.

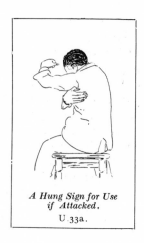

A Hung Sign for Use
if Attacked.
U 33a.

CHAPTER XII. *Concerns the Use of Signs connected with the Nose and Mouth.*

NDOUBTEDLY there are at least three signs connected with the nose, of which the first is probably a purely natural sign, and the second a vulgar form of insult, while the meaning of the third is somewhat obscure. The first consists in pinching together the nostrils of the nose and appears in most representations of the Raising of Lazarus, but although for the sake of uniformity and completeness I have included it in this book, it seems to be merely a natural sign rather than a mantric one, being just the ordinary action of anyone who smells an obnoxious odour.

The second sign is well known to most people, being used by vulgar little boys to show their contempt for someone. It consists in placing the thumb to the tip of the nose with the fingers extended. Sometimes the left thumb is placed on the little finger of the right hand to extend the sign. Although this sign is well known, I have never seen any explanation concerning either its meaning or its origin, but it is certainly very old and its origin lost in the mists of antiquity. I have deliberately mentioned it in the hope that some other student may be able to discover its origin and the reason for its significance.

The third sign is obscure in its meaning and consists of placing the index finger of the left hand on the right nostril, but sometimes the right hand is used, as in the example which occurs at Hampton Court.   The ceiling of the bedroom of William III, to which reference has already been made, contains a painting depicting Momus, the God of Sleep, and among the allegorical figures are two men, apparently conversing.   One is clearly making the Sign of Preservation and the other man answers it by placing the index finger of the right hand against his nostril.   It is obvious that in this case there is some definite meaning attached to the sign, but what it is I cannot say for certain.

When we turn to signs connected with the mouth we are on firmer ground and there are at least three. In the West the first is also an insult, for just as naughty little boys put their fingers to their noses, vulgar little girls put out their tongues. It is quite true that the fair sex have not the monopoly of this insulting gesture, for little boys also adopt it, but speaking generally, it is more often used by girls, who seldom use the corresponding boys' sign.   It is just possible therefore that each sign is connected with sex, and if so the instinctive wrath which descends on the heads of the impudent juveniles if detected in these actions by their parents, is perfectly intelligible, even if the parents themselves do not know the reason for their strong disapproval.

In the East, however, putting out the tongue has a more solemn significance.   It is a sign of Kali, the Destroyer, and according to the Hindu legends in her case was a Sign of Shame.   The legend is that Kali, the Avenger, descended to earth to attack the Demon hosts and in her ruthless slaughter slew men and devils alike.   Indeed, carried away by the lust of killing, it seemed to the horrified gods in heaven that she would destroy the whole human race. But, despite the appeals of the gods, nothing could stay her hand until her spouse, Shiva, threw himself in her path amid the corpses.   As Kali sped on, dealing death and destruction, she suddenly found herself trampling on Shiva, and the sight restored her balance.   She paused and put out her tongue in shame and confusion at realising to what length her fury had led her.

It is stated that among some savage tribes to put out the tongue to a person, far from being an insult, is a sign of respect.   It may

HORUS.

A STELE OF A PUNIC PRIEST.
From Carthage.

A14.

E.3.

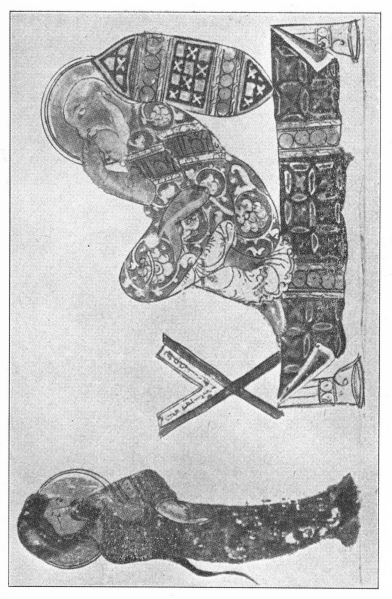

ERASISTRATOS AND HIS FAMILIAR SPIRIT.

A Miniature from Mesopotamia. 1222 A.D.

U.46.

be that in such cases the action implies that the person making the sign places herself at the service of the one she thus honours. In connection with the suggestion that these signs are related to matters of sex, it should be noted that in one aspect Shiva represents the phallus and is often depicted under the symbol of the lingum, while his female counterpart, Kali, is symbolised by the Yoni.

The second sign connected with the mouth appears to imply secrecy or silence. In Egypt it is associated with Horus, who in one sense symbolises man risen from the dead, and the illustration which appears opposite page 104 depicts a bronze figure of this God, crowned with the triple feathers.   Care is necessary not to mix this sign with the perfectly natural one of a child sucking his finger, and as the risen soul is often represented as a young child this difficulty is a very real one, for which reason I have rejected many examples where the figure making it is that of a baby.

Another excellent example is shown in the illustration opposite page 62, namely in the fresco at Pompeii, representing the Sacrifice of Iphigenia.   Herein one of the Greeks is clearly making the Sign of Secrecy, but even more significant is the figure of Diana, in the right hand corner, who also makes it.   It will be remembered that, just as the unfortunate girl was about to be sacrificed, Diana appeared in a cloud and carried her off to the Crimea, thus saving her from her threatened fate, but at the same time hiding her from her relations. Her exact hiding place long remained a mystery, until she was subsequently discovered and rescued by her brother.   In view of the fact that another sign is shown, namely that of Distress, there can be no doubt that the sign Diana makes is not a natural one, but is intended to convey to the onlooker the veil of secrecy in which for a time the Goddess enshrouded Iphigenia.

This sign, however, seems to have been regarded as particularly sacred and secret and was not lightly used by artists, perhaps because it was connected with the mystery of the Resurrection.   It will be noticed that in both these cases it is closely associated with a Divine Being. In the case of Horus its association with the risen man is fairly obvious, and even in the case of Iphigenia, although the legends say that she was not actually killed, her closeness to death, her temporary disappearance and her subsequent, but much later, return to normal life not only has a close analogy with the resurrection from the dead, but may well have been intended as an allegory thereof.

A third example, this time from Mesopotamia and dating from 1222 A.D., also shows the close connection of the sign with the Resurrection. The illustration opposite depicts Erasistratos raising his familar spirit from Hades. The magician makes the Sign of Secrecy, while the spirit who has been raised from the Underworld makes the sign which implies that he has ascended from the Underworld, to which place he must ultimately again descend. It should be noted that this latter sign often occurs in Christian art and generally in connection with the descent of our Lord into Hell and His subsequent ascension into Heaven. Therefore we see that once again the Sign of Secrecy is closely associated with One who has risen from the grave.

It may be asked, however, why secrecy and silence should thus be associated. The explanation seems to be that even if they return to earth the dead are supposed to be under a vow of secrecy not to disclose to mortal men much, if anything, of what transpires in the world beyond the grave, a fact which is brought out most strongly in connection with the third sign associated with the mouth.

Before passing to this sign, however, a fourth example of the use of the Sign of Secrecy is worth quoting. In a 16th century Indian painting, the original of which is in the Museum of Industrial Arts at Vienna, we see a number of travellers embarked on a ship which is just leaving port. Friends on shore are making various signs, such as that of Fidelity and Preservation, which the voyagers are answering in different ways. One, for example, is evidently full of evil foreboding, or sorrowful at his departure, for he makes the Sign of Distress, while another places his index finger on his lips as if to enjoin secrecy.

The third sign consists of placing the point of the thumb of the right hand just beneath the chin as if stabbing through the lower membranes of the mouth, so as to pin the tongue to its roof, and this also appears to be associated with the risen man, for not only have we an excellent example of it in another statue of Horus which is in my possession, but the following account of what takes place at the initiation of an Australian Bushman seems definitely to establish, not only the reason for the use of this sign, but also why the Sign of Secrecy has a similar association.

The ceremony I am now about to describe is the Initiation into the high office of a Medicine Man or Master of Ceremonies among the Arunta of Alice Springs, Australia. This is a very restricted Order, open only to the old men and jealously guarded, since not only has the Medicine Man great influence in the tribe, but it is he who presides over the initiation of all the lower ranks. The ceremony takes place in a cave, which the ordinary natives dare not enter, for they say it extends into the very centre of the earth and that there dwell the spirits of their ancestors, in a beautiful earthly paradise. The aspirant enters the cave and goes to sleep, and while asleep one of the spirits is said to drive an invisible spear through the man's throat and tongue, in such a way as to make the latter cleave to the roof of his mouth. Henceforward he has an actual hole in his tongue, and it is believed that if this hole should close up his magical powers would leave him. After this first operation has taken place they say that the spirit drives his spear through the man's head from ear to ear and kills him. He then carries off the body to the land of the spirits, cuts it open, takes out the internal organs and replaces them by new ones. Thereafter the man returns to consciousness and is received among the tribe as a Medicine Man.[1]

Doubtless the above is the version related to inquisitive members of the tribe who are beneath the rank of a Medicine Man, and what actually takes place is a dramatic representation of the journey of the soul to the realm of the departed, during which the candidate is attacked by members of the degree, dressed up to represent spirits. During the proceedings these "ghosts" pierce his tongue, which henceforth becomes the recognised hallmark of a Medicine Man. There seems little doubt, therefore, that when Horus places his thumb underneath his chin in this significant manner he is referring to the pierced tongue. As to secrecy, not only are the Medicine Men forbidden to relate exactly what transpires in the realm of the spirits, but a similar restriction is usually placed on the tongues of all initiates into all degrees. Thus, in the Congo there is a secret society known as *The Ndembo*, which avowedly performs a ceremony which represents the

---

[1] B. Spencer & F. J. Gillen, "*Native Tribes of Central Australia,*" pp. 523 sq.

death and rebirth of the candidate.   It takes some months to perform and when it is over the initiates, who are said to come from "The country of the dead," are not only forbidden to speak of their experiences but are supposed to have forgotten how to speak at all, and have to go through the farce of being retaught their mother tongue.[1]

The Bushongo, who inhabit the Belgian Congo, have a similar ceremony, representing the journey through the Underworld and resurrection therefrom.   All boys have to take this Rite, which starts by their being carried off into the Jungle, where for several nights, during the dark hours, the initiated men march round the camp whirling bull-roarers, which noise the boys are taught is the roaring of ghosts.   Later they have to pass through a tunnel where they meet four men, suitably disguised, who represent denizens of the Underworld, and ultimately emerge into daylight.[2]   These boys are similarly bound to secrecy.   It may be added that initiates of the Ndembo Lodge are taught a secret language, as is often done in these Rites, and this again would explain the significance of placing the finger on the lips, indicating not only the necessity for silence but the possession of a secret language.

---

[1] Dr. Bentley, "*Pioneering in the Congo.*"   Vol. I. pp. 282 sq. also J. H, Weeks, "*Among the Primitive Bakonga,*" pp. 172 sq.

[2] E. Torday et T. A. Joyce, "*Les Bushongo*" (Brussells 1910), pp. 82 sq.

THE RAISING OF LAZARUS.
By Piombo.
In the National Gallery, London.

M.15.

A SECOND CENTURY ROMAN SARCOPHAGUS.
In the Vatican Museum.

F.25.

CHAPTER XIII. *Deals with the Sign of Horror and shows how it is closely connected with Death.*

ERHAPS ONE OF THE most dramatic signs is that of Horror. It is made by turning the head over the right shoulder and raising the right hand, palm outwards, as if trying to shut from the eyes some horrible sight, while the left arm points outward and down, as if endeavouring to thrust something away.   A good example is seen in the painting of the Raising of Lazarus by Piombo, illustrated opposite page 108, although often the left arm is somewhat lower, as in the example on the Roman Sarcophagus shown opposite page 110.   Artists vary slightly in their methods of depicting this sign, but all its forms are such as to render it easily identifiable.

In order of seniority the earliest example is on a Minoan seal, (C.11) illustrated opposite page 16.   The next is a Roman example of the second century, being a Sarcophagus in the Vatican Museum and is referred to above.   Hereon is depicted a battle scene, in which the victors are apparently slaughtering men and women indiscriminately, and one woman is shown rushing from the scene of slaughter making this sign.

Coming to the middle ages a particularly good representation occurs in a bas-relief by Orcagna, at Florence, an illustration of which is in my possession. The composition is divided into two panels and in the lower the Virgin, either dead or dying, is surrounded by the Disciples and Apostles, while above she is seen seated within the vesica piscis and being drawn upwards towards Heaven by the angel host. It is in the lower panel that the artist has striven, most successfully, to depict the emotions of grief and horror of the on-lookers, and one in the extreme right of the composition averts his head and makes this sign.

Coming to the next century, namely, the fifteenth, the illustration opposite page 152 depicts the Raising of Lazarus. It is by Nicholas Froment and was recently acquired by the Louvre. Around the grave several of the onlookers are making signs and one woman, right in the background on the left hand side, adopts this position to show her horror. Doubtless this is Martha, who in the Biblical account clearly indicates her horror at the idea of opening the grave.

Another example of the 15th century is in a fresco of the Last Judgment at Sienna, painted by Giovanni di Paolo. This is interesting in that the man who is making the sign is seated, having just risen from his grave, and his horror is fully explained by the fact that just behind him a devil is carrying off another soul, at which appalling sight the unfortunate man averts his head and adopts this posture, whereas a third soul, nearer to our Lord, raises his left hand in the Sign denoting Preservation.

A different, but equally horrific, scene is represented in an illuminated manuscript of Valerius Maximus, written in French about A.D. 1485 and now in the British Museum. There are two scenes: one depicting the massacre of prisoners and another, below, representing people entering the room in which these have been butchered and by their gestures showing their horror. Although the sign occurs in both panels, the best representation thereof is made by a man standing near the King who has given the order for the slaughter. He averts his face and makes this sign, in horror at the appalling sight, whereas the king gazes on the scene, stern and relentless.

In the 16th century we find yet further examples, of which we have already alluded to one, namely, the painting of Piombo, now in the National Gallery and illustrated opposite page 108. This is the work of a Venetian artist and the picture was painted between 1517 and 1519. As some of the onlookers strip the grave cloth from the rising corpse, Martha averts her head in horror but Mary, who kneels at our Lord's feet with her back towards Lazarus, and has not seen the miracle, with her right hand on her breast, testifies to her faith in her Master and her firm belief in His power to bring her brother back to life. On the opposite side of our Lord a man is kneeling making the Sign of Prayer.

It is worth while comparing Piombo's representation of this scene with that by Froment. Whereas the former makes Mary adopt the Sign of Fidelity, the two women near our Lord in Froment's picture are making entirely different signs. The one nearest to Him has extended her hands at an angle of about 39°, palms upward, the significance of which sign seems to be some such idea as "It is hopeless; life is finished." If so, the artist has been careful to contradict her flatly by depicting the man slowly rising. It should be noted, moreover, that this woman is not looking at the grave but towards the Christ, and presumably has not seen the miracle. On the other hand, the woman nearer to us makes the sign we have met with often in these pictures, namely, that made by the familiar called up by Erasistratos, the Magician, as related in the last chapter. In other words, she has seen the miracle and in sign language is saying, "Although Lazarus descended into the Underworld he has reascended therefrom."

An entirely different scene, drawn from Pagan Mythology, is represented in the painting by Pitati, entitled *Diana Surprised by Actæon*. The original is in Hampton Court Palace and its reproduction opposite page 116 is by gracious permission of His Majesty, the King. There is also another picture of the same subject by this artist, in the library of Christ Church College, Oxford. This varies considerably in detail from the one reproduced, but in both cases the unfortunate man is shown making this sign. It will be remembered that the legend says that Actæon, a noted hunter, pryed on Diana while she and her attendants were bathing in a small lake in the woods, Seeing him, the goddess said in her wrath that he should be turned into a stag and subsequently be torn to pieces by his own hounds, which catastrophe ultimately occurred. In the picture the curse has just been spoken and the unfortunate man makes this gesture in horror as he feels his head change into the form indicated.

One last example must suffice. In the mosaic of the Transportation of the body of St. Mark from Egypt to Venice, which is depicted in the tympanum over one of the West doors of St. Mark's Cathedral, the body, which is in a hamper, has just been acquired by the Venetians from a group of Jews. One of the latter is holding his nose, while a second turns away with the Sign of Horror. Apparently the Venetian sailors are about to open the basket so as to make sure that they really have the right body. Seeing that St. Mark had been dead for a much longer time than Lazarus, it may be thought that the Jews had some justification for these dramatic gestures, a view which the artist seems also to have shared. The work is of about 1660 and is reproduced opposite page 102.

It will be realised that in every case this sign dramatically represents a feeling of horror and it is clear that the mediæval artists inherited it from ancient times. In this connection it should be noted that the Cretan seals usually appear to have on them symbols of a religious or quasi-religious nature, in some way connected with the religion of Crete and probably with the System of Initiation associated therewith. Several examples of Mantric Signs which appear on such seals have been referred to in earlier chapters of this book, and hence there seems little doubt that this sign is not merely a natural gesture but a mantric one which, like so many others, has been passed down by tradition.

A ROUNDEL OF STAINED GLASS OF THE 15TH CENTURY,
DEPICTING THE ANGEL APPEARING TO THE SHEPHERDS.

In the Victoria and Albert Museum.

L.67.

THE WEIGHING OF THE HEART OF ANI.

A18.

CHAPTER XIV. *Wherein are discussed Signs connected with the Hands and Shoulders.*

UITE A NUMBER of signs fall into this group, but perhaps one of the most important consists in laying the right hand on the left shoulder, with the forearm placed diagonally across the breast. Numerous examples of its use occur on the Egyptian monuments and in manuscripts, particularly those which contain the text of *The Book of the Dead*. An example of the former type can be seen at the Louvre and is entitled "A Stele with Magical Representations." Herein we have a small figure making the sign as he approaches a god. (Reference A.9.). This is not the only mantric sign which occurs in this stele, for several excellent examples of the Sign of Preservation are made by figures who are following in the wake of the Solar Barque.

Turning to the papyri, the illustration opposite page 114 is from the famous Trial of Ani and depicts the latter watching the weighing of his heart. This was the vital moment in the journey of the soul through the Underworld, for upon the result of the weighing depended whether the suppliant would pass to Paradise or be doomed to destruction. A third example occurs in the same papyrus and shows Ani being led by Horus into the presence of Osiris. The weighing of the heart is finished and the soul of the scribe awaits the decision of the Judge of the Dead.

In Babylon the sign was also used, as is clear from a stele engraved with the text of Khammurabi's Code of Laws. This is now in the British Museum and represents the King, who makes this sign as he receives the laws from Shamash, the Sun God. It should be remembered that many archæologists believe that the ten commandments promulgated by Moses are based indirectly on the Code of Khammurabi. The exact date when this king reigned is a matter of dispute, but it is probably not later than 2,000 B.C.

Turning to Roman times, a Sarcophagus of the 4th century A.D. which stands in the atrium of St. Mark's, Venice, is a particularly happy example, because on it are sculptured two rows of figures, both apparently symbolical of the deceased. In the lower row all the figures are making the Sign of Distress, doubtless to symbolise the distress felt by the soul as it leaves its physical body and passes into the unknown, but the upper row clearly implies a message of hope. Here the souls are all represented with the right hand on the left shoulder, and I suggest that the obvious difference between the two groups is that the second is intended to imply that the soul has passed through the gateway of death into Paradise. Indeed, as we pass down the ages we find numerous examples of the use of this sign by a soul rising from the grave, and although this does not entirely explain its full significance it gives us a useful hint which we shall find valuable when endeavouring to interpret the meaning of the gesture.

It is not until the 12th century that I have been able to find another example of the use of this sign, although doubtless many exist. On the right hand jamb of the great West door of St. Laurence's Cathedral, Genoa, appears a figure with the right hand on the left shoulder. It occurs among the ancestors of our Lord, who constitute a tree of Jesse. Thus David, who rises from Jesse, is flanked on either side by two smaller figures, of which the one on the left makes the sign we are considering, while the figure on the right makes the Sign of Preservation. In like manner the ancestor immediately beneath Our Lady also places his right hand on his left shoulder. This work is 12th century and is reproduced opposite page 226.

A 13th century example occurs at St. Mark's, Venice, in a mosaic depicting the martrydom of St. Bartholomew and St. Matthew.   In this case the sign is made by one of the onlookers who is watching the unfortunate saint being flayed alive.   Another representation from this century occurs in a portable alter which is now in the British Museum.   It was apparently a gift from an abbot, named Theodoric, to the Abbey of Sheida, near Cologne, Germany.   In this one of the small bas-reliefs represents the Virgin, flanked on either side by worshippers, one of whom is making this gesture.

The same sign can be seen in a 14th century stained glass medallion in the top of the tracery of the East window of Whichford Church. The scene represents the Crucifixion, with St. John to the left, who with his right hand is apparently cutting his throat, while his left arm is squared, thus combining two signs whose full significance we have already explained, whereas on the right side stands the Virgin, with her right hand on her left shoulder.

A miniature in a Book of Hours which belonged to Margaret of Foix, Duchess of Brittany, affords another illustration of the use of this sign, this time at about 1480.   In the upper part of the picture we see the Nativity and in the lower part the Flight into Egypt.   In both scenes various mantric signs occur, but the one we are considering is made by an onlooker as Joseph and Mary pass by on their way into safety.   The complete miniature is shown opposite page 128.

The fresco by Fra Angelico reproduced opposite page 140 has already been referred to in connection with the Sign of Reverence, but must be mentioned again owing to the fact that one of the women at the tomb is undoubtedly making the sign we are now discussing, although the artist has slightly disguised it by making it appear as if she were merely clutching her mantle.   Apparantly she is doing this in answer to the angel who says, "He is not here, but has risen." Another 15th century example can be seen in a miniature which appears in the Convenant of Christoforo Mauro, Doge of Venice, A.D. 1462, the original of which is in the British Museum.   In the picture we see the Virgin and Child flanked by two saints, and before her kneels a man, probably the Doge himself.   In answer to his prayer, the Christ Child makes this gesture.

In the 16th century fresco at Basle, illustrated opposite page 186, to which allusion has already been made, one of the souls rising from the grave has her left hand on her right shoulder, an unusual, but not unique, variation. She is surrounded by other figures making mantric signs, and so there can be little doubt that the gesture is symbolic. Other examples from this century are given in the list at the end of the book, among them being one from a bas-relief and another from a tapestry. Neither does the 17th century lack proofs of its survival, perhaps the most striking being the embroidered panel, now in the Victoria and Albert Museum, which shows Abraham entertaining the angels, while Sarah, who has overheard their promise, has her right hand on the left shoulder. This is shown opposite page 124.

So far we have only dealt with the simplest form of this sign but a most interesting and significant variation occurs to which we must now devote our attention, for in combination with the other it apparently gives us the full sign. This is made by stretching out the right hand and striking it with the side of the left, as if cutting it off, as is shown in the illustration opposite. This is a painting of the 15th century, representing Christ's descent from the Cross, the original being in the Louvre. After making this first movement, the right hand, which has symbolically been severed, is lifted by the left and a pretence is made of throwing it over the right shoulder. This posture is seen in the fresco on the South wall of the Chancel of Easby Church, reproduced opposite page 118. The original was painted in the 12th century. It is important to note that here again we have a scene of the Descent from the Cross, but in this case it is the Virgin, and not a man, who is making the gesture. The third stage of the sign, and the one most usually seen, is that we have been discussing at great length, wherein the left hand has been dropped once more to the side.

Before turning to consider the symbolic significance of this sign, or group of signs, at least passing reference must be made to the fact that the second stage thereof also appears in the 20th century bas-relief behind the Altar of the Holy Souls at Buckfast Abbey Church, the importance of which will be clear from the previous references made thereto. (See illustration opposite page 90).

The key to the meaning of the sign seems to be the gesture of

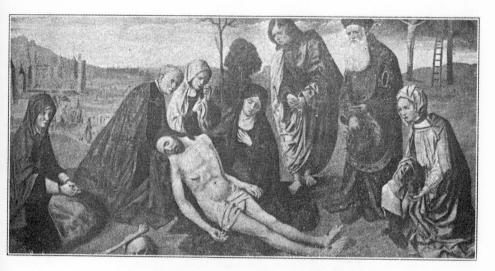

"THE DEPOSITION FROM THE CROSS."
A 15th Century Painting now in the Louvre.

L.44.

DIANA SURPRISED BY ACTÆON. By Bonifazio di **Pitati.**
At Hampton Court Palace.
By Gracious Permission of His Majesty The King.

M.18.

THE FRESCO ON THE SOUTH WALL OF EASBY CHURCH.

I.26.

flinging the right hand over the shoulder, which is clearly a sacrifice. Even to-day superstitious people who upset the salt throw a pinch of it over the left shoulder, and in West Africa it is customary to propitiate the spirits of the departed by throwing a libation of milk or other liquid over the left shoulder, on to the ground.   With this key we are at once able to interpret most of the examples quoted. In the Roman sarcophagus the implication is that the soul, having sacrificed his body by death, is able to enter Paradise.   In the Trial of Ani, the Egyptian, a perusal of the text indicates that in order successfully to pass the trial it was necessary for Ani to prove that he had made numerous sacrifices, some of the ordinary type offered to the Gods, and others of a more spiritual nature, which consisted of doing good to his fellow men, such as giving water to the thirsty, visiting those who were sick and in prison, and the like.   Ani's gesture, therefore, is intended as a reminder to the Judge, Osiris, that he has made such sacrifices and therefore trusts that he will be saved.   Khammurabi made the sign because, through his acceptation of the code of laws from Shamash, both he and his subjects would have to sacrifice much which to them had become dear, in order that they might conform to the prescribed higher precepts.

The scenes associated with the Descent from the Cross almost explain themselves.   At Easby the Virgin testifies that Christ has sacrificed Himself for the world, and doubtless also reminds the onlookers of her own sacrifice involved thereby, while in the other picture Joseph of Arimathea, for no doubt it is he, thus strikes off his hand to imply that the great sacrifice has been made.   When Christ makes the Sign it is to remind His worshippers of the great sacrifice *He* has made, and when the onlooker sees St. Batholomew being slain because of his faith he almost involuntarily testifies thus to the sacrifice the Saint is making.

The same sign is found in various parts of the world and always, apparently, with the same underlying meaning.   Thus in Africa, among the Chuke tribe of Kenya, the boy who is about to be initiated makes the Sign of Distress as a signal that the circumcision is to begin, a fact to which we have already alluded, but when the operation is finished and the sacrifice, for such it undoubtedly is, has been completed, he makes the sign we are now discussing, as will be seen

by consulting Article Number 39 and plate F in *Man*, 1915. A
similar use of the sign occurs among the Konde people, who live on
the shores of Lake Nyasa, and is associated with certain of their
ritualistic dances, its use being proved by an illustration in my
possession.

There is much dispute as to the original cause for the widespread
rite of circumcision and various suggestions have been put forward
by anthropologists. In my opinion, however, most of these suggestions are based on far too recent data. The most common theory is
that it is intended as a sanitary precaution, particularly in countries
of a dry climate, where sand abounds, as, for example, in Palestine.
Unfortunately for this theory, we find that the same Rite is performed
all over the world, often in districts where there is no sand and where
the climate can hardly be described as dry. It is, indeed, a mistake
ever to assume that a primitive rite owes its origin to practical con-
siderations, although an ancient rite such as this may be continued
by a race which has reached a relatively high stage of civilisation
because experience has proved that it has certain practical advantages. On the contrary, as a rule such ceremonies are either magical
or religious, and among primitive people magic and religion are so
intermixed as to render it difficult to distinguish one from the other.
Now it is very common for primitive races, such as the Bushmen of
Australia, to knock out a tooth at initiation or to cut off a tip of a
finger, both mutilations being avowedly intended as a sacrifice to
the spirits of misfortune, on the principle of sacrificing a part in order
that the whole may be safeguarded, and I think there is little doubt
that circumcision was originally a sacrifice to the Great Mother,
intended to safeguard the rest of the organ.

Thus we see that having made this sacrifice the Kenya boy is
ceremonially correct in making the Sign of Sacrifice. It should be
noted, however, that in this case he places his left hand on his right
shoulder, as does the woman in the fresco at Basle, while in India we
find another example of this reversal of the arm. This occurs in an
illustration of a bas-relief representing Vishnu sleeping under the five-
headed cobra, and just about to descend to earth in one of his Avatars.
Above him we see several of the gods making mantric signs, while
below are a row of six figures, one of them being an ogre who is about

to attack a man. It was against this ogre that Vishnu descended to make war. The ogre is opposed by a human being, who is drawing his sword to protect himself, and behind him stand three attendants, all of whom are making signs. The one furthest off is making the Sign of Preservation, the man next to him has both hands crossed on his breast, which is a sign we shall discuss later, while the man nearest to the human champion is making this Sign of Sacrifice. The import of the gesture in this connection is an acknowledgment that Vishnu is about to sacrifice himself by descending from Heaven and restricting his godhead, by assuming a human form. (See illustration opposite p. 200.)

Another Indian example is the so-called Teacher Group, a 13th century bas-relief from Konarak, near Orissa, which is now in the Victoria and Albert Museum. Here we have a Guru, who is a follower of Vishnu, and an aristocratic Hindu, probably of the fighting caste, has apparently come to him promising to be his disciple. Behind him is an attendant, who makes the Sign of Sacrifice with his right hand, probably to indicate the material sacrifice of rank and wealth which the would-be disciple has to make.

Another interesting Hindu example occurs in an 18th century painting in the State Museum at Berlin. It represent Krishna playing on his magic flute, surrounded by the Gopis, or female goat-herds. One of these women is making the Sign of Secrecy, a second, that of Resignation, a sign we shall explain in the next chapter, and a third is protending to strike off her right hand at the wrist by a blow from her left. It will be remembered that according to the legend the goat-herds were the earliest and most loyal of all Krishna's disciples and remained faithful to him throughout his whole earthly mission. If Krishna revealed his divine nature through his wonderful music, the significance of all these signs is clear. The woman making the Sign of Secrecy is warning her companions to keep their discovery a secret. The goat-herd with the Sign of Resignation implies that she is content to follow him wherever he goes, while the third woman is saying that she is willing to sacrifice everything for his sake.

A Persian Miniature now in the British Museum entitled, "A dispute between two Learned Men," also shows one of them making this sign, the implication being that this man thus alludes to the sacrifices he has made in his pursuit of truth, but his opponent replies by the gesture of striking off his hand at the wrist, which, as has been previous shown, is the first part of this threefold sign.

It is certainly not without significance that we are thus able to produce examples of the mantric use of this sign in its various stages among men of such different lineage and religious belief as Hindus, Persian Mahomedans, African Pagans and European Christians, but when we recollect that ancient Bablyon and Egypt also used it with the same inner meaning, we see at once that instead of the long arm of coincidence we have a really reasonable explanation, namely, a vast antiquity, going back probably to a period long preceding even the time of the Pharoahs.

THE ARRIVAL OF THE BODY OF ST. MARK AT VENICE.

A 17th Century Mosaic from the West Front of St. Mark's Venice.

N.5.

FROM "THE PSALTER OF ROBERT DE LISLE." C1322.

K.9.

CHAPTER XV. *Concerning a Gesture which we will call "The Sign of Resignation."*

ET US NOW consider this sign, which consists in crossing the hands over the breast with the tips of the fingers resting on the shoulders. (See illustration opposite page 132.) There is a tradition that the left arm should be uppermost, and although artists often ignore this small point (see illustration opposite page 122) there is probably some foundation for the tradition. It will be noticed that this sign is easily made from that of Sacrifice and, as the latter is usually made by placing the right hand on the left shoulder, in order to pass to this second sign one has merely to cover it with the left arm.

There is a peculiar fact connected with this sign which deserves a little consideration, the more so as the same peculiarity is noticeable in connection with two other important gestures, namely, that which has been called "The Sign of Heaven and Earth," and the one designated "The Sign of Completion." All three of these seem to appear in the 14th century, and it is certainly an interesting problem why this should be so, seeing that both the sign we are considering and that of Heaven and Earth were well known in ancient days and then seem to have vanished for a period of at least 1,000 years.

The Sign of Resignation constantly occurred in ancient Egypt, where the dead were buried with the hands thus crossed on the breasts, and the mummy cases almost always represent the deceased in this position.   For the dead it is a most appropriate sign, implying that they were resigned to their fate and laid down perfectly satisfied that the great judge would give to them the just reward of their deeds.   Thus it implied that they resigned their souls into his hands with perfect confidence.

Considering the vast influence of ancient Egypt on the early Christian Church, it is surprising to find that this gesture practically never appears on Christian sepulchral monuments.   Instead of being depicted with his arms crossed on his chest, alike in brasses and in sculptures in the round, the deceased is usually represented with his hands folded in prayer.   For more than a thousand years this sign practically vanishes and, although I have searched diligently,   I have been unable to find any example of its use until the 14th century. It is, of course, necessary to speak with a certain amount of caution, considering the vast field to be covered, but the remarkable difference noticeable when we reach the 14th century certainly calls for some explanation.   From that date until the end of the 17th century we find representations of the use of the Sign of Resignation in vast and increasing numbers, so much so that one might almost regard it and its companion sign, the Sign of Heaven and Earth, as characteristic of this closing period of the Middle Ages.

It is therefore worth considering whether its complete disappearance and sudden reappearance do not point to its being associated with some secret Rites of the Church.   In order to do so it seems necessary to point out that the Church did possess at any rate remnants of Secret Rites.   A considerable amount of evidence exists proving that in early days Christianity was to a large extent a secret society, a fact which partly explains the hostility with which it was regarded by some of the best of the Roman Emperors.   Civil governments at all times are apt to view with suspicion anything in the nature of a Secret Society inside their territory, and many of the monstrous charges made against the early Christians by their pagan opponents

THE TEMPLE OF RAMESES III. KARNAK.

A.32.

A 17TH CENTURY CANVAS PANEL EMBROIDERED WITH SILK AND WOOL.

Depicting the Sacrifice of Isaac, Abraham and the Angels, etc.

Original in the V. & A. Museum.

N.2.

can be traced to garbled and misunderstood accounts of their secret ceremonies. For example, the Christians were accused of sacrificing and eating children, a fantastic story, probably due to the fact that some spy had learnt a little about the Eucharist and the Christ Child. The Eucharist was undoubtedly to a large extent secret; Catechumens, i.e., unbaptised converts, were not permitted to be present at the Holy Communion, and the secret nature of the Mass still survives to some extent in the Greek Orthodox Church. In this Rite a curtain is drawn across the Sanctuary just before the Consecration, so that the act cannot be witnessed by the laity, and the Roman Catholic Church, although she has abolished the curtain, still has her "Secrets of the Mass" which are not revealed to those outside that ministry. Even to-day there are traces of an initiation in connection with Christianity. A person is admitted into the Christian Church by the ceremony of Baptism, and all baptised persons, except those who have been excommunicated, may be present at the Mass, but no one who has not been Confirmed is permitted to partake.

In the early Church, however, there were pass words and signs, the *Khi Rho* and the *Fish* being two of the best known, while certain words of power, written in the old, i.e., the Greek, language, still survive in the Roman Mass. When we turn to the signs we find that the use of the Sign of Blessing and the Sign of the Cross is widespread, so much so that they only require passing mention. The sign of Reverence is also used, namely, on Good Friday, at the Ceremony of the Adoration of the Cross, and at Venice, and probably in other large churches, it is customary during the Mass to pass round a peculiar grip among the Priests.

It is when we turn to the Monastic Orders, however, that we obtain some of the clearest evidence of the survival of what can only be described as remnants of the Ancient Mysteries. Most monks and nuns pass through a symbolic death and resurrection. In the majority of cases the novice is clad in white and laid in an actual coffin in front of the high altar, while the Mass for the Dead is sung. This is when he or she becomes "Professed," and previous to taking this degree the novice has passed through several preliminary grades. We find, moreover, that, at any rate during the Middle Ages, certain secret signs were known to the Monastic Orders, for Matthew Paris mentions them and adds, "Let us all endeavour to learn the necessary signs." [1]

The existence of such knowledge among the Mediæval monks may in part explain how it is that in the illuminated manuscripts which they wrote and illustrated in their monasteries we find such abundant use of these signs. As to the sculptures, it should be recollected that while many of these were carved by the monks themselves, others undoubtedly were carved by professional masons, but even here the knowledge may have filtered through to the Masonic Guilds from lay brethren. Most of the monasteries had lay brethren who were skilled craftsmen, and for a large monastery it was essential that among these there should be a number of masons, well qualified and expert in their craft.

The above facts cannot be brushed aside, they are too well known to students of mediæval history, and in view of them I would suggest that what happened in the 14th century was the release of some higher degree which up till then had been reserved for only a few centres, such as the Mother Abbeys of the various foundations. It is noticeable that during that period several important events occurred. At the beginning of the 14th century took place that sudden, and curious, attack on the Knights Templar, which swept them away. About the same time we have Dante writing his Divine Comedy, and on the other hand an immense increase in the veneration of our Lady, which led to the building of great Lady Chapels, almost as large as small churches. Before that date the Lady Chapel had been very little different in size from any other side chapel, but from the 14th century onwards it becomes a large building behind the High Altar, completely dwarfing all other chapels. It is not easy to say definitely what was the nature of the ceremony which was now permitted to be worked on a more extensive scale but, judging from the signs, it was connected on the one hand with the veneration of the Rose and the Blessed Virgin Mary, and on the other with the journey through Hell and the entry into Paradise. In other words, it would be a degree subsequent to the degree of death taken by all the "Professed." My reasons for this conclusion are that some of the earliest examples of this sign occur in manuscripts depicting Dante's Divine Comedy. Thus in the illustration reproduced opposite page 92, we

---

[1] See previous mention on page 23.

see four stages of Dante's journey into Paradise, and in the third and fourth he is shown making this sign. In the third it appears as if his instructor were opening his eyes and in the fourth he is clearly investing him with a rope or girdle.

Another 14th century example is a French Diptych, which is now in the British Museum and is illustrated in the Guide to Mediæval Antiquities in that collection. It is a beautiful ivory carving, and in one of the panels we are shown the Crucifixion, wherein our Lady is represented making this gesture, instead of one of the more usual signs made by her on such occasions, to which we have previously alluded. So far this is the earliest example of Our Lady in this position which I have found, although, of course, we have a whole series of works of art showing the Crucifixion, stretching back to the Dark Ages. Here we have the sign associated with the Virgin and with death, and if we had to translate her gesture into words they would be, "Not my will but Thine, O God, be done," that is to say, *resignation*.

A third example from the 14th century is the fresco in St. James's Church, Southleigh, near Oxford, to which reference has already been made in Chapter VIII. It is over the Chancel Arch and is a Last Judgment scene and, as is usually the case, contains a vast number of signs, all appropriately used, including Distress, Preservation, Sacrifice and Throwing the Hand over the Shoulder, but in addition it shows one of the earliest examples of the use of the Sign of Resignation. It is made by one of the souls, who rises from his grave on the right hand of the Judge, that is to say, to Salvation. So here again we get that other idea of a journey after death into Paradise. In the subsequent centuries we shall find many examples of the use of this sign in paintings of the Last Judgment, and so we will here and now point out how its use in such scenes links up with its original meaning in ancient Egypt. The souls who rise from the dead in this attitude intimate thereby the perfect confidence with which they resign their cause into the hands of the just Judge.

Turning to the 15th century, a painting of the Assumption of the Virgin, in the Uffizi Gallery, Florence, by Perugino, shows Our Lady going up to Heaven in the Vesica Piscis, a symbol sometimes represented by the Rose, and beneath her a monk is making the sign, and in a second painting by the same artist, also at Florence, namely, one showing the Crucifixion, we see another monk in a similar attitude. Thus these two pictures indicate a close association of the sign with, firstly, the Monastic Orders; secondly, death; thirdly, the Virgin; fourthly, the Vesica Piscis and fifthly, entrance into Paradise.

Now let us revert to our original proposition. At the beginning of the 14th century the Templars were suppressed, and although greed and jealousy were no doubt the predominant causes of their downfall, there seems little doubt that there was a certain amount of truth in the charge that they had been working some Rite of which the Church Authorities strongly disapproved. It is possible that the Rite was really heretical, but even if so it may have been not very dissimilar from a perfectly orthodox Rite of the Church which was higher than those they were entitled to work. If I am correct in my thesis, beyond the degree of death by which all monks were "professed" there lay one or more higher degrees, which dramatically represented what befell the Christian after death, but these degrees could only be worked at the Mother Abbeys and the branches thereof, often separated from the Mother Abbey by considerable distances, were not permitted to work them. Lest this thesis may appear unreasonable to those not fully conversant with monastic regulations, let me add that even to-day certain Houses of the Monastic Orders of the Roman Church in this country have to send their members to the Mother House on the Continent to take certain final steps before they become fully professed. No doubt the purpose of such regulations is to retain discipline and control over such subordinate houses, and to make sure that the ceremony is performed correctly and with dignity, a thing not always possible in a small House where only a few people would possess these higher degrees. But it has its obvious disadvantages, involving expense and long delay in the case of a deserving candidate. In the Middle Ages, however, what with defective transport, bad roads and, above all, constant wars on the Continent, it must often have been impossible for the monks in many parts of England ever to obtain these degrees. I suggest that the Templars, faced with this difficulty, had been working them without due authority. Therefore, after their suppression, the Papacy gave permission to the larger abbeys to work certain degrees under due safe-

THE TRANSFIGURATION, BY FRA ANGELICO.
At St. Mark's Monastery, Florence.

L.26.

"THE NATIVITY" AND "THE FLIGHT INTO EGYPT."
A French Miniature made for the Duchess of Brittany.   Circa A.D. 1480.
Original in the Victoria and Albert Museum.

L.47.

guard, with the natural result that far more people obtained them, and the artists among them could not resist the temptation to work these signs into their pictures, as private hints to the initiated. At any rate, until a better theory is established, this one is deserving of very careful consideration, and if followed up may lead to the discovery of other facts which will either confirm or contradict it. If it be asked why the Virgin and the Rose should be closely associated with such a degree, I would suggest that one explanation may be that all through the Middle Ages the Virgin is represented as the special intercessor with our Lord, the Just Judge, on behalf of sinful man, therefore the soul who had to pass through Purgatory to Paradise was well advised to seek her assistance. Thus in any dramatic representation of such a journey stress would naturally be made on the desirability of so doing. As to the Rose and the Vesica Piscis, from the very earliest times these have been associated with the female principle and therefore later with Our Lady, who was regarded as the crown of womanhood.

As will be seen from the list at the end of this book, the 15th century supplies quite a number of examples of the use of the Sign of Resignation, but I feel that more than passing reference is due to two paintings by that great artist, Fra Angelico, both being frescoes at the Monastery of St. Mark's, Florence. The Transfiguration of Our Lord, to which we have already had to allude on several occasions because of the appearance therein of more than one mantric sign, gives an example of the use of the Sign of Resignation under somewhat unusual circumstances. The Biblical account makes it clear that the only persons present at that event were the three apostles, Moses and Elijah and our Lord, but the artist has allowed himself more than the usual artistic privilege by inserting in addition the figures of St. Dominic and the Virgin. The former, of course, was his patron saint, but the appearance of the latter must be due to the special devotion with which she was regarded by this Monastic Order of which Fra Angelico was a member. It is significant that it is she who is making the sign we are considering and that the glory round our Lord is in the form of the Vesica Piscis. (See illustration opposite page 126.)

The other fresco by this artist to which I alluded shows the Last

Judgment, in which Christ is seen coming in glory in the midst of a double vesica piscis, which itself is surrounded by two more circles, consisting of saints and angels, thus making an outer double vesica piscis. (See illustration opposite page 192.) At the bottom of this emblem stands an angel bearing the cross and making the Sign of Heaven and Earth, as it is called in Asia. To the right of our Lord, but outside the mystic symbol, is seated the Virgin, making the Sign of Resignation and, strangely enough, in relatively the same position as she occupies in the fresco of the Transfiguration, while opposite to her is another saint, making the Sign of Prayer and occupying the same position as does St. Dominic in the other picture, who also makes the latter sign.

The careful correspondence between these two pictures shows clearly that the artist intended to convey a deep symbolic lesson, and although we may be unable to unravel its full significance the close connection between the Virgin, the vesica piscis and this sign is self-evident. Exoterically, at any rate, the gesture indicates the complete confidence of the Virgin in the judgment of our Lord, while it is possibly intended to remind Him of her patience and resignation throughout life, on the strength of which she claims permission to plead for erring man. That Fra Angelico attached great significance to this sign is further proved by his painting of the Deposition from the Cross, wherein an old man in the foreground is making it.

It is in this century that we get another theme wherein this sign begins to appear, namely, the Nativity. In the earlier representations, the Signs of Preservation and Reverence are the ones most closely associated with this scene, but in the 15th century, although these still continued to be employed, in addition we find the Sign of Resignation, usually made by one of the angels. For example in the illustration reproduced opposite this page, (L.47), which is from a French Book of Hours of about 1480, the infant Christ is making an excellent example of the Sign of Preservation, but an angel in the background makes the gesture we are discussing. In a similar scene painted inside an initial D, which is French work of 1450, and of which I have a reproduction, although the original is in a private collection, we have the Virgin and St. Joseph kneeling in front of the infant Christ and between them two tiny angels. Again the Christ Child is making the Sign of Preservation and one of the angels that of Resignation. The interpretation here appears to be twofold. Firstly, the angel signifies his resignation at the loss which Heaven sustained by Christ's descent to earth, and, secondly, he acknowledges Christ's own resignation to His Father's will in thus putting aside his Godhead and taking upon Him our frail mortality.

A 15th century wood block by the Florentine School which is now in the British Museum gives us a further extension of the use of this sign. It depicts our Lord rising from the tomb; the Roman soldiers are making the Sign of Reverence as He ascends, while on either side stand a pair of angels. The one on His right has his hand to his throat with the gesture meaning, "True till Death," while the corresponding angel on the left makes the sign we are discussing, thus once more bringing it into close relation with death which, as we have seen, was its original significance in Egypt.

For students of the ancient sign language perhaps the greatest treasure of the 16th century is the Sforza Book of Hours, which is now in the British Museum. Some of the miniatures were painted in Italy at the very end of the 15th century, but the book was either damaged or never finished, for quite a number were added some twenty years later by a Flemish artist. We have at least three miniatures in this book containing the Sign of Resignation, all of them Flemish. The first represents the Nativity and it is the Virgin who makes the sign, whereby the artist probably intended to imply that by prophetic powers she foresaw the future sufferings of our Lord and her own sorrow, and thus signified her resignation in face of the trials which awaited her. Perhaps a more striking example is the miniature depicting St. Clare repelling the Saracens, which is illustrated opposite page 130. Here again we have that monastic touch which, as we have seen, is so often associated with the use of this sign. St. Clare advances to meet the approaching Saracens, bearing in her hands a Monstrance containing the Sacred Host. Behind her are gathered the other nuns, one of whom places her left hand to her throat to symbolise that she is willing to be faithful unto death, while a second falls on her knees and by this sign shows her resignation to whatever fate it may please God to send to her and her sisters.

In the background appears the West end of the Church attached to the monastery, adorned with sculptures, in the top panel of which is a representation of the Virgin and Child, accompanied by two saints, and the Child is depicted making the Sign of Preservation. According to the legend, at the sight of the Monstrance the Saracens were stricken with terror and fled, and in the miniature some of them, who had climbed up the front of the building in order to force an entrance through the windows, are seen falling from it. The third example is of St. Albert of Trapani and in it one onlooker is making the Sign of Reverence and an angel in the background makes the the sign we are considering. (See M.19, opposite this page). In a *Deposition from the Cross*, by Andrea del Sarto, at Florence, one of the women makes this sign while the Virgin holds our Lord's arm with a peculiar grip.

The next illustration to which we will devote attention is reproduced opposite page 132 and is from a Printed Book of Hours of about 1527, the original of which is in the Victoria and Albert Museum. As it contains the Sign of Distress and our Lord is making the Sign of Preservation, it has, of course, been mentioned previously, so here all that is necessary is to point out that once again Christ's Sign of Preservation is answered by crossing both arms on the breast, this time made, not by an angel, but by the Virgin herself. The example is a particularly good one as from the nature of the medium we can see distinctly that the left hand is placed over the right.

Let us next turn to the illustration opposite page 186, which represents the Last Judgment, by Hans Dyg (1519). We have already alluded to the fact that all the souls who are rising are making mantric signs and have promised that towards the end of the book we will endeavour to interpret the complete series as a definite whole. We will therefore content ourselves now with mentioning that the woman in the foreground who makes the Sign of Resignation does so with the right hand uppermost. It is, however, worth pointing out that in order that the figures in the foreground might be reproduced on a reasonably large scale we have had to omit the upper half of the fresco, which shows our Lord coming to judge the world, surrounded by saints and angels. On His right kneels the Virgin, and as is so often the case she has her hands crossed on her breast in order that she may form the Sign of Resignation.

"ST. CLARE REPELLING THE SARACENS."
A Miniature from *The Sforza Book of Hours.*
Now in the British Museum.

M.35.

"ST. ALBERT OF TRAPANI."
A Miniature from *The Sforza Book of Hours.*
In the British Museum.

M.19.

THE NATIVITY.

From a Printed Book of Hours. Circa 1527 A.D.

M.3.

In the 17th century a mosaic over the West door of St. Mark's Cathedral, Venice, made in 1660, shows a number of mantric signs and is reproduced opposite page 120.   It represents the arrival of the body of St. Mark at Venice and one of the sailors in the boat is making this gesture.   But to English people a more interesting example is an embroidered panel now in the Victoria and Albert Museum and reproduced opposite page 124.   It depicts various Biblical scenes connected with Abraham, including the Sacrifice of Isaac.   As he kneels before the pile of wood the latter makes this significant gesture to show his resignation to the fate which appears to be in store for him.   It is hardly necessary to point out how appropriate is the use of this sign in this case, for not only is it associated with death but testifies to the willing sacrifice of Isaac.   Despite the fact that Isaac is usually represented as a boy, the Biblical account makes it clear that he was a full grown man, quite strong enough to make a vigorous resistance to an old man like Abraham, with whom, it must be remembered, he was absolutely alone.   Hence his acquiesence in the terrible fate threatening him is a fine example of resignation to the will of God, and as such was seized on by Divines as a prototype of Christ and His sacrifice upon the Cross.

Any readers who have visited the Engandine Museum at St. Moritz will remember that it contains a wonderfully panelled room, taken from a 17th century Chateau in the neighbourhood.   The panels are divided by twisted pillars, each of which terminates in a caryatide.   Above them is a frieze and above this another series of panels, divided by figures of little boys, who in their turn support an elaborately carved roof.   Now the striking thing about the room is that practically all the caryatides, and likewise all the boys above them, are making mantric signs.   Thus the first but one on the right as we enter the door makes the sign we are discussing, which sign is also shown by one of the small boys in a different part of the room, (See N.3, opposite page 170).   We also get the Sign of Heaven and Earth in more than one place, to say nothing of a host of other signs. One cannot help wondering therefore whether at some time this room was intended for some Rite of a quasi-religious nature.

Considering that, as we have seen, the light of tradition was almost obscured in the 18th century, it is satisfactory to find that this

sign was not entirely forgotten and it is probably not altogether
accidental that it is used in connection with Dante's entry into
Paradise.   Two illustrations by John Flaxman, engraved by Piroli
in 1793, are now in the British Museum.   In one Beatrice and Dante
are seen viewing the Virgin at a distance, surrounded by angels;
Beatrice has her hand to her throat in a significant manner, as have
several of the angels, while the Virgin makes the Sign of Resignation.
In the other engraving the Virgin is seen seated surrounded by saints,
two of whom are making this sign, while in an outer circle of angels
several of them are also making it.

At St. Mark's, Venice, is a mosaic, inserted over one of the West
doors about 1830 in order to complete the series.   It is illustrated
opposite page 134 and has been alluded to in a previous chapter.   It
depicts our Lord in Glory, and on His right kneels the Virgin Mary,
making the sign.   Thus have we bridged the centuries and just as in
the 14th we showed the sign associated with Dante and with the Virgin,
so in the 18th and 19th we find the same associations.   So far, however, we have dealt only with Europe, but its use is not by any means
restricted to this Continent, for I have been able to collect examples
from Asia and Africa.

On the Abyssinian Cross illustrated opposite page 178, on the
left hand arm as we view it, will be seen depicted the Virgin adoring
the infant Christ.   Near by is the upper part of a man, who makes
this gesture, while nearer to the centre is a full length engraving of
an angel in the same significant posture.   We thus see that the
Abyssinian Church follows the same tradition as that of Europe.

When, however, we turn to the illustration opposite page 218 and
look at the carved Yoruba Gates from Oyo we can no longer restrict
the use of this sign to the Christian Church, for, among other mantric
signs this one will be seen, made by a little figure at the bottom of the
third board from the left as we look at the picture.   Moreover, in
an illustration of a Konde Dance in my possession, to which allusion
has been previously made, one of the onlookers is also making this
sign.   It is quite possible, of course, that it has reached Central
and West Africa from the banks of the Nile, although in the author's
opinion the more probable explanation is that the Egyptians brought
it forward from the days when they were no more civilised than were

the blacks of West Africa when discovered by the white man. In other words, that this was originally one of the magical signs associated with the primitive initiatory rites of the early ancestors of men.   If it were only Africa and Europe which we had to consider, an Egyptian origin might suffice, but as Asia also supplies examples of its use we are driven to the conclusion that its origin must date back to a more primitive period.

In Asia an interesting example of the use of this sign occurs in a Persian manuscript of the 15th century now in the Musée des Arts Décoratifs, Paris, entitled, *Humay and Humayun*.   Here we have four Persians standing in a garden, one of whom appears to be a visitor, greeting the other three, who are women.   It is the man who makes the sign, and with its aid it is not difficult to interpret the meaning of the picture.   The young man has made a proposal of some sort to the lady, probably an amorous one, and indicates that now his fate is in her hands.

The 17th century painting of The Deposition from the Cross, to which allusion has been made previously, contains a particularly good example of the Sign of Resignation, made with the left arm uppermost. [1]   Its appropriateness is so obvious that it need not detain us, and the same is true of another Christian subject, this time Indian work of the 17th century.   Here we have the Virgin, apparently wrapping up the infant Christ, while a servant, for such she obviously is, makes the sign we are considering.   This picture clearly shows European influence for the servant is dressed in Western clothing, whereas the Persian painting has nothing to suggest European influence and may be merely a Mahomedan version of the Bible story, for the Mahomedans accept Christ as a great prophet.

A purely heathen picture from India, however, will dispose of the theory that the sign is merely imported, and I can produce at least three examples.   Thus it occurs in an 18th century Indian painting of Krishna playing on his flute, the original being in the Berlin Museum.   In this we not only have a good representation of the Sign of Resignation, made by a woman, but a second woman is pretending to strike off her hand.

Two sculptured slabs will finally dispel any doubt in our minds

---

See Illustration opposite page 136.

as to whether this sign has been imported from Europe.   In an early Buddhist bas-relief of the pre-Christian era, representing the Worship of the Sacred Tree, we have a fine example of the Sign of Preservation and near by, on a separate piece of carving taken from the same building, is depicted a man making the sign which is the main theme of this chapter.   Nor does it stand alone, for if we turn to the illustration opposite page 200, of Vishnu sleeping under the sacred Cobra, we find one of the figures in the bottom row making this gesture, flanked by another who makes the sign of Heaven and Earth.   In this case Vishnu was about to descend to earth to help mankind in its struggle against a great ogre.   The figure making the sign thus intimates that he is resigned to his fate, which appears to be an early death, since the earthly champion could hardly hope for victory if unaided.   He is seen drawing his sword, but the figures on either side of him show by their gestures that they know that Vishnu is about to descend to help them.

Thus, at any rate so far as the old world is concerned, we find this sign in use and, wherever we can interpret it, with the same significance, namely, resignation to fate or to the will of God.

"OUR LORD IN GLORY."

A Mosaic on the West Front of St. Mark's Venice.   19th Century.

P.2.

THE DEPOSITION FROM THE CROSS.

A Persian Miniature of the 17th Century.

U.15.

CHAPTER XVI. *Tells us of the Sign of Heaven and Earth and its use in Europe and in Asia.*

AST AND WEST alike know the sign we are now about to consider and in Asia it is called either *The Sign of Heaven and Earth* or *The Sign of the Witness*. The latter name arises from an ancient legend connected with Buddha, which is as follows:—

The Lord Buddha was accused of immoral conduct by a wicked woman, whereupon he pointed with his right hand to heaven and his left to earth and called on Heaven and Earth to witness the falsity of the charge. Hence it is that in many statues, bas-reliefs, and paintings of the Buddha he is depicted making this sign. In the Hung Society of China it is called *The Sign of Heaven and Earth* and this seems to be the underlying principle behind all its variant uses.

In Europe it usually has a more precise significance, particularly in Christian art, and implies that someone has descended from Heaven to earth and afterwards reascended, or, alternately, that someone has descended into the grave and thence ascended into Heaven. Occasionally it would appear as if the stress is laid upon the *ascending*, implying that someone first ascended to Heaven and then descended to earth in order to help mankind.   It is not surprising therefore to find that in Christian art it is closely associated with the resurrection of our Lord, although, as we shall see, it occasionally occurs in connection with other incidents, such as the Raising of Lazarus.

In the East, where the doctrine of reincarnation is firmly established, it seems sometimes to imply that the character making it has first ascended to heaven and subsequently descended to earth and been reincarnated thereon.   It is indeed probable that when made by Buddha, the Witness Sign originally referred to the fact that he, having achieved the beatific vision, or ascended into Heaven, condescended to descend once more to earth in order to preach his gospel to humanity.

The sign has several minor variations, the most important being (1) the one hand extended upwards as far as possible, palm open and fingers close together, while the other is pointing to earth.   (2) The index finger only of the one hand pointing upwards, and that of the other, pointing downwards.   Sometimes in this position the hands are placed in front of the body, with wrists close together, and the index fingers pointing up and down respectively.   There is, however, another variation, difficult to recognise in painting or sculpture, whereby only the right hand is used.   In this case the hand first points upward and then down.   In one or two cases, to which I shall refer later, a man is seen pointing downwards only or upwards only, but despite the existence of this variation I am of the opinion that here we have a case of the sign being divided.   Pointing downward denotes that the man is dead, buried in the earth or passed into the underworld, while the upward gesture would indicate "He is not here, he has ascended."

Having thus made clear the various sub-forms of the sign and their symbolical significance, we will now draw attention to a peculiarity of its use in Europe.   In Asia it seems always to have been known, but while we have definite evidence that it was known and used in Christian Rome, thereafter we have a complete hiatus until it reappears in the 14th century, at the very same time as the Sign of Resignation is found.   Indeed, all that has been said in the previous chapter about the probable significance of the temporary disappearance of the Sign of Resignation, and its reappearance in large numbers·

in the 14th and 15th centuries, holds good of the Sign of Heaven and Earth, which seems in some mysterious way to be associated with the other sign, and therefore probably with the Mystery Rite which we have suggested explains the reappearance of the Sign of Resignation. The appropriateness of such a sign in connection with a Rite dealing with the descent of the soul into the Underworld and its subsequent ascent into Paradise is obvious, and strengthens the arguments in favour of the view that such was the drama and symbolism of the initiation degree connected with the other sign.

The earliest example of the use of *The Sign of Heaven and Earth* which I have found appears in a bas-relief from Babylonia, now in the British Museum, depicting the adoration of the Sacred Tree by two semi-divine beings. The figures are pointing upwards with their right hands and downwards with the left, but whereas the hands pointing upward are outstretched, those pointing down in each case hold a large bracelet-like object, strongly reminiscent of the discs used in the worship of Priapus in ancient Rome.

Although I have been informed that some frescoes of Horus show him making this sign, I have been unable to find an example. I think, however, that my information is probably correct as in the nature of the case one would expect to find this sign associated with that God, who to a large extent represents the risen Osiris who has returned to earth.

In Greece the sign is associated with the Eleusinian Mysteries and a bas-relief from that site, circa 450, which is reproduced opposite page 176, shows the neophyte before the hierophantess making this sign with the two torches which she holds. The hierophantess no doubt symbolically represents Ceres and is showing to the initiate a bunch of ears of corn, a symbol of the body, which is planted in the earth and rises therefrom to a more glorious life. Exoterically, the upturned torch was explained as symbolising life and the down-turned one reminded the neophyte of death and of the underworld, through which in symbolism she had passed during the ceremony of initiation. Many other examples of upturned and downturned torches could be quoted, but they are almost too well known for us to waste space upon them. It is sufficient to say that this action is merely an alternative form of the sign we are discussing and, further, that even as near home as Scotland at the present day on certain occasions, such as All Hallows Eve and St. John in Winter, processions occur in which torches are carried, and at some particular spot are turned down and beaten out. Often the people who perform this ancient rite have forgotten its old meaning, but for all that it undoubtedly originally referred to the dead who had passed into the Underworld.

A very important and striking example of the use of this sign in the Roman period is to be seen in the ruins of the Church of St. Mary Antiqua, which stands in the Forum at Rome. On the right hand side as we enter the building from the Forum there is a fresco of the three Maries, each of them holding a child. Christ, of course, is in the centre, with St. John the Evangelist on one side, and St. James on the other. St. James makes the Sign of Preservation while St. John makes an excellent example of the Sign of Heaven and Earth. The date of the painting is 5th century A.D. Then comes the strange silence, 900 years during which this sign vanishes, or at any rate wherein I have so far found no example of its use.

A 14th century carved, ivory diptych, now in the Louvre, contains among other scenes a representation of the Crucifixion. From the attitude of Christ it is clear that He is dead, and an onlooker points his hand upward to signify that He has ascended into heaven. It is possible that the other hand, which is partly covered by the figure of St. John, makes the rest of the sign, but it cannot be said for certain whether this is so (See illustration opposite page 138). Another example, also in the Louvre, appears on the ivory coffer reproduced opposite page 70. We have previously alluded to these scenes, showing how in the first one the attendant, finding her mistress dead or dying, makes the Sign of Preservation; in the second, she throws up her hands in distress as the lady's lover commits suicide on discovering the death of his loved one. In the third scene a man has entered the room and is drawing out the sword from the lover's body, hoping to save his life, but the maid points her right hand to heaven and her left the earth, wrists close together, intimating thereby that the man's well-meant efforts are too late and the lover is dead: "His body to the earth, and his soul to heaven," would be the words she would utter.

AN IVORY DIPTYCH OF THE 14TH CENTURY.
Now in the Louvre.

K.7.

THE RESURRECTION, BY FRA ANGELICO.
At St, Mark's Monastery, Florence.

L.51.

A third, and somewhat unusual, example occurs on some panels from orphreys, embroidered during the second half of the fourteenth century, the originals of which are in the Victoria and Albert Museum. They contain scenes from the life of the Virgin and in one of them St. Anne and St. Joachim, mother and father of the Virgin, are both making this sign as they watch her beginning to walk. It will be remembered that according to the legends, which enlarge somewhat on the Gospel narrative, St. Joachim was informed by an angel of the coming birth of his daughter and that she should be the mother of the Messiah, and it seems as if the two parents were making these signs to testify to her semi-divine nature and also prophetically to indicate her death and assumption into heaven.

In the 15th Century, stained glass panel of the Nativity shown opposite page 108, the angel is making this sign, while Fra Angelico supplies no less than three examples of its use. In his fresco of the Resurrection, reproduced opposite page 140, to which we have previously alluded, the angel makes this sign as the women look into the empty tomb. The implication of the gesture indicates more than the actual words in the Gospel, for it means that He has descended into Hell and from thence has ascended into Paradise. In his picture of the Last Judgment, reproduced opposite page 192, to which also we have previously referred in connection with the Sign of Resignation, the angel bearing the cross, at the lowest point of the Vesica Piscis, has her two hands so arranged as to make this sign over her centre.

Finally, in his painting of the Descent of the Holy Ghost which, like his other two, is at Florence, not only is one of the Apostles making the Sign of Reverence, but a female saint, probably St. Mary Magdalene, is making the Sign of Heaven and Earth, while a second woman near her is likewise pointing her right hand upward, although we cannot say for certain what she is doing with her left since it is hidden. It is also worth nothing that whereas in both of the other pictures the Christ is in the centre of the Vesica Piscis, in this case the Apostles and Saints are standing shoulder to shoulder, so as to form a perfect vesica piscis, into the midst of which the Holy Ghost is descending in the form of a dove. It is also significant that the Virgin stands in the centre of the back arc, as if *she* were presiding at the assembly. These facts should be considered in connection with the indications

I have already given that the other sign, namely that of Resignation, is closely associated with the Rose, or vesica piscis, and with the Virgin.   It is possibly for this reason that the artist has restricted the use of the sign to the two women, also it must be admitted that in the other two pictures the angels making it have a distinctly feminine cast of features.

A similar association with women occurs in the last example which we will quote from the 15th century.   In the Raising of Lazarus, by Nicholas Froment, now in the Louvre and reproduced opposite page 152, a woman, probably Mary, kneels at the foot of the grave making this sign, just as Lazarus rises from it. She is in striking contradiction to another woman who makes another sign, of which the interpretation appears to be "It is finished," i.e., "all is over," and to which we shall refer in the next chapter.   No doubt Mary is saying, "Although he has descended into the Underworld, or grave, yet at Thy will, O Master, he has ascended once again."

Turning to the 16th century we have a curious and interesting variation of the Sign in a painting of the Descent from the Cross by the Master of "The Death of Mary," an unknown Flemish painter of this epoch.   St. Mary Magdalene is making the Sign of Distress and a monk in the left hand corner points with his left hand to earth, implying that he has descended into the Underworld.   Note, he correctly uses the left hand, but his right hand does not point upwards.   Possibly the artist meant to imply that he had no hope of the resurrection, a justifiable view seeing that from the Gospel narrative it is clear that none of the Apostles envisaged the wonderful end of the grim tragedy. But the monk clutches in his hand a lily, the counterpart of the Rose, emblem of the female principle, and the lily points up to heaven, a subtle little point, cleverly conveying to the onlooker the fact that although the apostles did not know that Christ had ascended or would rise from the grave, yet the dumb flower, emblem of the Virgin Mary, knew quite well.

The miniature of the death of St. Peter Martyr, from the Sforza Book of Hours, is reproduced opposite page 142 because it contains a peculiarly interesting example of the use of this sign.   As the unfortunate man is stricken down by the murderer he points one hand to heaven and the other to earth, clearly implying that although his body would descend into the earth, his soul would ascend into heaven. The reason the hands are reversed is evidently for the purpose of clarity, for had the right hand been raised and the left pointing downwards the sign would not have been so clear, as a glance at the reproduction will show.

In the 17th century the famous carved room in the Museum at St. Moritz supplies an interesting variation of the Sign. Not only are the hands reversed, but the left hand is crossed over the upper half of the body and the right arm over the lower part. (See illustration opposite page 170). Above, on the cornice, can be seen one of the little boys making the Sign of Resignation. Furthermore, in the same room, in the corner of the door, two of the caryatides come close together so that they almost appear to be speaking to each other. One points to earth and the other answers her by pointing to heaven. Here again we have the female figures making the sign. Unfortunately, the corner of the room to which I am now alluding does not appear in the section reproduced in this book, but I have a photograph of the figures.

After the 17th century all signs become rare, yet in the private chapel of the Archbishop of Coire appear two paintings of cherubs, one in either corner of the wall, just beneath the ceiling, one of whom makes the Sign of Preservation and the other that of Heaven and Earth. Between them, on the floor, stands the altar, wherein is a tabernacle containing the Host. Thus He who descended and ascended is present to Preserve His worshipppers, for such of course is the meaning of the symbol, this being the doctrine taught by the Roman Church.

Outside Europe, Asia and America supply examples of the use of this sign, but on the other hand it should be noted that so far I have been unable to find evidence of its use among the more primitive races. One of the earliest Asiatic examples is a painting from Mesopotamia, of 1222 A.D., reproduced opposite page 106, the original being in the Sarre Collection, Berlin. The picture, to which we have already referred in connection with the Sign of Secrecy, represents the Magician Erasistratos and his Familiar, or the ghost he is in the habit of calling up from the Underworld. The spirit makes an excellent example of this sign to indicate either that he himself has come from the Underworld and ascended to earth at the behest of his master or, alternatively, that he is replying to a question of the magician concerning the whereabouts of another spirit.   In any case, the close association of the use of this sign with the Underworld and the raising of a spirit therefrom is in consonance with the examples of its use we have seen in the West, which, be it noted, are all a century later than this Eastern picture.   This fact is of some importance, for the accusation against the Templars was that they had imported heretical and even non-Christian ideas from Asia, as a result of their contact with the infidels, or in other words, it is quite possible that they were illegally working a high degree dealing with this theme which they had obtained either from Asiatic Gnostics or unorthodox Mahomedans.   I have previously suggested that, as a counterblast to such a movement, the Pope gave permission for the working of the equivalent Christian degree in far more centres than had been the case previously.

Passing to India we find the sign well known and usually associated with Vishnu, the Preserver. Several peculiarities concerning this god must therefore be mentioned, for they show that the association of this sign with Him is perfectly reasonable.   Vishnu is fabled to have descended to earth nine times in various avatars and on more than one occasion is said to have been slain and then brought to life again.   Furthermore, as Krishna he is said to have descended into Hell and rescued therefrom his earthly brothers, who had been murdered.   Finally, after having accomplished his work on earth in each avatar, he reascended into Heaven.   In one illustration of the God which is in my possession He stands inside a truncated vesica piscis, a fact which should be compared with the use of this emblem in Mediæval Europe.   On either side, and actually carved on this emblem, stand two attendants, one of whom is making the Sign of Heaven and Earth.

Another illustration reproduced opposite page 144, depicts Vishnu in his lion incarnation coming out of the vesica piscis, which is carved on a pillar, and again we have a little attendant making the sign. The third example is shown opposite page 200 and to it we have alluded on more than one occasion.   It represents Vishnu sleeping under the five-headed cobra, and about to descend to earth in order that he may help mankind against the ogre.   A woman in the bottom

"THE DEATH OF ST. PETER, MARTYR."
A Miniature from *The Sforza Book of Hours*.
Now in the British Museum.

M.34.

THE LION INCARNATION OF VISHNU.
A Sculpture on a Pillar in a Hindu Temple.

U.39.

row of figures, and note, it is a *woman*, makes the sign. The fact is the more significant as she is the only woman in the whole series of figures in the lower register.

We have already mentioned that statues of the Buddha are constantly depicted making the Sign of Heaven and Earth, which among the Buddhists is called the Sign of the Witness. Two examples, however, namely, a painting and a bronze figure, are illustrated opposite pages 158 and 146. In the Chinese painting of the five Buddhas, it is the right hand, top figure which is making the sign,

Quetzalcoatl Challenged by the God of Death.

T.15.

and in doing so has placed his wrists close together in front of the centre of the body. The other example is of the child Buddha, clad in a curious apron and giving the other form of the sign, namely, one hand fully extended to heaven, and the other stretched downwards as far as possible and pointing towards the earth. I have a photograph of a somewhat similar figure of the Child Buddha, in precisely the same position, but standing on the lotus and having his hair done in a kind of scalp lock.

If we pass to Central America we shall find evidence not merely that this sign was well known to that strange, ancient people, the Aztecs, but further that it was definitely associated both with a Rite of Initiation and with the Mexican preserver, Quetzalcoatl. A series of illustrations from Mexican codices which are reproduced in the Bulletin of the Smithsonian Institute, U.S.A., depict incidents in the life of this god, wherein the sign occurs. For example, Quetzalcoatl, who had descended to earth in order to help man, is shown on a kind of ship, being challenged by the God of Death.[1] The latter points upwards, as if to say, "Your place is in Heaven and not on earth, where I am ruler," and Quetzalcoatl answers by pointing to Heaven and to Earth, by which simple gesture he summarises the whole of his legend-

Teaching a Candidate a Sign.
From the Mexican Codices.
T.16.

ary career. This god is said to have descended to earth, taught the Mexicans many of the arts of peace, fought with a great giant, by whom he was severely wounded, and then journeyed to the West, where he immolated himself on a great funeral pyre on the sea shore. Thence he descended into the Underworld through which he travelled for four days, finally reascending to Heaven, where he took up his residence in the Star Venus.

The second picture to which I wish to allude is reproduced above, and shows a Red Indian Initiate being taught the Sign of Heaven and Earth by the Mexican hierophant. The initiate places his hand on his lips in the Sign of Silence, while the Hierophant points to Heaven and Earth. Having previously pointed out the close

1 See Illustration on page 143.

connection between the Sign of Silence and the man who symbolically has risen from the dead, we can see that the teaching of this further sign is a natural corollary.

One last example from Mexico must suffice. In this a man is being taught a grip. The right hand of the Hierophant is grasping the *left* wrist of the candidate, who meanwhile is carefully pointing that hand downward, i. e., making the sign "He Descended." Not only is the index finger extended, but the hand has had to be twisted in such an unnatural position that it is impossible to avoid the conclusion that in this case we have a grip and sign combined, as a glance

A Candidate Being Taught a Grip.
From the Mexican Codices.
T.17.

at the illustration below will prove. Thus Mexico strongly supports my theory that this sign is connected not only with a legend of the journey through the Underworld, but with an actual Rite, wherein this journey is dramatically represented.

Probably the Codices which contained these drawings were intended for use in these Rites, enabling the Master of Ceremonies to memorise and explain the chief incidents therein and their connection with the hero. This aspect of the case compels us to consider very carefully the position of the right arm of the God of Death in the picture on page 143. It is bent at the elbow in such a way as to indicate that the hand is laid on the left shoulder to make the Sign of Sacrifice. The fact that the figure is drawn in profile makes this position somewhat complicated because of the need to show the other sign, but fortunately this is not the only example which occurs, for in the illustration shown opposite page 212, we are shown Quetzalcoatl descending from Heaven to earth by means of a ladder while in the sky above the other Gods make this same Sign of Sacrifice and point slightly downwards as if to say, "See, he is sacrificing himself by descending to earth."

Thus in Mexico we have a whole series of Signs starting apparently with that we have called "True till Death" but which perhaps in this case is more truly indicative of mortality. It occurs on the famous vase found at Chama wherein the candidates are seen with nooses round their necks and carrying human bones. Probably the whole ceremony implies the allegory of birth into a mortal body which will inevitably lead to death. Next we have the Sign of Preservation, which would naturally be connected with a degree representing the journey of life, and then the Sign of Distress made by a skeleton, which obviously connects with death. Lastly, we have the Sign of Sacrifice, which in Europe seems to be linked with the risen man, as is the Sign of Secrecy, while the Sign of Heaven and Earth is not only connected with the resurrection, but with the divine Salvator. In short, these Signs in outline give us the material for a complete rite of five degrees.

A CHINESE, BRONZE STATUE OF THE CHILD BUDDHA WEARING AN APRON.

U.28.

STATUE OF ATTIS IN THE MUSEUM AT AVIGNON.
3rd Century work.

F.26.

CHAPTER XVII. Which shows that Saint and Sinner alike use the Sign of Regret.

ESPAIR OR REGRET is indicated by resting the side of the head on one hand while supporting the elbow of that arm by the other hand, the arm of which lies across the body. It is more usual for the head to rest on the right hand, but if for convenience in balancing the picture the other hand seems more satisfactory, mediæval artists seem not to have hesitated to use this variation. A good example of the correct use of the sign occurs in the statue of Attis reproduced opposite page 148, the original of which is in the Museum at Avignon, the date of the work probably being of the 3rd century.

The fact that Attis makes this sign is of considerable importance seeing that he was one of the divine heroes of the great Mystery Rite of Cybele, being, indeed, but another form of the god Adonis, who in Syria was known as Tammuz. According to one form of the legend Attis died from a self-inflicted wound, but according to a later version he was killed by a wild boar. In either case he was the lover, and apparently also the son, of the great Earth Mother. Symbolically he represents the corn, which is planted in the earth that it may rise again as a plenteous harvest. He is thus the ancient Vegetation God, whose death and resurrection played such an important part in the old religious Mystery Rites. The initiate into these Mysteries was identified with this god and it was believed that because he rose from the dead the initiate might likewise hope for life beyond the grave. The Cult of Attis, or Adonis, was for a long time a serious rival of Christianity, particularly in Rome, and his Mysteries spread throughout the Roman Empire.

The reason Attis makes this sign is probably to indicate his regret at the hasty action which caused his death, for the meaning of the sign seems always to be *regret*, and could often be translated into some such phrase as "Alas, alas, my work (or life) has been in vain." The latter phrase is particularly applicable when the man making the sign forms part of a Judgment scene and often we find the lost souls making it. Perhaps not unnaturally, it is also constantly made by the Virgin in scenes representing the Crucifixion, more particularly in pictures and sculptures made before the 14th century, after which date the Sign of Resignation often replaces it. An early Mediæval example of the Virgin making this sign occurs in an ivory panel of the 11th century, now in the British Museum. The Virgin makes the Sign of Regret, while St. John answers it by striking off his left hand with his right. Above are two angels, each making the same gesture as the Virgin, one with the *left* hand touching the face and the other the *right*, the variation obviously being in order that the balance of the picture may be maintained.

In a 12th century manuscript, wherein there is another picture of the Crucifixion, we find the Virgin once more making the Sign of Regret, while St. John, with his hand to his throat, makes the gesture which we have previously explained indicates "true till death." This picture is reproduced opposite page 36. Another example from the same century occurs in the sculpture in the tympanum over the West door of the Cathedral of St. Laurence, Genoa. The scene represents the martyrdom of that saint, who is being baked on a gridiron, and one of the onlookers makes this sign to indicate his sorrow and regret at the terrible fate of the holy man.

In a mosaic of the same period reproduced opposite page 38 the original of which is in the Cathderal of Torcello, near Venice, we see three of the lost souls amid the fires of Hell, and one of them makes this sign which, as we have said, in such cases may be well translated, "Alas, Alas, my life has been in vain." In the sculpture over the West door of the Church of St. Trophime, Arles, among the numerous figures may be seen one who is making this sign. It is a Last Judgment and whereas on one side of the door appear the saints in glory, the unfortunate man making this sign is apparently among the lost.

When we come to the 13th century we find the same tradition maintained, for in a German portable altar, which is now in the British Museum, there is a small sculpture of the Crucifixion in which the Virgin by this gesture shows her sorrow and regret, and she appears also in the same position in the panel representing the Crucifixion among the mosaics which adorn the cupola of the Baptistery at Florence. Among the same mosaics is also that interesting scene to which we referred earlier in the book and in which this sign occurs. It depicts the sons of Jacob bringing to him Joseph's coat of many colours, smeared with blood. Joseph rests his head on his right hand, whose elbow he supports with his left, as he hears the doleful story, while the Mother of Joseph throws up her hands to heaven in her bitter grief and distress. This is shown opposite page 74.

Passing from the 13th to the 15th century, we find in an alabaster carving, now in the Victoria and Albert Museum, one of the apostles making this sign as Christ is lowered into the tomb. It is worth noting that our Lord's hands are crossed downwards over his loin cloth, a sign which is often used in the East but very seldom in the West, while St. Mary Magdalene makes the Sign of Preservation, perhaps to show that through His teaching Christ has converted her and so saved her from destruction. More probably, however, the artist intended to convey the suggestion that St. Mary Magdalene firmly believed that although apparently dead, our Lord would in reality be preserved and rise again, for it must be remembered that she was subsequently the first person who saw and recognised the risen Christ. It is quite possible that the Apostle who is making the Sign of Regret is meant to represent Thomas, the Doubter.

As usual a last Judgment supplies another excellent example, and is reproduced opposite page 150, being an early 15th century example of the Flemish School.   There is, however, something rather unusual about the figure making the sign.   A careful examination of the picture will show that his grave is exactly under our Lord's feet, that is, occupying the central line of the picture.   Every other figure clearly represents a soul either lost or saved, and many of them are making appropriate mantric signs.   This man himself is bending over towards the lost, with the side of his head resting on his left hand, but instead of completing the sign with his right arm he is making therewith the Sign of Sacrifice, and it would appear as if the artist has deliberately left the exact fate of this soul in doubt.   On the one hand a man says, "Alas, my life has been in vain," but literally, on the other hand, he pleads Christ's sacrifice for the lost sheep.   The combination of the two signs is unique and interesting.

In the painting of the Last Judgment at Basle, reproduced opposite page 192, which is 16th century work, we once more find a lost soul by this characteristic gesture proclaiming that his life has been in vain, while in a long, narrow painting, No. 132, at Hampton Court Palace, which represents *the Departure of Æneas*, we see Dido thus testifying to her regret at the loss of her lover.

Subsequent to the 16th century I have so far found no examples of the use of this sign until we come to the 20th, but doubtless they exist.   The last modern example occurs in a scene of the Crucifixion in the Chapel of St. Benedict, Buckfast Abbey, illustrated opposite page 54.   Here the Virgin makes the Sign of Regret while St. John answers with the Sign of Preservation.

From all these examples it will be seen that, as I said at the beginning of the chapter, the sign undoubtedly implies regret and sorrow.   It has the same implication outside Europe, and an interesting variation occurs in a Persian Miniature in the British Museum which shows Joseph being pulled up out of the pit.   An onlooker makes the combined form of the Signs of Secrecy and Regret. Furthermore, on a lacquered, Persian Book cover of the 17th century, now in the Victoria and Albert Museum, a group of onlookers are depicted gazing at a dead man and some of them are making this sign. (See U.3 and U.58 in the list at the end of this book).

THE LAST JUDGMENT
By the Flemish School.

"THE RAISING OF LAZARUS."
By Nicholas Froment.
In the Louvre Museum.

L.13.

CHAPTER XVIII. *Wherein is described the Sign of Completion and examples of its use.*

LANCING AT THE illustration opposite page 152, we see a good example of this sign. It is made by extending the hands downwards at an angle of about 39 degrees, with the palms upwards, and is so well shown in the illustration that no further description of it is required. Again, in a miniature from a manuscript now in the Vatican library, probably painted about the end of the 15th century, which depicts the Crucifixion, St. John, who makes the sign, by his gesture echoes the words of our Lord, "It is finished." Indeed, this sentence more nearly represents the significance of the gesture than any other phrase I can suggest, although under certain conditions a more colloquial form of speech might be considered as more appropriate, e. g., "That ends the matter," or "that business is finished."

The earliest example of the sign I have been able to trace occurs in a 9th century ivory carving of German work, now in the Louvre, which is reproduced opposite page 204. It represents the Judgment of Solomon and we have previously alluded to it in the chapter dealing with the Sign of Distress, for this sign is being made by the distracted mother of the infant whom Solomon has ordered to be divided. The other woman, who wrongfully claimed the child, casts her hands outward in the Sign of Completion, implying that that finishes the controversy. Although the right hand makes the sign absolutely, the left is not quite as well carved, but the same might be said of a good deal of the work in this early ivory, which is a somewhat crude specimen.

Examples of this sign are not plentiful, and although there is not such a complete hiatus as occurs in the case of the *Sign of Heaven and Earth* and its companion the *Sign of Resignation*, yet it is rather significant that I have been able to find more examples of it in the 15th and 16th centuries than in all the previous centuries put together.

It is not until the 12th century that I have been able to discover another picture showing its use. This occurs in the famous mosaic of the Last Judgment at Torcello Cathedral near Venice. We have already reproduced the lowest right hand register of the design, but this represents only a tiny fragment of the whole scheme. In the top panel we see Christ Harrowing Hell and bringing forth the Patriarchs, by whom He is greeted with various examples of the Sign of Preservation. The figures in this section are larger, and are apparently by a different hand than those in the rest of the design, which consists of four more rows of figures and depicts the Last Judgment in its various phases. It is to this section that the smaller part already reproduced belongs. In the top register of the Last Judgment Christ appears within the Vesica Piscis, seated on the Rainbow Bridge and making the sign we are considering. In so depicting Him the artist had two objects. Firstly, to show the nail wounds in His hands, and secondly, to communicate to the onlooker a new interpretation of the sentence He said on the Cross, "It is finished." By this simple piece of symbolism the artist conveys to his audience a tremendous moral in as terse a manner as it is possible to conceive, and in order that modern students may fully comprehend it a little expansion seems necessary. Christ first reminds the whole world of that pregnant phrase uttered when He gave up the Ghost for the Salvation of Mankind. From that time until the Day of Judgment He has stood in the presence of the Almighty pleading His sacrifice, but now the time of pleading is ended. It is finished. He Himself has assumed the position of Judge and it is now too late to plead to Him the Sacrifice of Calvary. Finally, it exoterically indicates the end of the world. In this mosaic the artist has managed to convey far more than is usual, but then he was dealing with a tremendous theme and his chief object was to strike terror into the hearts of his beholders.

When we turn to the 15th century we find the lesson intended is a much simpler one. We have already shown why St. John makes this sign on Calvary, but the intimation conveyed in the picture of the Resurrection of Lazarus by Froment, to which we alluded in the opening of the chapter, perhaps needs a little elucidation. The woman who kneels on our Lord's right hand means to imply that it is useless to trouble any further about Lazarus, for all is over, but we have gone into this in a previous chapter in connection with the other signs.

Our last example in Europe is from a woven tapestry depicting the Three Fates. It is 16th century Flemish work, now in the Victoria and Albert Museum, and is shown opposite page 172. The three Fates may represent *Time Past, Time Present* and *Time to Come*. In this example *Time Past* and *Time Present* each stand behind a prostrate woman and place one foot on her body. *Time Past* places her left foot thereon and makes the sign we are considering, by this gesture implying, "what is finished *is* finished." *Time Present* has her right foot on the prostrate body and makes the Sign of Preservation, an appropriate gesture, in one sense symbolising life itself. But *Time to Come* has neither foot on the woman and makes no sign, the future is wrapt in mystery, for the Fates give no indication of what is in store for man. The significance of the position of the feet will be dealt with in a subsequent chapter and we will now turn to consider illustrations showing the use of this sign overseas.

Two Indian examples prove that knowledge of it is not restricted to Europe. The first is an 18th century picture in the Stchoukin Collection at Moscow and is reproduced on page 102 in Kuhnel's *La Miniature en Orient.* It is entitled "Les Acrobates" and represents a wrestler throwing his opponent over his head. A man standing out in the ring, apparently the referee, makes this sign, as if to say, "That contest is finished."

The other example is reproduced opposite this page, and is entitled "A Visit of a Prince." In addition to the two signs which we have already discussed, the pair of men in the middle of the picture are making the Sign of Completion, having seen that the Prince has promised by the gesture of Preservation to protect the petitioner. We might translate their signs as meaning, "That is a happy conclusion to the matter."

From the above it will be seen that in every case where this sign appears it means, and can only mean, that something is finished and done with, for which reason I call it the "Sign of Completion."

THE VISIT OF THE PRINCE.
A late 16th Century Indian Miniature.

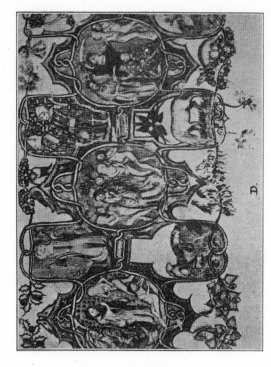

A. and D.   PARTS OF A BORDER IN THE PSALTER OF THE ST. OMER FAMILY.
B. and C.   DITTO FROM THE ARUNDEL MS.

14th Century work, now in Brit. Mus.

K.20.

CHAPTER XIX. *Wherein are gathered together numerous Miscellaneous Signs.*

SO FAR WE HAVE dealt with the most important and well known mantric signs, but there are a large number which, although less frequently used, clearly belong to the same type, and I am including them in this chapter in the hope that other students will be encouraged to make further research into the matter and, as a result, not only will fresh examples be discovered but a clearer interpretation of some of the more obscure ones be obtained.

I have moreover included in this chapter not merely hand signs but a few examples of grips, which in certain cases are clearly associated with particular signs, such, for example, as the peculiar one which accompanies the sign of "True till Death," to which I refer later. In addition, there appear to be a number of leg signs, of which by far the most important consists in advancing the left leg in front of the right. I devote some space to this sign, but this seems an appropriate moment at which to draw attention to the strange position of the feet of the four men shown in the illustration of the mosaic of "The Last Judgment" at Torcello, which appears opposite page 38.

The first and third of the men are apparently making a tau

cross; the right foot being turned outward and the heel thereof brought
more or less into the hollow of the left foot. The tau cross is a very ancient
symbol, representing the phallus, and hence it often stands for our
animal passions.   In this case it seems to imply that these two men
are telling us that they owe their unhappy fate in Hell to the fact that
during their lives they had not brought their animal passions under
control.   The second man has his right leg crossed over his left;
its exact meaning in this case is obscure, but it evidently alludes to
the position in which Knights are often depicted on their sepulchral
monuments, namely, with one foot crossed over the other.   This
attitude is characteristic of monuments of the 12th and 13th centuries, but thereafter is seldom employed.   It is usually stated to
imply that the knight was a Crusader, but this interpretation is very
doubtful.   At any rate we may safely say that it refers to the manner
in which Christ's legs were crossed on Calvary, and so implies a prayer
by the dead man, wherein he invokes our Lord's death as a plea for
his own preservation.   The fourth man has his legs in a double crossed
position.   What this implies I do not know, but seeing that the other
three are clearly making symbolic gestures with their feet, it seems
probable that this also had a significance which to-day is lost.   We
will, however, now turn back and consider the remaining hand signs.

THE SIGN OF WATER.

This is the name given by *The Hung Society* to a sign
associated with that important occult centre, the reins.
According to the Chinese system of correspondences, the
reins are associated with the element of water, and, as will
be seen by turning to the illustration on page 57, the sign is made
by crooking the elbows and placing the hands on the side of the waist
line.   Usually the thumbs are forward and it is probable that even in
cases where this does not occur it is merely due to carelessness on the
part of the artists.

The fact that this sign is known and used by *The Hung Society*,
both as a mantric sign in connection with water and as a sign of recognition, justifies us in paying more attention to the few examples I
have found in Mediæval art than would be the case if these occurred
alone.   At the same time, in view of the limited number of the

latter, it is dangerous to be too dogmatic as to the meaning of the gesture. It would appear, however, as if in some way it implies an admission of weakness on the part of the person making it. The first examples in Europe which I propose to quote occur on the 12th century font in Eardisley Church, Herefordshire, and in a border of the Psalter of the St. Omer family, now in the British Museum. The figure from the latter is reproduced opposite page 156 and an important factor in considering its significance is the fact that the whole border is crammed with figures, many of whom are making mantric signs, including such easily recognisable examples as the Signs of Distress and Sacrifice. The Eardisley font is of special importance because the figure is that of our Lord at the moment of His Baptism, and He is standing in water. This and the fact that it appears on a font shows that it *has* a hidden connection with water.

A third example, which is not perhaps so good, but which I do not feel justified in ignoring, occurs on a Norman font at St. Buryan's Church, near Helston. The figures are angels, supporting blank shields, and their hands are similarly placed against the side of the waist, but in such a manner as to make it appear at first sight as if they are merely supporting the shields. The fact, however, that the thumbs are turned forwards most ostentatiously, whereas the more natural position would be to turn them backwards and support the shield with the fingers, makes it probable that the sculptor was privately giving a hint to those entitled to know, e.g., the clergy, a possibility which is strengthened by the fact that the sculpture is on a font, and so once more connects the sign with water.

Furthermore, its use is not restricted to Europe and Asia but certainly occurs both in Africa and Australia. On page 638, Vol. II, of *George Grenfell and the Congo*, by Sir H. Johnston, is a photograph of a roadside fetish shrine, painted with six figures. The original is on the Zomba plateau in the Congo, and of the six figures three are making the Sign of Distress and one the Sign we are now considering. The Australian example comes from the Solomon Islands, for shell carvings from Rubiana, now in the British Museum and reproduced in its *Handbook of Ethnology*, page 128, depict little figures making this sign. These carvings seem to be charms and so in this case the Sign is connected with quasi-magical religious beliefs.

Another important sign used by *The Hung Society* is called "The Sign of the Element of Wood"and likewise appears on page 90. It consists in crossing the hands downwards over the Solar Plexus and is chiefly found in Asia, although it is not entirely lacking in Europe, where we will seek for it under the title of

HANDS CROSSED DOWNWARDS.

A second example from China occurs in the old painting of the Five Buddhas, all of whom are making mantric signs and to which allusion has already been made. (See illustration opposite). Here we see one of the Buddhas making this sign and it is probable that the arrangement of the figures is connected therewith, for they are so set out as to form the Cross of the Equinox, better known in Europe as a St. Andrew's Cross. Now it is certainly significant that the figure who makes this sign with his hands, itself a St. Andrew's Cross, is placed in the centre, and the hands are actually at the centre of the whole cross.

Passing to India, a 16th century painting, now in the State Museum at Berlin, entitled "A Visit to the Hermit," shows an attendant standing by with his hands carefully crossed downwards, and another Indian painting of 1820, of which a reproduction is in my possession, shows the Emperor Bahadur and his Court, wherein at least three men are standing in this position. Indeed, one of them is thrusting himself forward and holding his hands out so obviously as to lead one to suppose that he wishes the Emperor to see his humble attitude, for that the sign is connected with humility seems probable. A somewhat similar scene of a King in Council appears in a Persian miniature, a reproduction of which is also in my possession, and here once more we have three members of the Court most carefully making this sign.

In Europe so far I have found but few undoubted examples, but a good one occurs on the monumental brass of Abbot de la Mare, at St. Alban's Abbey, circa 1360, wherein the Abbot is represented with his hands crossed thus . (See picture opposite page 160). Another is found in a Book of Hours, circa 1500, now in the British Museum, in the section dealing with the meditation on death. Here is depicted the figure of a naked man lying on his tomb, his hands crossed downward.

THE FIVE BUDDHAS.
A Chinese Painting.

U.38.

THE BRASS OF ABBOT DE LA MARE.

St. Albans Abbey.   C. 1360.

A 15th century alabaster scuplture representing the entombment of our Lord gives us yet a third example. The original is in the Victoria and Albert Museum and we have alluded to it previously in connection with the Sign of Regret, which one of the apostles is making. In this case it is the dead Christ Whose arms are thus crossed downwards, and this fact gives us a key to the inner significance of the gesture. It seems to imply impotence or helplessness, and therefore, in the cases we have just been considering, we can see that the courtiers are weak and helpless in the presence of their King, who holds their lives in the hollow of his hand. If this be so, the Hung Society's association of the sign with the element of wood is not quite so far-fetched as it might at first sight appear. We must recollect that it is a sign of one of the five Chinese elements, of which the others are, metal, fire, earth and water, each of which in turn may be regarded as stronger than wood and usually destructive of it.

THE SIGN OF THE VESICA PISCIS.

This is such an important sign in the Hung Society and throughout the whole of Asia that it deserves to be recorded here, even though I have been unable to find many examples of its use in the West. It is, indeed, such an obviously significant gesture that I cannot help feeling that further research nearer home will sooner or later reveal others, the more so as the symbol itself is so extensively used in Christian art, Saints, particularly the Virgin, and Christ, often being depicted in it.

An interesting example occurs on an 11th century Byzantine Ivory Carving, probably intended for the cover of a book, which is now in the Victoria and Albert Museum (H.10). It consists of a portrait of St. John the Baptist within a circle, and above him are two more circles containing portraits of Saints, with a similar pair below. St. John himself is making the combined Signs of Blessing and the Vesica Piscis, that is to say, his first two fingers are raised and his third and fourth bent over so as to meet the thumb, instead of being pressed into the palm of the hand by the thumb as is usual when the Sign of Blessing is made.

The Saint in the left hand bottom corner, as we look at the carving, makes an even more interesting sign, for it is really the Sign of the Horns and that of the Vesica Piscis combined. The Index and little fingers are held straight out, while the second and third are bent so as just to touch the tip of the thumb.   In short, this Christian Saint, is making precisely the same sign as Kwan Yin, the Chinese Goddess of Mercy, who with her left hand makes the Sign of the Horns and with her right the combined Horns and Vesica Piscis.   (See illustration opposite page 164).

Four illustrations of its use by the Hung Society are here re-produced, enabling my readers to see the correct form, although it should be added that there are many minor variations.   The illustration below shows it as used by a somewhat disreputable offshoot

The Sign of the Vesica Pisces as used by the Hung Society.

U.33b.

of the Hung Society, known as *The Three Dots Brotherhood*, of Singapore.   I regret to say that the majority of the members of this Society belong to the criminal class and this is one of their signs of recognition.

The illustration opposite page 162 depicts a sign to be used when a fight is in progress.   If one of the men fighting is a member of the Hung Society the onlooker turns the palm of his right hand inward, to indicate that this particular man is within the Society and so entitled to assistance from other members, but if the man is not a

member the palm is turned outward, to show he is outside the Society.
It will be noted that the position of the right hand approximates to
the Sign of Preservation, and the general similarity is further increased
by the position of the left hand on the breast.   It is important,
however, to note the position of the finger and thumb in this hand,
which touch and form the Vesica Piscis, thus implying that the makel
is within the womb of the Hung Society.   That this is not fancifur
is shown by the ritual, wherein again and again the initiate is informed
that he is a brother of every other member of the Hung lodge because
by the ceremony he has been reborn from the *same womb*, and they
speak of their lodge as their "Mother,"just as a European might speak
of his "Mother City."

The third example, illustrated opposite page 206, depicts the
great three-fold sign in common use by the Society when any member
wishes to disclose the fact that he is a Hung Brave.   The three
signs form a definite sentence, which is interpreted as, "I am a Heaven
and Earth Society Man."   The first position, with the thumb and
both fingers extended, represents Heaven and all there is between,
i.e., Heaven, earth and man, or the whole universe, for it is a saying
of the Hung Society that man is begotten of heaven and earth, and
the triangle and the number three are highly venerated by them.
The second position simulates the Vesica Piscis, and is said to stand
for earth.   In many ancient mythologies Heaven and the gods are
declared to be masculine, and mother earth, feminine.   The third
position, which is here said to represent man, is really the mantric
symbol of the horns, and more correctly belongs to our next section.

The last example occurs among the illustrations opposite page 210.
These include the Nine Finger Sign and various methods of indicating
membership of the Society, of which the correct manner of passing a
tea cup is extremely important.   In the left hand, bottom illustration,
we see a member passing a tea cup in rather a peculiar manner while
with his left hand he makes the Sign of the Vesica Piscis.

But it is not only the Hung Society which attaches particular
importance to this Sign, for in all countries where the Buddha
is venerated statues occur in which he makes it.   A glance
at the Chinese picture reproduced opposite page 158, showing the
five Buddhas, will reveal one of them in this attitude.   Nor is the

reason far to seek.   The emblem stands for the feminine and mother-ing power, and in the case of the Buddha may be construed as an appeal to the onlooker to take refuge in Him, Who has found the way.   A constant Buddhist phrase is, "I take refuge in Buddha, the law and the Assembly," just as a Christian might say, "I take refuge in Christ."   A Japanese statuette of Buddha in my collection shows him making this sign with both hands, and in the Pagodas of Burma I have seen many Burmese statues in a similar position.

A strange and unusual example comes from India, being a portrait of Shir Muhammad Kavval, a 17th century Indian miniature, now in the British Museum, wherein this gentleman is most carefully and ostentatiously making this sign.

THE SIGN OF THE HORNS.

We have previously alluded to the widespread use of this sign as a protection against the evil eye and have shown that it is one of the signs of the Hung Society, an example having just been given.   Before proceeding further, however, it may be desirable in the interests of those who have not read my three-volume work on this great Society, to say that although, owing to the fact that a large number of disreputable characters have taken refuge in this Society and exploited it for evil purposes, the experience of the British authorities in Singapore has led them to have no high opinion of its members, the rituals of the Society itself, which are translated in my book, show that it was once a great religious and mystical body, working one of the most magnifi-cent rituals it has ever been my privilege to study.   It seems to have been founded, or at any rate re-organised, in the 4th century by Eon, a great Buddhist monk and Saint, and after many vicissitudes was re-organised in the 17th century by Chinese patriots who were anxious to overthrow the Manchu usurpers and restore the genuine Chinese dynasty of the Mings.   Naturally, therefore, the Manchus viewed it with little favour and tried to suppress it, by putting to death any member thereof they caught.   The Society raised insurrection after insurrection, including the famous Taiping revolt, and, finally, in 1912, under the leadership of Sun Yat Sen, it achieved its self-imposed task of hurling the last of the Manchu Emperors from the throne.

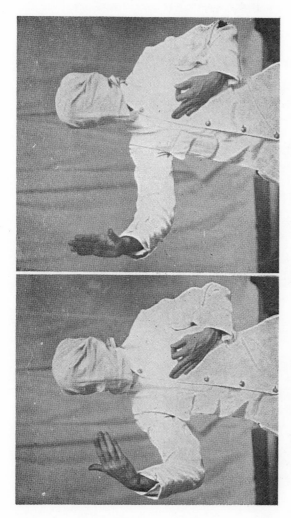

TWO SIGNS OF THE HUNG SOCIETY FOR USE WHEN A FIGHT IS IN PROGRESS.
Showing a variant form of the Sign of Preservation combined with the Sign of the Vesica Piscis.

U.31.

A CHINESE BRONZE STATUE OF KWAN YIN
Making the Sign of the Horns.

U.12.

Since that date it seems gradually to have turned into an anti-alien Society of Communist tendencies, and has been responsible for much of the trouble in South China.

Such, in brief, is the Hung Society and yet, despite its tragic history, the ritual has been retained with all its lofty teaching almost unaltered. These facts must be compared with the survival of similar signs under the safe keeping of the Mediæval Church and, also it is rumoured, under the protecting banner of certain Western Secret Societies. Although the Hung Society possesses this sign, it is also associated with the exoteric form of Chinese Buddhism, for the statue of Kwan Yin, reproduced opposite page 164, shows her making it. Kwan Yin is the Goddess of Mercy, but was originally a form of Buddha, and doubtless she is represented making this sign as a hint that she will ward off evil from her devotees.

Opposite page 56 is a picture of a statue of Shiva, the original being in the author's collection and, as we have pointed out previously, he is making a combination of the Sign of Destruction and the Sign of the Horns. He is often found in this attitude in Hindu temples and it is more than probable that this peculiar form of the sign has a definite esoteric significance for the Hindu priests, and others conversant with the esoteric side of symbolism.

In Europe, as has already been stated, this sign is still used to ward off the evil eye and has been explained as referring to the crescent moon. It is not, however, a popular sign with the Church authorities, probably just because it is so closely associated in the lay mind with magic. But for all that we do find examples of its use in ecclesiastical surroundings. No farther afield than Westminster Abbey it can be seen, for one of the figures which adorn the North West corner of the exterior of the transept is undoubtedly making it. It is perhaps dangerous to lay too much stress on its appearance here, as, of course, this part of the Abbey was ruthlessly restored in the 19th century, but there is reason to believe that even if this figure is not original it was copied from an older one, and, since the statue is placed very high up, it is quite probable that it is a pre-Reformation one. The appropriateness of the sign in this position cannot be denied. According to Mediæval tradition the North side of a Churchyard was considered to be the gathering place of evil

spirits, and the import of the statue therefore is that the Saint is avert-
ing these evil influences from the Abbey itself.

An extremely interesting example of the use of this sign occurs
in the miniature from a 12th century manuscript which is reproduced
opposite page 166.   The original is in the Vatican library and the
crowned figure in the chariot is the Emperor Otto III.   The small
bishop in the foreground is making the combined signs of Preservation
and the Horns, an almost unique example, and the import of the
gesture is, "May God preserve the Emperor from the powers of evil,"
Students of Mediæval art will find a further point of interest in the
picture, for it shows one of the earliest representations of a bishop's
mitre, a vestment which, so far as we can trace, was only introduced
in the 12th century and, as will be seen from the picture, was at first
quite a low cap.

The Martelli Mirror illustrated opposite page 4 is a striking
15th century example of the use of this sign in Renaissance Italy,
and, having been dealt with in the opening chapters, need detain us
no longer.

THE SIGN OF OBLIGATION.

In a photograph in "Travels in West Africa," by M. H. Kingsley,
a number of Bantu natives are shown seated in a circle, and all of
them hold their hands in a peculiar position.   The two hands are
placed in front of the body, one above the other, the back of the lower
being towards the earth, and the other being held parallel to it, a
few inches above, but with the back of the hand facing upwards.
Thus the two palms face each other and are separated by some two
or three inches of space.   This photograph is described in the letter-
press as "Making a magic charm."

If my readers will now turn to the illustration opposite page 158
of the Chinese painting of the Five Buddhas they will perceive that
the Buddha in the right hand bottom Corner is making this sign.
It is also made by one of two travellers who have been accosted by a
beggar, in a scene depicted in a Persian miniature from Hafiz-Diwan.
The miniature was painted in the 16th century.

But, in addition to Asia and Africa, Egypt, Crete and Greece
supply examples of its use.   Thus a bronze statue of Hathor represents

the Goddess in this attitude, while a votive figure from Crete, reproduced in Bossert's *Alt-Kreta*, shows a man in precisely the same
position.   On a painted Greek Amphora of c. 550 B.C., which is now in
the British Museum, a number of women are dancing with satyrs,
and practically all of them are clearly making mantric signs, such as
the *Sign of Preservation, Touching the top of the Head*, etc.,   and
two figures, a satyr and a woman, hold their hands in the position we
are discussing.

Its use in Greece makes it the more surprising that I have not
been able to find examples of this sign in the art of Mediæval Europe,
but, of course, they may be still awaiting discovery.   Nevertheless,
they cannot be numerous or I should certainly have found them, and
its partial, if not complete, disappearance may very likely be due to
the fact that to some extent this sign represents a Sign of Prayer,
which in Mediæval times was already generally represented by the
hands placed together in a vertical position.

I cannot help thinking that this sign originated in some form of
obligation or oath.   For example, placing the hands on either side of
some relic, just as to-day one thus holds the Bible while taking an oath.
If so, this gesture would, on the one hand, be the outward sign of
acquiescence in an oath, and, on the other, imply a prayer to the
Deity to keep the swearer firm in his promise.

THE BECKONING SIGN.

In modern Europe it is usual to beckon by moving the right
hand upward and downward, but the ancient form of the sign, which
is still used in the East and among primitive races, is to swing the
hand downward.   It is thus used by the Australian Bushmen and
by the modern Red Indians, who, however, use it more to imply
respect to a great chief than as an indication that they wish someone
to come to them.

In the *Eddas* we are told that Odin used this sign to summon
into his presence the dwarfs, when he called them before him to punish
them for the murder they had committed, and in Asia, particularly
in Mahomedan countries, it is employed as a sign of respect and
veneration to a superior.   It seems possible also that the polite
gesture made by a gentleman in the 17th and 18th centuries to a lady,

wherein he took off his hat, swung it downwards and then brought it to rest over his heart, to which we have previously alluded, is a combination of the mantric form of the Beckoning Sign and that of Fidelity.

THE SIGN OF ADORATION.

As previously mentioned, this sign must not be confounded with the Sign of Distress, and it is excellently shown in the Vignette of Praising Ra at Sunset, illustrated on page 12.   Therein the upper row of gods are making the Sign of Preservation, but the four figures in the lower register make the true form of the Sign of Adoration as used in Egypt, namely, the two arms bent, with the palms turned outward and thrust slightly forward.   Many representations of the Virgin in the Middle Ages portray her making this sign.

THE SIGN OF THE PILLARS.

This consists in holding the hands well apart, while in each is grasped a straight object, such as two wands or a pair of candles.   It is admirably shown in the fresco of the Sacrifice of Iphigenia, reproduced opposite page 62, wherein will be seen a small statuette of Diana making this sign, and it appears probable that it refers to the two great pillars which played such a prominent part in the construction of the ancient temples.

It will be recollected that in the Bible considerable emphasis is laid on two pillars which stood in front of the entrance to King Solomon's temple, and such pillars were characteristic of Syrian and Egyptian sacred edifices.   Thus at Heirapolis, the modern Membij, Lucian tells us that there were two large phalli, thirty fathoms high, which stood at the door of the Temple of Astarte.[1]   Furthermore, in the famous shrine of Astarte at Paphos, in Cyprus, two lofty pillars appear, each terminating in a pair of ball-topped pinnacles, with a star and crescent shining between the tops of the columns.   These details are shown on gold models found in the tombs of Mycenæ, circa 1200 B.C., and also on coins of the time of the Cæsars.   To this day in Burma similar phalli, or pillars, flank the entrances to the Pagoda platforms, and their use in Europe survived well into the Middle

---

[1] See *De dea Syria*, 8.

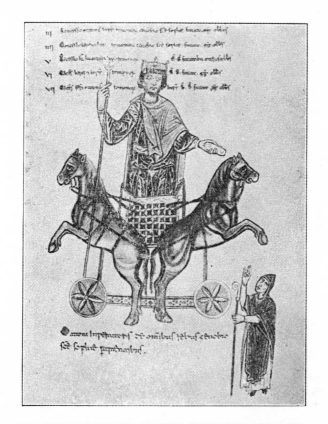

THE PROCLAMATION OF THE EMPEROR OTTO III.
From a 12th Century MS. in the Vatican Library.

I.28.

THE DESCENT OF SHAMASH OR OF DAMUZI.

B1.

THE RESURRECTION OF SHAMASH OR OF DAMUZI.

B.2.

Ages, for at Coire Cathedral, Switzerland, two such pillars are still standing in front of the West entrance, and, as will be seen from the illustration which appears opposite page 186, they are not only a good distance in front of the edifice, but make no pretence of supporting an arch or canopy. Somewhat similar pillars are placed on either side of the door leading to the Treasury at the Cathedral of St. Mark, Venice, and in like manner stand entirely clear of the building. It is probable that they have several meanings, the basic one being that they were the Pillars of the Dawn, and hence symbolically represented the gateway of birth and rebirth. A glance at the illustration opposite page 168 of the Resurrection of Tammuz shows the Gates of the Dawn being drawn back by two attendant Deities, but it must be admitted that any later artist might reasonably regard them as the pillars which supported the gates rather than as the gates themselves.

In Judea it was customary for Kings to be crowned between the pillars in the porchway, one of which was supposed to represent the royal, and the other the priestly, power then conferred on him. Later, such pillars became symbolical of justice and mercy respectively, which fact leads us to our second point, namely, that in Mediæval art Kings are often represented holding in one hand the sceptre of Mercy and in the other the sword of Justice. To this day a sceptre of Justice and a sceptre of Mercy form part of the symbolism and regalia of the King.

This leads us to interpret the sign as one implying justice combined with mercy, but undoubtedly it also had a highly esoteric significance, as is proved by the fact that in ancient Crete we find statues of priestesses making it, although holding in their hands, not rods, but serpents. A particularly striking example is illustrated in Sir A. Evans's Book, *The Palace of Minos at Knossos*, wherein is shown an altar shelf with ceremonial objects found thereon. In the centre is an equal armed cross, and on either side are statuettes of Priestesses, wearing double aprons and making this sign by holding in each hand a serpent. The Cult of the Serpent and Cross is, of course, one of the oldest Cults in the world and definitely phallic.

In Christian art the two pillars are often replaced by the one pillar of the scourging of our Lord, and in pictures of the Last Judgment it is usual to see Him seated on the Rainbow and flanked on one side by an angel holding the cross and on the other by another holding this pillar. Finally, we must not omit mention of the numerous cases in which a Saint is depicted flanked on either side by an angel each holding in his hand a single candle.

THE NINE FINGER SIGN.

This is one of the great mantric signs of the Hung Society, and a glance at the illustration opposite page 210 renders any further description of it unnecessary. The mere fact that it is an important Hung Sign justifies its inclusion here, even if I had not reason to believe that it is used in the West, despite the fact that so far I have discovered no definite illustrations showing its use in Europe.

EROTIC SIGNS.

In addition to the signs we have just been discussing, there exist both in Europe and Asia a number of Erotic signs, of which Mr. N. M. Penzer, in his *Ocean of Story*, gives a fairly detailed account. These constitute almost a Sign language in themselves, but they hardly fall within the pervue of this book. I nevertheless mention them as showing the widespread nature of the Sign Language and the various uses to which it has been put. Even in the case of this group, however, it must be remembered that since early religions were largely connected with the Fertility Cult, it is possible that signs which are now discreetly passed over in silence once had a more exalted and honourable connection with religion than is the case to-day.

GRIPS.

From very early times we find that the popular form of greeting was to grasp hands, so much so that the ancient Egyptians used a picture of two men clasping hands as a hieroglyph with the phonetic value of *heter*, as will be seen from *The Egyptian Language*, by E. A. Wallis Budge. It is popularly supposed that this action was taken so as to prove that you could not stab the other man, but the theory seems far-fetched, for in practice it would be quite as easy to stab a man with your left hand while grasping his right, as it would be if he was standing quite apart. Be that as it may, it is clear that there were several types of hand grips and probable that they all had an inner significance, because in certain cases they are clearly associated either with a particular mantric sign or with an important symbolical action. Thus, when Osiris is being raised from the dead, we find that his wrist is grasped by Anubis, or sometimes by a lion-headed god, in a peculiar manner. The living god lays his hand on the wrist and holds the dead man's hand and arm in this manner instead of taking only the hand. We might therefore call this *The Strong Grip* or *The Grip of the Resurrection.* Thus in the Roman Sarcophagus from Arles reproduced opposite page 96, we see St. Peter raising the daughter of Tabitha with this grip, and it is also being taught to a Mexican Initiate, as will be seen by turning to the illustration reproduced on page 145.

Another early grip is that shown on the Stele from Athens, which appears opposite page 176 and is closely associated with the sign "True till Death." As will be seen, it consists in pressing the first knuckle joint of the right hand. It is a popular grip on Greek sepulchral monuments, and also occurs on the Greek stele to which allusion has previously been made, which is now in the British Museum, and wherein the same sign is portrayed. (D5.)

A 19th century example occurs at St. Peter's Rome, for in a Mosaic of St. Peter raising the beggar at the Gate of the Temple, he is shown using this grip, while St. John makes the Sign of Fidelity and a woman the Sign of Distress. Here the suggestion seems to be that the person is being led out of darkness into light, or in some way is being reborn to a new life.

In a 13th century French Manuscript, entitled *Biblical History Moralised,* now in the British Museum, among the illuminations several examples of grips appear. One of particular interest consists of placing the right hand under the elbow of the opposite party while taking that person by the fingers with the left hand. The same grip also occurs in a picture of the Descent from the Cross, by Andrea del Sarto, at Florence. Furthermore, on the capitals behind the high altar in the Church at Saintes-Maries-de-la-Mer, South France, two figures are shown making yet another grip, the work being c. 1200 A.D., and a representation of this same grip appears in the fresco of the Last Judgment by Paolo, which is now at the Gallery of Fine Arts, Sienna, wherein an angel is raising a soul from his knees by gripping him under both the armpits.

Among many races various grips are used, each having a peculiar significance, and when in Algiers recently I saw Arabs greet each other in the manner depicted on the Greek Stele, i.e., by pressing the first knuckle joint of the right hand, and I also saw them use a second grip, wherein the man pressed the *second* knuckle joint, but the exact significance to them of these two grips I was unable to discover.   I have, however, placed on record these and other grips in the hope that some of my readers may be moved to collect further examples, from a careful comparison of which it may be possible to establish their sequence and significance, as I have endeavoured to do with regard to the Mantric Signs.   In view of the examples of different periods to which I have drawn attention and the fact that in some cases the grips are clearly associated with the use of Mantric Signs, it seems probable that they were connected with the Ancient Mysteries and were intended to convey a symbolic meaning.   They were also of practical utility, seeing that they could be employed by initiates at times and places when the use of signs would be impracticable.

LEG SIGNS.

Before concluding this chapter mention must be made of a definite symbolic sign associated with the feet.   It is a widespread custom to depict a divine champion of man attacking some symbol of evil, such as a serpent, and when doing so advancing the left foot first. Thus in ancient Egypt we find numerous representations either of a god, or of the deceased, attacking a serpent while he tramples on it with his left foot.   For example, in the Papyrus of Ani the deceased is shown spearing a serpent and at the same time trampling on its tail with his left foot, while a similar scene occurs on the Papyrus of Mes-em-neter and is reproduced by E. Wallis Budge in *The Book of the Dead*, Vol. II, opposite page 167.   The same attitude occurs in Mediæval pictures of our Lord harrowing hell, which latter is represented as a serpentine monster.   A Byzantine bronze pound weight, inlaid in Silver with two military saints, shows one of them attacking a creature like a leopard and planting his left foot firmly on its body. The work is 6th century and the original is in the British Museum. It is reproduced on page 171.

A curious and striking example of this piece of symbolism occurs

A 17TH CENTURY PANELLED ROOM.
Now in the Engandine Museum, St. Moritz, Switzerland.

A FLEMISH TAPESTRY SHOWING THE THREE FATES.
Original in the V. and A. Museum.
M.7.

THE REVELATION OF ST. JOHN.
From a 14th Century Manuscrpt.
Showing the Sign of Preservation.
K.17.

on the 16th century tapestry of the *Three Fates*, reproduced opposite page 172, wherein one of the Fates is seen stepping on a woman with her left foot, while the 17th century wood block from the *Azoth Philosophorum*, reproduced opposite page 174, shows that even at that date this attitude was intended to have a symbolic meaning. The plate is an Alchemical, and possibly a Rosicrucian, manifesto, full of symbolism, with which, however, we are not here concerned.

Now Apuleius, in *Metamorphosis*, Book I, 1st Episode, says that Aristomenes was unlucky because he started left foot first, while Major Sanderson tells me that in Java, when entering the rice store,

A Byzantine Bronze Weight with two Military Saints Inlaid in Silver.
6th Century.
G.11.

a woman must enter with her *right* foot first, or she will offend the rice spirit and that a Muslim enters a house or Mosque right foot first to show that he comes in peace. He suggests that when attacking the serpent of evil the champion wishes to insult and defy him, and therefore steps off left foot first. A medical friend of mine, however, told me that there is a good practical reason for such an action, which is also the justification for the military practice of starting with the left foot. The left leg being nearer to the heart than the right, less effort, and therefore less strain on the heart, results in passing from the static to the moving stage by starting with the left foot.   At any rate, the same attitude is adopted by the gods in India when attacking a representative of the evil powers, for I have seen statues of Kali trampling with her left foot on an ogre she has overthrown, and of Krishna in like manner trampling on Kaliya, the serpent of evil. Symbolically, therefore, it implies subduing, or trampling under foot, the powers of evil.

One last curious example of a sign connected with the foot deserves passing mention.   In the Zurich Museum is a caste of a bas-relief, the original of which is in a monastery at Shaffhausen. Herein is depicted a man with a halter round his neck; the index finger of his right hand is laid on his lips and with his left hand, the fingers of which are apart as if to form a pair of shears, he is pretending to cut off his left foot at the ankle.   The exact significance of the action is problematical, but it has clearly some connection with the Mediæval practice of striking off the foot of a criminal.

This, then, concludes the series of important Mantric Signs which have come down through the ages, but the question as to the full significance of their existence will be considered in the next chapter.   It is clear that they are largely religious, even to some extent magical, and if my contention is correct not only is the interpretation of them of the greatest assistance to students of Mediæval art, but their continued survival points to something even more important, namely, that in their essentials the Ancient Mysteries continued right through the Middle Ages, practically down to the present day, taking refuge under the banner of the Church and under various disguises, among which it is possible we may include Knights Templar, Mediæval Masons and that mysterious body, the Rosicrucians, concerning which much has been written but little is really known by the ordinary man of the world.

CHAPTER XX. *Shows how the Sign Language links the Ancient Mysteries with the Modern World.*

ANY TIMES IN the course of this book it has been suggested that the Mantric Signs were originally associated with the Ancient Mysteries. If this be so, their continued survival right through the Middle Ages indicates that at least some fragments of this ancient system of instruction either survived independently or became incorporated in other organisations whose open existence cannot be disputed.

Our knowledge of the Mysteries is unfortunately very fragmentary, due in no small measure to the nature of the obligation imposed on candidates and the general atmosphere of secrecy which at all times enshrouded them. Nevertheless, we are not so entirely ignorant of their teaching and methods as may be supposed by many. In Classical Greece there were several Mystery Cults besides the famous one of Eleusis, and it is quite clear that not only had most of them a close affinity with those carried out at Eleusis, but that they also belonged to the same type of ceremony as still takes place among primitive races to-day, although no doubt to some extent shorn of many of the more barbaric elements which form such a noticeable feature of the Rites of the African and Australian natives.

It is indeed in the nature of things that, as the Greek race evolved, both Religion and Rites should develop from their primitive form into a more complex and ethical system of instruction.   Doubtless also intercourse with ancient Egypt and with nearer Asia, in both of which districts Mystery Rites flourished, would tend to hasten the evolution from the primitive to the more complex systems. In the Egyptian Book of the Dead, wherein are embedded definite fragments of the Egyptian Mystery Rites, traces of the primitive and savage beginnings are obvious to every student, and we find side by side the most exalted spiritual teaching, crude anamistic ideas and savage customs, doubtless retained because the conservative Priests did not venture to throw out these older elements, which had behind them the sanction of centuries.

Although we cannot produce much evidence of the Primitive Rites of Greece and Egypt from which their Mystery System evolved, owing to the vast period of time which has elapsed, we can find in Africa, even to-day, Rites which there is little doubt may be regarded as being, if not the ancestors, at any rate close blood relatives, of the primitive ceremonies out of which the more sophisticated Mystery Rites were evolved.   All over Africa we find two sets of such Rites, the first and most widespread being a ritual of the initiation of a boy or girl into adulthood, a ceremony which generally includes circumcision and a dramatic representation of death and rebirth.   This Rite is open to and generally encumbent on all young people when they reach the period of adolescence, but less information is available concerning the ceremonies connected with a girl than about those connected with boys, and less importance is attached to the female counterpart of the male Rites.   (See the Kenya Boy illustrated opposite page 186).

The other type of Rite shows a nearer approach to the Mystery Cults of Classical Days.   Definite secret societies exist, such as *The Ndembo* of the Congo, into which men and women are admitted by a series of initiation ceremonies, but all members of the tribe do not necessarily enter such a Society, and in many cases membership thereof is definitely restricted to quite a small percentage of the whole

A PLATE FROM THE "AZOTH PHILOSOPHORUM."
17th Century.

N.10.

THE INITIATE BEING PRESENTED TO CERES.
A Bas-relief of the Eleusinian Mysteries.

D.7.

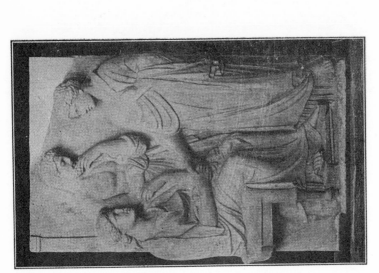

A STELE FROM ATHENS,
Now in the National Museum, Athens,
Circa 450 B.C.

D.4.

tribe.   In a sense, therefore, such societies as *The Ndembo* mark a higher stage of social evolution towards a proper Mystery Cult than do the Initiation Rites of a boy into manhood.   If we take the latter as representing the most primitive form of all these Rites, we shall be justified in regarding it as the elementary basis from which not only Mystery Cults but probably most forms of exoteric religion have subsequently branched off, and thus it is specially significant that in these Rites we find profound attention directed to certain Mantric Signs.   For example, in the Rites of the Yao Tribe, in Nyasaland, we get circumcision, a grave and a dramatic representation of resurrection therefrom, and the passing between two pillars, marking the ceremony of rebirth.   Symbolically the boy dies as a boy; his foreskin is buried as representative of his old self, and he is reborn between the pillars as a man and an adult.

I have previously pointed out that during these very ceremonies the men employed on them make the Sign of Preservation, and the two pictures of the designs which play an important part in the ceremony, illustrated opposite pages 86 and 88, show that therein is incorporated the Mantric Sign of Distress.   Now this is far from being an isolated case, for similar examples of Mantric Signs appear among the Australian Bushmen, notably the Sign of Reverence, which is connected with one of their higher degrees, and these people likewise have a dramatic representation of death and resurrection[1].

Among the people of New Guinea the same theme plays a prominent part in the initiation of a boy into manhood, in some cases the boy being swallowed alive by a mythical Monster, really the House of Initiation, whose doorway is formed like the head and jaws of a kind of dragon.   They are subsequently spewed out of this "mouth" as fully initiated men.   The Bullroarer used during these ceremonies (see illustration opposite page 82) and the Dancing Belt which is worn only by an initiated man, and which is illustrated on the same page, prove once more the association of the Sign of Distress with a Rite of Death and Resurrection.

Another example from this area is the use of the Sign of Reverence among the natives of Melville Island, North Australia.   Here Mr. Spencer[2] saw several boys and a girl initiated together, an unusual

---

1 A. W. Howitt, *Native Tribes of South East Australia.* pp. 554-56.
2 B. Spencer, *Native Tribes of the Northern Territory.* pp. 69-109.

feature, as the two sexes are generally initiated separately.   The old men went round the ground in procession before the ceremony commenced, and while so doing held their left hands as if to shade their eyes from the light, although at the time the sun was obscured.   Obviously, this was because the ground was "Holy Ground."   Later, the girl and her boy companions were thrust into a small hut, which was attacked by a body of men and the candidates symbolically slain. Subsequently the initiates were hidden in the forest and afterwards rediscovered, buried under a pile of bushes.

These examples from among the primitive tribes of Australia and Africa must suffice, but if we pass to America we find designs made in sand similar to those made by the Yaos, and for a like purpose, namely, in connection with Initiation Rites.   A characteristic one is that made by the Navaho Indians, called *The Design of the Grinding Snakes*, wherein appear figures making the Sign of Distress. Now the Navaho Indians are of interest as representing a primitive branch of the same race as the ancient inhabitants of Mexico and Central America.   We have already not only pointed out that the Divine hero, Quetzalcoatl, makes several important Mantric Signs, but have also shown pictures of candidates actually being taught such signs, as will be seen on page 144, where the Sign of Heaven and Earth is being given.   Another example occurs on the famous vase found at Chama, clearly depicting an initiation ceremony, wherein a candidate, with a rope round his neck, is being taught the sign, "True till Death," whose appropriateness under the circumstances cannot be denied.

The Ancient Mexican peoples are of especial interest to us in this connection because they had advanced a considerable way along the path of civilisation, but not as far as the ancient Greeks or Egyptians, and so form an interesting stage in the process of social evolution. From them to ancient Egypt is a natural migration, and there is no question of the existence of Mystery Rites in the latter country, for the testimony of Iamblicus, the Disciple of Pythagoras, concerning them, in his work, *The Egyptian Mysteries*, does not stand alone; Heredotus, and more especially Plutarch, in his *Isis et Osiris*, 12. 20, give us quite a considerable amount of information, although we should have liked it to have been fuller.   From them we learn, however, that the main basis was the story of the Death and Resurrection of Osiris. Recent research has amplified these contemporary accounts by showing that there were many grades or degrees in these Rites, some of which, symbolically, took the candidate after death through the Underworld, and fragments of this have become embedded in the famous *Book of the Dead*.

Marshall Adams[1], in his two books on the subject, and M. W. Blackden, in his *Ritual of the Mystery of the Judgment of the Soul*, have disentangled quite a section of the actual ceremony, with rubrics and spoken parts complete. Thus we are on sure ground with regard to the Egyptian Mysteries, and in *The Book of the Dead*, which contains fragments of the actual ceremony employed during these Rites, we get numerous examples of the use of Mantric Signs, such as the Vignette entitled, *Praising Ra at Sunset*, reproduced on page 12, wherein we have the Sign of Preservation. Examples of the Sign of Sympathy, of Distress, Tearing out the Heart, and so forth, are also to be found in this same work, as well as on the monuments and frescoes of ancient Egypt, as will be seen by turning to the section dealing with Egyptian signs.

Of the Eleusinian Mysteries but few pictorial representations survive, and it is surely significant that in one of the very few that do exist, namely, the bas-relief illustrated opposite page 176, we see the candidate making the Sign of Heaven and Earth at the particularly dramatic moment when she stands before the hierophantess, who symbolises Ceres, and is shown the ear of corn. The drama of Eleusis related how the God of the Underworld carried Proserpine into his dismal abode and, in symbolism, the candidates searched for her and journeyed through the Underworld. We have shown that, right through the subsequent ages, this Sign is always associated with death and resurrection, and here also we have it definitely linked with this particular form of the Mystery drama.

Passing from heathen to Christian times, we must always bear in mind the fact that during the first three centuries Christianity had much in common with the Ancient Mysteries. It was certainly a semi-secret cult, viewed with hostility by the State and performing most of its ceremonies in the underground recesses of the Catacombs,

---

[1] Marshall Adams *The Book of the Master*.
,, ,, *The House of the Hidden Places*.

surrounded by elaborate safeguards to protect it from the outside world.   That it had secret words, such as Ikhthus (the fish), which served as passwords for the initiates, is not disputed, and that certain of its Rites were definitely secret and its followers divided into Grades, I have already shown.   Thus Catecumens were not allowed to be present at the Mass, and those who were not confirmed were not permitted to partake of the Sacrament.   Just as in the Ancient Mysteries there was a ceremonial bathing as part of the Initiation of a candidate, so in the Christian Church the Rite of Baptism played an exceedingly important part, far more important than it does in modern Christianity.   Something of the secret nature of the Mass survives even to-day in the Roman Catholic and in the Greek Orthodox Churches.   In the former there are certain secret, we might almost say Mantric Prayers, which the laity not only do not hear, but cannot even read in the printed rituals, while in the latter the actual Consecration takes place behind a veil.

When the Church became established, the Mysteries were not discontinued at once, and in some places lingered on as late as the 6th century, as, for example, in Egypt.   But long before that date they gradually begin to disappear, and it is significant that it is just about this time that the hermits of the earlier Church begin to be gathered together into Monasteries and we get the establishment of definite Monastic Orders, with rules and Ceremonies of Initiation. To this day these ceremonies include a dramatic representation of death and resurrection, and that Mantric Signs were always connected with them is proved by the statement of Matthew Paris, "We monks have our signs, etc.," to which I have previously alluded.[1] Even in the exoteric form of worship traces of the old Rites lingered long, for the ceremony of the Easter Sepulchre, representing the burial and resurrection of our Lord, appears to be a Christianised version of similar ceremonies performed in connection with the Rites of Adonis and of Attis.

But although the Monastic Orders seem, to a large extent, to have taken over all that was best in the Ancient Mysteries, there is good reason for believing that these Mysteries also survived independently of the Church, and in some cases actively hostile to it.   The organisa-

---

[1] See page 23.

A GILT BRONZE CROSS FROM ABYSSINIA.

S.6.

A FRESCO OF THE RESCUE OF ŒDIPUS.
From Pompeii, Circa 70 A.D.

F.3.

tions of the Witches in Italy and Scotland, and the ceremonies performed thereby, seem to have been a distorted and somewhat degener-
ate form of some of the less reputable Mystery Cults.   In addition we
get that curious organisation, the Knights Templar.   As a quasi-
monastic Order they were entitled to work a definite ritual of initiation
for their candidates, and concerning the main details of this ritual
there has never been much dispute.   It was not to this that
the Pope and the Inquisitors took exception, but to certain secret
ceremonies which had not been authorised by the Papal Authority.
In addition, the fact that so many of these signs were employed perfectly intelligently by the Mediæval Masons suggests that there also
traces of the Mysteries may have lingered long.   It is generally
believed that the Masons, who were a particularly close guild, had
ceremonies of initiation, consisting of more than one Grade, and even
as late as the beginning of the 19th century the Operative Stone
Masons, who subsequently developed into the modern Trade Union,
had such a ceremony, as Postgate shows in his valuable work, *The
Builders' History*.   Fragments of these rituals can still be seen at the
Offices of the Amalgamated Union of Building Trade Workers[1].
Obviously, the whole of the ritual was not put into writing; no doubt
their obligations forbade the compilers thereof so to do, but that the
ceremonies were connected with a dramatic representation of death
and resurrection is clear, as the following quotation will show:—

"Give these strangers light.—Strangers mark well this shadow
      whcsh know (*sic*) you see
  'Tis a faithful emblem of man's destiny.
  Behold this head once filled with pregnant wit
  These hollow holes once sparkling eyes did sit,
  This empty mouth no tongue or lips contains
  Of a once well furnished head see all that now remains.
  Behold this breast where a generous heart once moved
  Filled with affection, loving, and behold
  Mark well these bones the flesh hath left its place
  These arms could once a tender wife embrace.
  These legs in gay activity could roam
  But alas the spirit fled and life is gone."

1 "The Builders," Crescent Grove, South Side, Clapham Common, S.W.

That an actual skeleton was shown to the candidate is clear from the portion of the ritual here quoted, and until fairly recently such a skeleton was still part of the regalia of one of the oldest Trade Union Lodges of Masons which still survive. My informant, Mr. William Williams, who until 1921 was General Secretary of "The Operative Stone Masons and Quarrymen," a Trade Union now absorbed into the Amalgamated Union of Building Trade Workers, told me that when he visited Hulme Lodge, Manchester, some 14 or 15 years ago, he asked if any of the old relics and regalia which had been used in the lodge when initiation into it was a formal and ritualistic affair, still survived. He was told by old members that the last relics were a skeleton and an axe, but that both of these had recently been cleared away and could not then be traced.

He also informed me that the Quarrymen at Portland still kept up certain secret rites and ceremonies, but were very secretive about them, so much so that neither he, nor any of the great Trade Union Officials, had ever been permitted to witness them. It should be noted that the men I am now discussing are genuine quarrymen and builders, and not members of the organisation known as "Speculative Freemasonry."

It may at first seem strange that Operative Stone Masons should have even faint traces of a kind of Mystery Cult, but on closer examination the strangeness will disappear. In Pagan times, when owing to the increase of civilisation it ceased to be the custom to hold big religious meetings in secluded places in the jungle or desert, temples and temple halls were substituted, as was undoubtedly done in Egypt, and in the case of some of the Temples, especially in the great Pyramid at Giza, there are clear indications that the buildings were erected in a particular manner so as to make them suitable for initiation ceremonies. The same thing occurred in Greece, where there were special halls for this purpose at Eleusis, and in the Roman Empire quite a number of the Halls of Mithra have been discovered.

Now if men had to build edifices of this nature, with peculiar arrangements for representing dramatically a journey through the Underworld, as appears to have been the case in Egypt and Greece, it would have been important to the Priests that such men on the one hand should know something of the peculiar nature of the ceremonies to be performed, and on the other should be bound by oaths of secrecy not to disclose to the uninitated world outside any casual information they might obtain during the process of their work. The simplest method to ensure this would be to initiate them, at any rate in part, into the Mystery Rite, the buildings for which they had to erect. It is not surprising therefore that in Roman times we find the Roman College of Architects had some form of Mystery Rite of their own, as is proved by a curious inlaid table top found at Pompeii, and now in the Naples Museum, whereon are depicted a skull, a combined square, level and plumb line, and a beggar's mantle, opposite to which is a royal robe, together with other emblems whose significance is fairly evident. They imply that man must die, casting off his earthly body as an outworn mantle, but will receive in its place a glorious spiritual body, which may be likened to the robes of a King. It should be noted that the men who worked this Rite must have included those who painted the fresco of the Rescue of Œdipus, wherein is depicted a woman making the Sign of Preservation, (see illustration opposite page 180) and also the fresco of the Sacrifice of Iphigenia, which shows the unfortunate girl making the Sign of Distress (see illustration opposite page 62). At this time the Guild of Architects was exceedingly strong and powerful and a very close corporation, and no one would have been permitted to do mural decorations in Pompeii unless he were a member of the local Guild.

These same men adorned what we should call their "lodge room" with a bas-relief on the outside wall, depicting the ordinary masons tools, but having in the middle an upturned urn, as if the ashes of the dead had been scattered to the four winds, a characteristic Roman symbol for death. Why should they in this instance, and in the case of the inlaid table top, associate their working tools with the emblems of death if they had no cult of their own? As a matter of fact, it seems as if all the great Trade Corporations, or Guilds, in ancient Rome had Cults, each no doubt differing a little from the others, and it is possible that other Guilds besides the Masons worked a ritual of death and resurrection, but if so I have so far been unable to find any conclusive evidence, such as that I have quoted in favour of the Guild of Architects. It must not be forgotten, however, that in the Middle Ages most of the Trade Guilds had a kind of Cult of a

Patron Saint, and often enacted a Miracle Play or Drama. The close similarity of such Miracle Plays, or Mysteries, as they were called, to the dramas of the Ancient Mysteries, is obvious, and even in the 20th century actors in the Russian Miracle Plays make use of similar Mantric Signs at appropriate points.

As late as the 17th century, and, of all places, in Holland, such signs were still being used in connection with Mystery Plays, although probably their significance was nearly lost and the Sign carelessly made. The woodcut reproduced below is a facsimile of one forming part of a series of graphic illustrations to an old school book entitled,

A 17th century Dutch Woodcut of an old Morality Play, "The Prodigal Son."

N.7.

"Orbis Sensualium Pictus: or a Picture and Nomenclature of all the Chief Things that are in the World; and of men's Employment therein. Originally written in Latine (sic) and high Dutch." It represents a scene in one of the old Morality Plays, namely, *The History of the Prodigal Son*. The original Latin description is given and it is also translated into English, as follows:—

"In a Play-house, which is trimmed with Hangings, and covered with Curtains, Comedies, and Tragedies are acted, wherein memorable things are represented; as here, the History of the Prodigal Son and his Father, by whom he is entertained, being returned home.

"The Players act, being in disguise; the Fool maketh Jests.

THE WEST FRONT OF ST. TROPHÍME'S, ARLES.

I.44.

THE CIRCUMCISION.
A Fresco by Fra Angelico at St. Mark's Monastery, Florence.

L.53.

"The chief of the Spectators sit in the Gallery, the common sort stand on the ground, and clap the hands if any thing please them."

This woodcut is of interest for more than one reason, and shows that at that early date which, from the style of the costumes, must have been about the period of Charles I, already some kind of scenery had been evolved.   But for our immediate purpose the main point of interest is the man standing in the background, who is making the Sign of Preservation at the very moment when the father is raising the returned prodigal from his knees.   It is more than probable that the Fool, who is shown in the foreground, is taking off the man who is making the sign.

Reverting, however, to the Roman College of Architects, it is important to note that on the collapse of the Roman Empire her Guild System was practically destroyed by the barbarian invaders, but a Roman College of Architects which had taken refuge in Comacina, a small island in the midst of Lake Como, survived.   This place was never taken by the Lombards, and when in due course these Northern invaders came to realise the advantages of order and civilisation, their King, Rothares, decided to encourage building by placing the control of it in tried and competent hands.   Therefore on November 22nd, 643. he issued an edict, or charter, wherein he recognised the authority of the masons of Comacina over all the masons in his Kingdom of North Italy.

Comacine work is easily recognisable in North Italy, South Germany and South France by certain characteristic signs, which we may almost regard as the Trade Mark of the Guild, among the most obvious of which are the endless knot and the lion of Judah.   A good example of their work is at Arles Cathedral, where the lions of Judah can be seen at the foot of the Saints who support the great arch of the West front.   Unfortunately, the picture reproduced opposite page 182 merely shows the tops of the heads of two of them, in the right hand bottom corner, but there are a whole series.   It will be remembered that we have several times referred to this church as containing sculpture work showing the use of Mantric Signs.

Another good representative piece of Comacine work is the pulpit at Ravello, wherein Jonah is depicted making the Sign of Preservation, and we have a fine example of the endless knot.   (See illustration

opposite page 98).   It was from the Comacine Masons that the various
Northern Masons learnt the rudiments of architecture and building,
in the course of years organising their own National Guilds, such as
The Freemasons, in England, *The Companionage*, in France, and *The
Steinmetzen*, in Germany.   But although the Builders' Guilds probably
played no inconsiderable part in keeping alive the tradition that certain signs should be employed in sculpture and pictorial art to depict
certain emotions, it is probable that it was the Church herself, and more
especially the Monastic Orders, who retained the fullest knowledge of
the inner significance of such gestures, and saw to it that when pictures
were painted on the walls of the Churches, or bas-reliefs sculptured
therein, the correct signs were employed.

In the Middle Ages the pictures and scupltures which adorned the
churches had a practical as well as an artistic use.   The laity could not
read but, like all semi-educated people, they seem to have been
particularly appreciative of pictorial art, and we know that frescoes,
stained glass and sculptures alike were not chosen arbitrarily, but
according to a definite symbolic system, and arranged round the building so as to supply "a poor man's Bible," as it is called.   Scenes from
the Old Testament were not given so as to trace the history of the Jews,
but selected because they were considered to be prototypes of certain
events in Christ's life, or at any rate symbols of them, and no doubt
the clergy would constantly refer to these pictures during the course of
their sermons.

Under such circumstances the fact that in one scene of the Crucifixion the Virgin is making the Sign of Regret and in another the Sign
of Resignation, would enable the Priest to vary the text of his sermon
and to make it vivid to his audience.   Such scenes, in short, spoke by
means of their symbolism, and it was incumbent on the clergy to see
that the symbolism was not forgotten by the Masons.   It does not
necessarily follow that the clergy disclosed to the laity the exact
significance of all these signs.   It is indeed highly improbable that
they did.   It is a characteristic defect of all hierarchies to endeavour
to enshroud themselves in mystery and try to keep to themselves various fragments of secret knowledge, but when explaining a picture the
presence of a particular sign would enable the priest to translate its
meaning correctly.   If considerable importance were not attached

to this knowledge, why does Matthew Paris lay such stress on the necessity of knowing the Signs?

It is quite possible that a few of the simpler signs, such as those of Preservation and Distress, were known to the more enlightened of the people, for certainly they are known, or at any rate used, by some of the laity in the Roman Catholic Church to-day, as is shown by the use of the Signs of Preservation, of Sacrifice and of Resignation by the little Italian girl at Carthage, which is described on page 26. In the main, however, these signs were doubtless known only to the few, among whom would be the clergy, the monastic orders in particular, and possibly the great Building Guilds. Certain it is that in the Primitive Initiatory Rites of savages, in the Mystery Rites of Egypt, Eleusis and Attis-Cybele, (see illustration opposite page 148) in Mediæval ecclesiastical art and in that modern representative of the Mysteries, the Hung Society of China, we find the use of these mantric signs. When moreover we see that we can show, century by century, these signs descending through the ages, down to the present day, we are, I consider, justified in claiming that they are proofs of the survival of at any rate portions of the Ancient Mysteries and the teachings which they enshrined.

Before leaving this subject mention must be made of a group of men who have always been suspected of being at least indirectly connected with the survival of these Ancient Mysteries. These are the Alchemists, from whom it is probable that the far-famed Rosicrucians were an offshoot. The writings of the alchemists are obscure and difficult to follow, because in most cases they were speaking in cryptic language under the veil of symbols, and in many cases we have lost the key which would enable us to interpret their meaning. The plate from the *Azoth Philosophorum*, however, reproduced opposite page 174, is clearly intended to be symbolical.

The figure with the two heads probably represents Man natural and Man regenerate, surrounded by the seven planets and trampling with his left foot on the dragon which crouches over the winged globe. The fact that the figure bears in its hands the square and compasses, suggests some inter-relationship between these philosophers and the Masonic Guilds, while the emphatic way in which the left foot is planted first proves that to them this mantric sign had a very definite inner meaning. Possibly the dragon who is thus being attacked symbolises exoteric religion and the popular ideas of right and wrong, which the alchemists thought should be overthrown so that the light of the sun and of the planets could once more shine on the world shrouded in darkness.

To such men as the Alchemists many of the rules laid down by the Church, as for example, her severe edict against heresy, must have seemed as a sore impediment to the spread of the Truth and Light.

A FRESCO OF "THE LAST JUDGMENT."
By Van Dyg.

In the Town Hall, Basle.

M.9.

THE CATHEDRAL, COIRE.
Showing the Pillars.

"THE LAST JUDGMENT."
Two leaves of a Triptych of Coloured Limoges Enamel.
French work of the early 16th Century.
Now in the Victoria and Albert Museum.

M.54.

CHAPTER XXI. *Wherein we arrive at the conclusion of the whole matter.*

NOW IT SEEMS desirable that before concluding this book we should endeavour to show how as a result of our knowledge of the meaning of these signs we are able to interpret a picture, and discern the sentiments contained therein more fully than would otherwise be possible. In the fresco shown opposite page 186, we see the devils carrying away the damned, while above, although not reproduced in this book, our Lord is depicted coming in Glory surrounded by angels and saints.

The man in the foreground, who makes the Sign of Preservation, calls upon our Lord, as the Saviour and Preserver of mankind, to preserve him in this hour of peril, while the woman whose hands are crossed on her chest in the Sign of Resignation is symbolically saying, "Thy will, O Lord, be done." Behind this woman stands another, who is apparently making the Sign of Sacrifice, thereby reminding Christ that He sacrificed Himself to save mankind and by that sacrifice she craves forgiveness. The Pope, who stands beside her, and is easily distinguishable by the fact that he wears the triple tiara, makes no mantric sign, although the expression on his face and his general attitude bespeak clearly enough the abject terror in which he stands, owing to the fact that he has already been touched by one of the demons. Coming once more to the foreground, we can see that the man with his back turned towards us is appealing to Christ in the clouds, and in so doing displays his deep distress. He has not, however, entirely lost all hope, which is the sad fate of the man in the right hand corner as we look at the picture. The latter we can almost hear saying, "Alas, alas, my life has been in vain, for God has rejected me and I am about to be cast out amid the rubbish."

Before disposing of this picture it is worth while drawing attention to the fact that there are five people making mantric signs, and as five is such an important number in symbolism, it seems probable that its choice is deliberate. Furthermore, they are arranged, as it were, in a series of gradations of hope. The man who makes the Sign of Preservation may be considered as typifying hope with a certain amount of confidence in it. This hope is further increased by being based on the strength of Christ's definite promise that through His death mankind should be saved, as is shown by the woman who is making the Sign of Sacrifice, while the other woman, who is making the Sign of Resignation, has really passed beyond hope, into complete confidence. But there is the other, or descending, side of the story. The man next to the woman who makes the Sign of Resignation still hopes, but there is a quality of desperateness and distress, bordering almost on despair, intermingled therewith, and finally we come to the picture of vain regret of hopelessness, of knowledge of rejection. Yet the whole composition by its very proportion of four to one bespeaks the hopeful and confident belief of the artist that at the Day of Judgment the majority of mankind will be saved.

The Triptych in coloured Limoges enamel reproduced opposite belongs to the early part of the 16th century. The original is owned by J. Pierpont Morgan, who has placed it on loan at the Victoria and Albert Museum. In the centre we see our Lord in Majesty, having on His right the Virgin, who is making the well known Sign of Prayer. Seeing that the Catholic Church continually speaks of the Virgin as the intermediary between man and Christ, ever pleading his cause, and further that she will intercede more especially at the Day of Judgment, we see at once why the artist depicts her making this sign. She is pleading for the dead who are rising, whereas St.

John the Evangelist, the beloved apostle, makes the Sign of Resignation, as if to answer that the Lord of all will assuredly do right. Beneath these central figures the dead are seen rising from their graves and some of them are shown making the Signs of Resignation, Preservation and Distress, while exactly the same series of three signs appears in a panel on the left of Christ, wherein the demons are shown carrying off the damned to hell.   Readers can for themselves apply the same principles that were used when interpreting the signs used on the fresco at Basle, but they should note one interesting little point, namely, that among the damned the signs are distributed in a series of three pairs, namely, two of distress, two of Resignation and two of Preservation.

It is, however, when we have before us a complete series of pictorial representations made at about the same date and under the control of some guiding Master hand, that we are able to perceive how important is a comprehension of the meaning attached to the various mantric signs. Many students of Mediæval art are aware of the fact that at Fairford Church the glass was designed as a complete scheme, which has fortunately survived, with most satisfactory results, and to a large extent the same is true of the stained glass at King's College, Cambridge.   In like manner at Rheims Cathedral, France, there exist a whole series of tapestries of the 16th century, depicting incidents in the life of the Virgin.   Some sixteen survive, although one or two are little more than fragments, and we cannot of course say for certain whether there may not have been others in the series which have completely vanished.   However, even if this be so, we are still left with a very fine set of tapestries and it is interesting to note that in most of them certain mantric signs occur, as can be seen by referring to the complete list at the end of the book.

Now there is one peculiarity of these tapestries to which special attention is directed because it is characteristic of the whole system of symbolism which runs through Mediæval art.   We have seen that as early as the time of the frescoes in the Catacombs, it was customary for Christian artists to draw on the Old Testament for certain symbolical scenes, supposed to be the prototypes of the chief incidents in the Gospels.   In these tapestries we find that each central and predominant picture is accompanied by two or more symbolic scenes, usually chosen from the Old Testament, and it is interesting to note how the figures in the latter, by their symbolical gestures, are brought into close connection with the corresponding figures in the central theme.   It is not that in every case the signs are the same, on the contrary, although always appropriate, the artist is usually careful to indicate a slightly different sentiment by the use of varying gestures in one or two cases.   It is even possible that thereby he intended to indicate the subtle difference between the prototype and the Christian equivalent.   For our purpose we have reproduced the tapestry depicting the Death of the Virgin.   The incident is not mentioned in the Canonical Gospels, but for all that in legend and in the Apocryphal Gospels it plays an important part.   In fact, my readers must realise by now that to the Mediæval Christians the legends and the Apocryphal books were almost as important as the incidents depicted in the Canonical ones.

In the tapestry itself, which is reproduced opposite, we see the central and main picture enclosed within a Renaissance arch, which is flanked on the lower right and left corners by figures of Saints, Patriarchs and Sages.   Within the arch we see a room and the Virgin lying dead upon a bed, with her hands crossed downwards.   A man in the foreground, possibly St. John, makes the Sign of Resignation, as does also a woman at the foot of the bed.   Above the arch, we see a group of seven Angels, the middle one of whom is making the Sign of Distress, a second the Sign of Prayer and a third that of Preservation.   The angel on the right of the one making the Sign of Distress is making the Sign of Adoration, enabling us clearly to distinguish the subtle difference between the two signs.   So much for the main picture, but in the two top corners are subsidiary scenes, taken from the Old Testament.   That on the left as we look at the picture, represents the death of Sarah, the wife of Abraham, that on the right, the death of Miriam, i.e., the sister of Moses.   In both cases the dead woman has her hands crossed downwards, the Sign of Impotence, exactly corresponding with the position of the hands of the Virgin, also in both examples there is a seated woman, who makes the Sign of Resignation.   Moreover, in the picture of Sarah there is a woman making the Sign of Prayer, exactly corresponding with a man in the left hand, bottom corner of the tapestry, while in the scene of the

THE DEATH OF THE VIRGIN.

A Tapestry from Rheims Cathedral.

M.52.

THE LAST JUDGMENT.

The Upper Part of a Fresco by Fra Angelico.

At St. Mark's Monastery, Florence.

L.50.

Death of Miriam, the man with the head-dress points to Heaven and Earth, in the Sign which I have thus named, corresponding with the attitude of the man in the right hand, bottom corner of the tapestry, and to the man wearing a head-dress on the extreme bottom left of it, both of whom make the same sign, the latter very much more perfectly than the former.

Thus all told there are three Signs of Heaven and Earth, four Signs of Resignation, one of Distress and one of Preservation in this tapestry, not to mention Signs of Prayer and Adoration. Now every one of these Signs is appropriate to the scene, for what could be more suitable on such an occasion than that an onlooker should remind the mourners that, although the body of the dead woman will be buried in the earth, her soul will mount upward to the Heavens, while to another mourner the sentiment uppermost would naturally be, "Thy will, O Lord, be done." As to the Signs of Prayer, no doubt they are intended to indicate that these onlookers are praying for the soul of the deceased, while the angel who makes the Sign of Preservation does so in order to remind the whole world that it was through the Virgin that He,. Who brought them Preservation and Salvation, came to the human race.

Another such series, in this case consisting of frescoes, occurs in the paintings by Fra Angelico at St. Mark's Monastry, Florence, wherein, as we have shown, the artist consistently employs mantric signs to convey various inner meanings. If we glance at the reproduction of the detail of his picture of the Last Judgment which is shown opposite page 192, we shall see that he has arranged a triangle of signs. On the left, the Virgin, making the Sign of Resignation; opposite her St. John with the Sign of Prayer, and in the foreground an angel making that of Heaven and Earth. Around our Lord the angel host have built up a glowing Vesica Piscis as the Lord of all the world comes to Judge the earth. The action of the angel bespeaks his proclamation, "He who ascended in glory now descends as He then promised, also in Glory, this time to judge the earth!" while St. John the Baptist prays for sinful man and the Virgin reminds Him of her sacrifice on their behalf as a plea for mercy. This should be compared with the other examples of this artist's work, which are reproduced on pages 126, 140, and 184.

Having thus shown how in many pictorial examples the Mantric Signs are built up into an almost complete narrative, it may be of interest to draw attention to the fact that their use occurs in almost every form of pictorial art, and on almost every material, just as they are to be found in every age and every clime. Among the examples I have scheduled in this book we find that they appear in the following materials:—-

Egyptian Papyri; sculpture and stone; frescoes; on mummy cases; in bronze statues; on seals; in terracotta and clay figures; on a gold ring from Mycenæ; on Greek painted vases; on sepulchral stele; on a Carthaginian clay lamp; on mosaics of every age; on carved sarcophagi; on the silver casket of Projecta; on statues of the Gods, such as Attis and Hanuman[1]; on ivory carvings and caskets; in illuminated manuscripts; on a bronze weight; on Cloisonné enamels; on tapestries; on "Champlevé" enamels; on Limoges enamels; on fonts; on stained glass; on altar crosses; on engraved glass; on engraved gems, such as the Crystal of Lothair; on an engraved, bronze bowl; on embroidered vestments; on carved woodwork; in pictures painted on wood or canvas; in early printed books; on tiles; on monumental brasses; on a shield of parade; on a bronze mirror; on native wooden beads; in native engravings on pebbles and boulders; in sand pictures intended for native Rites; in woven hangings and baskets; in funeral vases in the New World, and are actually made to-day by men in primitive Initiation Rites and in existing Secret Societies, such as the Hung. It would indeed by hard to find any substance under Heaven on which men can engrave, paint, sculpture or write on which I have not found examples of the use of this language.

If we divide art into its two main groups of symbolic and naturalistic, we shall find that in the case of the former a complete understanding of its meaning is only possible if we master the inner significance of this Ancient Sign Language, which has been handed down from generation to generation, usually under the protection of religion, and is still in use to-day in every quarter of the world.

---

[1] See illustration opposite page 220.

Schedule of Examples of the Use of Mantric Signs, arranged Chronologically.

REF. No.	TITLE AND DESCRIPTION.	SIGN CONTAINED THEREIN.
EGYPT.		
A. 1.	Praising Ra at Sunset. From the Leyden Papyrus now in the British Museum.†	*Preservation.* *Adoration.*
2.	Pediment of a Temple. B.C. 1333. Now in the Bath Museum.*	*Preservation.*
3.	Fresco from Thebes. B.C. 1500. Initiates being given food. Now in the British Museum.	*Tearing out heart.*
4.	Figure on Cartonage of the mummy of Heru-netch Tef. B.C. 500. Now in British Museum.	*Preservation.*
5.	Several figures engraved on the stone sarcophagus of Queen Ankhnes-Neferabra, of the 26th dynasty. Found at Thebes: now in British Museum.*	*Preservation.*
6.	Several figures on the tablet of Ptahnekhtu of the 19th dynasty. British Museum.*	*Tearing out heart.*
7.	Copies in Brit. Mus. of painted reliefs in the Temple built at Bet al Wali, in Nubia, by Rameses II., Circa 1330 B.C., to commemorate the conquest of Nubia. In the scene of the Libyan War Rameses is shown in the act of slaying a prisoner who makes the Sign of Distress, while in the scene representing the Syrian War a warrior being attacked makes Sign of Preservation.*	*Distress.* *Preservation*
8.	A bas-relief in the Louvre depicts Pharaoh making the Sign of Distress to a god who is seated under a canopy.	*Distress.*
9.	A bas-relief now in the Louvre depicting magical ceremonies.	*Sacrifice.* *Preservation.*
10.	The Ceremony of "Opening the Mouth" depicted in "The Book of the Dead." Original in British Museum.	*Sympathy.*
11.	The Tenth Hour in "The Book of Gates," now in British Museum.	*Preservation.* *Distress.*
12.	Horus with the scalp lock. Original in Author's possession.	*Secrecy.*
13.	Figure 91 in *The Egyptian Language*, by Budge. A determinative hieroglyph for anything connected with the mouth.	*Secrecy.*
14.	Horus crowned with three feathers. Original bronze statue in author's possession.†	*Secrecy.*
16.	The Creation. The God Nu bearing in his hands the Boat of Ra, accompanied by a number of deities making the sign. Budge, *The Egyptian Religion*, Vol. I. Op. p. 24.	*Fidelity.*

A.17.	Horus introducing Ani into the Hall of Osiris. Ani makes sign. Budge. *Book of the Dead.* Vol. I. Frontis.	*Sacrifice.*
18.	Weighing the Heart of Ani. Ani makes sign. Papyrus of Ani, now in British Museum.†	*Sacrifice.*
19.	The Hymn to Ra when he Rises. Budge, *Book of the Dead.* Vol. I. p.3.	*Egyptian Sign of Prayer or Adoration.*
20	Hieroglyphic character meaning *adoration* Budge, *The Egyptian Language,* p. 43.	*Adoration.*
21.	The Funeral Procession in the Chapter of "Coming Forth by Day." Papyrus of Ani. British Museum.	*Sympathy.*
22.	Funeral Ceremony at the Tomb. Anubis supports mummy, before which his wife and daughter kneel making this sign. Papyrus of Ani.† (*Book of Dead* p. 40).	*Sympathy.*
23.	Adoring the Boat of Ra. Papyrus of Nebseni: in British Museum.	*Adoration.*
24.	Papyrus of Ani. Ani spearing a serpent.	*Left foot first.*
25.	Papyrus of Ani. Ani adoring Ra in the boat.	*Adoration.*
26.	The Turin Papyrus. Vignette of the chapter of "Giving a Heart to Osiris". *Book of the Dead.* Vol. II. p. 138 and 140.	*Preservation.*
27.	Papyrus of Nefer-Uben-f. Vignette. Budge, *Book of the Dead,* Vol. II. p. 141.	*Tearing out heart.*
28.	Papyrus of Mes-em-neter. Vignette of a Man Spearing a Serpent. Budge. *Book of the Dead,* Vol. II. p. 67.	*Left foot first.*
29.	The Papyrus of Kerasher, Ptolemaic period, in British Museum. Isis and Nepthys wailing over the body of Osiris which Anubis is about to raise.	*Sympathy.*
30.	Statue of Hathor.	*Sign of Obligation.*
31.	Papyrus of Nebseni. British Museum.	*Tearing out heart.*
32.	Temple of Rameses III at Karnak, with colossal figures making Signs.†	*Resignation.*
33.	A Painted Stele in the Cairo Museum of the 21st Dynasty, depicting two scenes. Above, a woman in front of a table of offerings adoring Horus. Below, a landscape with tombs. In front of the tombs a woman makes Sign of Sympathy or Sorrow.	*Adoration.* *Sympathy.*
34.	A Vignette at the top of Chapter CLXXXII, *Book of the Dead,* from the Papyrus of Mut-hetep. The deceased lying upon a bier. In the upper and lower registers	*Sign of the Pillars.*

"THE RAISING OF THE MASTER."
By Geurcino.

N.8.

DRIVING OUT THE MONEY-CHANGERS.
By Guercino.
In the Palazzo Rosso, Genoa. 17th Century Work.

N.9.

Ref. No.	Title and Description.	Sign contained therein.

are a number of Dieties who hold in either hand pairs of Snakes, Knives, etc.

A. 35. Statue of Amen-Hetep. B.C. 1600. In British Museum.   *Resignation.*

36. Statuette of Tutankh Amen. In the Cairo Museum.   *Resignation.*

37. Interior of the Coffin of Soser, painted with the Twelve Signs   *Distress.*
of the Zodiac and the Goddess Nut, who makes the 'Sign of Distress. Thebes A.D. 710.

38. Fresco showing a Lion raising a Mummy with the Lion   *Lion Grip*
Grip while Isis, looking on, makes the Sign of Preservation   *Preservation.*
vation Orig. unknown.

BABYLONIAN.

B. 1. Descent of Shamash, or of Damuzi, into the Underworld.
British Museum.†   *Preservation.*

2. Resurrection of Shamash, or of Damuzi. British Museum.†   *Preservation.*

3. Stele with Scene representing King Khammurabi receiving   *Sacrifice.*
the Code of Laws from the Sun God. British Museum.

4. Worshipping the Sacred Tree. British Museum.   *Heaven and Earth.*

5. A Sumerian Seal of a Viceroy of Ur-Gur. B.C. 2500. See   *Preservation.*
Plate I, op. p. 562, Encyclopaedia Britannica, Vol. XI. 11th ed.

6. Assyrian Cylinder Seal representing a woman worshipping   *Preservation.*
Ishtar, who makes the Sign of Preservation in reply. Ref. as 5.

CRETAN.

C. 1. A Votive Figure reproduced in *Alt-Kreta*, by Bossert   *True till Death.*

2. A Votive Figure of a Woman. Ref. as above.   *Fidelity.*

3. Votive Figure of a Man. Ref. as above.   *Preservation.*

4. Figure of a Priestess wearing a double Apron and holding in   *The Sign of the*
her hands two serpents, *The Palace of Minos in Knossos*,   *Pillars.*
by Sir A. Evans.

5. Votive figure of a woman. Bossert, *Alt-Kreta*.   *Distress.*

6. Figures of two Cretan Priestesses from Minoan Seals. *The*   *Preservation.*
Palace of Minos in Knossos, by Evans.†

7. A similar Figure on a Seal as above.†   *Horror.*

8. A Votive Figure of a Man. As above.†   *Reverence.*

9. Votive Figure of a Woman. As above.†   *Reverence.*

10. Altar Ledge with objects from a Temple Repository. In   *Sign of the*
Centre, a four armed cross, flanked on either side by a   *Pillars.*
statue of a priestess; one making the Sign of the Pillars   *It is finished.*
with two serpents, the other, the sign, "It is Finished."

REF. NO.	TITLE AND DESCRIPTION.	SIGN CONTAINED THEREIN.

C. 11. A Priestess on a Minoan Seal. †   *Sign of Water.*

   12. A Minoan Seal Showing the Worship of the Sacred Axe. †   *Preservation.*

   13. A Mycenæan type of Gold Seal showing the Great Mother and   *Sign of Water.*
her Lover. †

GREEK.

D. 1. A Gold Ring from Mycenae. Dussaud, *La Civilisation*   *Preservation.*
Préhellénique.

   2. Athenian Black Figure Hydria or Water Jar. B.C. 550.   *Preservation.*
Women drawing water from a well. British Museum. †

   3. Black Figure Amphora. B.C. 500. In British Museum.   *Touching top of*
Head. Sign of
Obligation.
Preservation.

   4. A Stele from Athens now in the National Museum, Athens.   *True till Death*
c. 450 B.C. †   *and grip associ-*
ated therewith.

   5. A Sepulchral Stele of Archagora. In British Museum.   *True till Death*
and grip associ-
ated therewith.

   6. A Corinthian Pottery Vase. B.C. 650. In British Museum.   *Preservation.*

   7. Bas-relief of the Eleusinian Mysteries representing the   *Heaven & Earth*
initiate being presented to Ceres, and holding torches up
and down. †

PHŒNECIAN.

E. 1. Seven Steles of Punic Priests. C. 800—400 B.C. Found at   *Preservation.*
Carthage. †

   2. Five ditto in the Bardo Museum, Tunis. *   *Preservation.*

   3. One Stele showing a Priest between two Pillars. In Bardo   *Preservation.*
Museum, Tunis. †

   4. Seven Steles of Punic Priests in the Algiers Museum. *   *Preservation.*

   5. Several ditto. Setif Museum, Algeria.   *Preservation.*

   6. Several ditto in British Museum, London.   *Preservation.*

   7. Several Tombstones of the Laity in the museums at Algiers,   *Distress.*
Setif and the Bardo, Tunis, with the emblem of the
Crescent, Caduceus and a figure making the Sign.

   8. Caste of a similar tombstone now in the Bardo Museum.   *Distress.*

   9. A Funeral Statue, Carthage.   *Preservation.*

  10. Two Drawings of Punic Tombstones now in Constantine   *Distress.*
Museum, showing the Hand of Fatima, Caduceus and
Sign of Distress. †

Ref. No.	Title and Description.	Sign contained therein.
E. 11.	Statuette of Venus and Cupids in terracotta. †	Preservation.
12.	Fragment of a Carthaginian Figure showing Greek influence. A. L. Delattre, La Nécropole des Rabs.	Preservation.
13.	Lamp connected with the worship of Tanit, found at Carthage, illustrated in book named in 12. †	Distress.
14.	Another fragment of a Carthaginian Figure wearing a Phrygian hat; probably Tammuz. A. L. Delattre, as above.	Preservation.
15.	Statue of a Punic Priest found at Carthage.	Preservation.

ROMAN.

Pre-Christian.

F. 1.	Mosaic in the Museum at Djemila, Algeria, depicting the triumph of Amphitriton. In the border, a figure in a boat makes the Sign of Distress, evidently frightened at the appearance of the God and his accompanying Nymphs. *	Distress.
2.	Statue of Ceres in the Bardo Museum, Tunis. *	Preservation.
3.	Fresco of the Rescue of Œdipus in the House of the Tragic Poet, Pompeii. †	Preservation.
4.	The Sacrifice of Iphigenia, from Pompeii, now in the Naples Museum. A. D. 70. †	Distress, Secrecy. Sign of the Pillars.

Post-Christian.

10.	Mosaic of the 4th century now in the Bardo Museum, Tunis. *	Distress.
11.	A similar Mosaic, Daniel in the Lions' Den, in the Museum, Algiers. *	Distress.
12.	Three Sarcophagi of the 5th century in the Museum at Arles, showing (a) Jonah and the Whale. Jonah and two deceased make fidelity.	Fidelity.
	(b) Daniel in the Lions' Den.	Distress.
	(c) Daniel in the Lions' Den. †	Distress. Regret.
13.	Fresco in Church of St. Mary Antiqua, in the Forum, Rome. 5th century. Depicting the three Maries holding three Babes. St. John makes Sign of Heaven and Earth, and St. James, Preservation.	Heaven & Earth Preservation.
14.	Roman Sarcophagus at Arles, 4th century, showing the Nativity.	Preservation.
15.	Ditto at Arles, 4th—5th century, showing the Raising of the Daughter of Tabitha. †	Lion Grip. Preservation. Pulling Beard.

REF. No.	TITLE AND DESCRIPTION.	SIGN CONTAINED THEREIN.
F.16.	A 4th century sarcophagus in the Catacombs, Rome, depicting Daniel in the Lions' Den. Daniel and deceased both make sign.†	*Distress.*
17.	Fresco of Paradise in the Catacombs. 3rd Century. Three Souls making Sign of Distress.	*Distress*
18.	Fresco in the Catacombs. 3rd century. A man in a ship, representing the Church, makes Sign of Distress.	*Distress.*
19.	Grafita in the Catacombs of St. Calixus. 3rd—4th century. Souls making Sign of Distress.	*Distress.*
20.	Fresco ditto, of Abraham sacrificing Isaac. Both make sign.†	*Distress.*
21.	Ditto, 3rd—4th century, in Catacombs. Showing the Sign of Distress.†	*Distress.*
22.	Gilded Glass Disc with Scriptural subjects, found at Cologne. 4th century. Now in British Museum. Depicts Daniel in the Lions' Den; Three Children in the Furnace and the Widow of Nain. All make sign.†	*Distress.*
23.	Fresco of St. Cecilia in the Catacombs of St. Calixus. 5th—6th century.†	*Distress.*
24.	The Silver Casket of Projecta. Sign of Fidelity made by her husband. (A wedding casket). In British Museum.	*Fidelity.*
25.	A 2nd Century Roman Sarcophagus in the Vatican Museum.†	*Horror.*
26.	Statue of Attis, now in the Museum of Avignon. 3rd century.†	*Regret.*
27.	Tomb in St. Mark's Cathedral, Venice, 4th century. Top row figures make Sign of Sacrifice. In bottom row, Distress.	*Sacrifice.* *Distress.*
28.	Tomb of the Empress Helena in Red Porphry, in the Vatican Museum. Roman soldiers slaughter their enemies but spare one man, who makes Sign of Preservation.†	*Preservation.*
29.	A Christian Gem of the 4th century depicting the Good Shepherd and the Soul. Former makes Sign of Preservation, latter Distress.†	*Preservation.* *Distress.*
30.	Coptic Bone Plaque of the 3rd or 4th century depicting a woman making the Sign.	*Destruction.*
31.	Panels from an Ivory Casket known as the Werden Casket, showing the Virgin entering the Temple to drink the bitter water. The Virgin makes the Sign. Original in the Victoria and Albert Museum.	*Destruction.*
32.	A Fresco of the Baptism of Christ in the Cemetery of Ss. Peter and Marcellinus. F. Bond, *Fonts and Font Covers.* p. 8.	*Distress.*

THE CRUCIFIXION.
An 11th Century Carved Ivory Panel from Cologne.

H.14.

AN INDIAN BAS-RELIEF OF VISHNU ASLEEP UNDER THE COBRA.

U.40.

DARK AGES. 6th—10th CENTURY.

G. 1. Illuminated Greek MS., gr. No. 699 in the Vatican Library, showing the Virgin, Christ, John the Baptist, Zachariah and Elizabeth. Virgin makes sign. 9th century. — *Preservation.*

2. Carved ivory seal of Godwin, in British Museum. On the reverse demi-figure of Godgytha, the Nun, making sign, thereby indicating preservation by entering the nunnery. 10—11th century. — *Preservation.*

3. A Crystal Medallion engraved with the story of Susannah and made for Lothiar, King of the Franks. 9th century.† — *Preservation. Distress.*

4. A French Carolingian Ivory Carving. Early 10th century, No. 69 in British Museum. Depicts scenes from the Life of Christ. Two shepherds make sign when the angel appears. Our Lord speaks to apostles and onlooker makes sign. — *Preservation.*

5. A Byzantine Ivory Triptych of the 10th century now in the Louvre. Christ is seated between two figures who both make signs.† — *Preservation. Fidelity.*

6. An Ivory panel of the 9th century depicting the Judgment of Solomon, now in the Louvre.† — *Fidelity. Distress. "It is finished."*

7. Byzantine Ivory Carved Box, now in the British Museum, representing Daniel in the Lions' Den. 6th—8th century.† — *Distress.*

8. A 6th century Coptic Fresco from Wadi Saga, now in the British Museum, depicting the Three Children in the fiery furnace, flanked by large figures of St. Cosmas and St. Damian, between whom stand three other figures, representing their brethren. All eight figures make the sign.† — *Distress.*

9. Use of the Sign of Distress mentioned twice in the Eddas.* — *Distress.*

10. The Beckoning Sign described in the Eddas.* — *Beckoning Sign.*

11. Byzantine Bronze pound Weight with two Military Saints inlaid in silver, 6th century. Now in British Museum. One Saint attacking a monster advances left foot first.† — *Left foot First.*

12. Cloisonné enamel and gold Cross Reliquary. Byzantine work of the 9th—10th century. Figure in centre of cross makes Sign. Original in Victoria and Albert Museum. — *Distress.*

13. A Carolingian Ivory Carving showing the Last Judgment. Late 8th century. Now in the Victoria and Albert Museum. Souls rising from graves make the Sign of Preservation. — *Preservation*

REF. NO.	TITLE AND DESCRIPTION.	

G.14. On the Font at Cudworth, Warwick, c.900, in the N.E. corner is a figure in cope and morse making the Sign of Preservation. — *Preservation.*

15. Coptic Mummy Cloth embroidered with pictures of the Saints. C.600 A.D. Original in British Museum. Exhibit 30,806. — *Regret.*

16. Fresco of Christ in the Catacombs of St. Calixus, Rome, below that of St. Cecelia (See F. 23). IXth Century work. Christ makes sign.† — *Preservation.*

17. A 9th Century ivory from Bamberg Cathedra[l] now in the Royal Library at Munich, shows the Baptism of Our Lord. As the Dove descends several Angels made the Sign of Preservation. — *Preservation*

11th CENTURY.

H. 1. Guide to the Bayeaux Tapestries. Published by the Victoria and Albert Museum. Plate 1. Edward the Confessor sends Harold and a friend to Normandy. Two latter make sign. c.1080 A.D.† — *Preservation.*

2. Ditto. Plate 2. Harold Swears Allegiance to William. Two onlookers make sign. — *Preservation.*

3. Ditto. Plate 5. Harold Crowned King. Members of the Crowd make sign. — *Preservation.*

4. Carved Ivory panel of the Crucifixion. Illustrated p. 292, *Guide to the Mediæval Antiquities.* British Museum. Virgin makes Sign of Regret. St. John strikes his wrist. — *Regret. Sacrifice (1st position.)*

5. Bas-relief in the Cloisters of St. Trophime's Arles, depicting the Stoning of St. Stephen.† — *Distress.*

6. Ivory Statue of the Virgin and Child. Now in the Louvre. — *Preservation. Fidelity.*

7. The Bayeaux Tapestry. c.1080 A.D. The Normans crossing to Pevensey. Man in the Bow of one Ship makes sign. Reproduced in Vol. III, Encyclopardia Britannica. Op. p 557. — *Distress.*

8. Norman Font in St. Buryan Church, near Helston. — *Sign of Water.*

9. Byzantine Relief in Ivory showing the Last Judgment. 11th —12th century. Original in Victoria and Albert Mus. — *Sacrifice. Preservation.*

10. Byzantine Ivory Panel of St. John the Baptist and Four Saints. In Victoria and Albert Museum. The Saint in left hand bottom corner makes sign. Compare with Hung Society. — *Vesica Piscis and Horns Combined.*

REF. NO.	TITLE AND DESCRIPTION.	

H. 11. A Byzantine Ivory showing The Crucifixion, Deposition and Entombment. The Dead Christ is depicted with hands crossed downward. Original in the Victoria and Albert Museum. — *Hands crossed downwards.*

12. A Carolingian Ivory Carving Showing the Nativity. The Virgin makes the Sign True till Death. Joseph pulls his beard. In Victoria and Albert Museum. — *True till Death. Pulling Beard.*

13. A Spanish Ivory Carving of the Deposition from the Cross. The Virgin makes the Sign of Preservation. In Victoria and Albert Museum. — *Preservation.*

14. An Ivory Carving of the Crucifixion, from Cologne. The Virgin makes the Sign of Regret, an onlooker that of Preservation, a man in the foreground, the ordinary Sign of Distress (3rd position) and St. John, the Sign of Distress by wiping the forehead. In Victoria and Albert Museum. † — *Regret. Preservation. Distress (3rd postion.) Distress—the rare variation.*

15. Byzantine Ivory Carving of the Raising of Lazarus. Sign made with the right hand. — *True till Death.*

16. Font at Kirkburn, Yorks., shows a figure inside the Vesica Piscis making the Sign of Distress. See F. Bond. *Fonts and Font Covers*, p. 161. — *Distress.*

17. "The Mortal Sickness of Edward the Confessor." Two on-lookers make the Sign of Preservation — *Preservation.*

18. "A Saxon Banquet" from the Collon MS. in the British Museum. — *Preservation.*

12th CENTURY.

I. 1. Illuminated B from the Winchester Bible. Upper section, Christ shown Casting out a Devil. The onlookers make Sign of Preservation and devil that of Distress. Lower section, Christ depicted Harrowing Hell and the rescued shown making Sign of Preservation. † — *Distress.* *Preservation.*

2. Mosaic of the Last Judgment in the Baptistery at Florence. † — *Preservation. Distress.*

3. Greek Illuminated MS. No. gr. 1162 in the Vatican Library, depicting the Ascension of Our Lord. The man next to the Virgin makes sign. — *Preservation.*

4. Mosaic in Apse of St. Clement's, Rome. Virgin on left of cross makes Sign of Preservation, an apostle makes that of Fidelity — *Preservation. Fidelity.*

5. The Seal of Joanna, daughter of Henry II. Ills. op. p. 167, *Guide to Mediæval Antiquities*. British Museum. — *Preservation.*

6. Illuminated Greek MS. of Simon Metaphrastes: in the British Museum. A female saint makes Sign. — *Distress.*

201

REF. No.	TITLE AND DESCRIPTION.	SIGN CONTAINED THEREIN.

I. 7. An Engraved Bowl showing scenes from the Legend of St. Thomas. Original in British Museum.†

Distress.
Preservation.

8. Illuminated "P" in the Pudsey Bible, Durham, c. 1180 A.D. Photo in the Victoria and Albert Museum. Showing Solomon instructing a youth, who makes Sign.

Preservation.

9. Mosaic in Torcello Cathedral, near Venice, showing The Last Judgment. Containing 12 signs. Viz. seven Preservation, one Regret, two True till Death, two Distress, and one "It is Finished."

Preservation.
Regret.
True till Death.
Distress.
"It is finished."

10. Photo of Lower Right Hand Section of Above showing Souls in Hell.†

Preservation.
True till Death.
Regret.

11. Illuminated "O" from the Winchester Bible, Winchester, 1154—89 Photo in Victoria & Albert Museum.

Preservation.

12. Mosaic of the Creation of the World in St. Mark's Cathedral, Venice. Contains five Signs of Preservation and one Fidelity.

Preservation.
Fidelity.

13. Photograph of a miniature of the Crucifixion and our Lord in Glory, in the Victoria and Albert Museum. Our Lord in Glory makes Sign of Blessing. In scene of Crucifixion, Virgin makes Sign of Regret and St. John, True till Death.†

Blessing.
Regret.
True till Death.

14. Illuminated letter from the Pudsey Bible, Durham. c. 1180. Photo in Victoria and Albert Museum.

Distress.

15. Greek Illuminated MS. of the Gospels with Miniature of the Death of the Virgin. In British Museum.

Distress.

16. Illuminated "U" from the Winchester Bible, Winchester. 1154—89. Photo in the Victoria and Albert Museum, shows Christ casting out a devil. Onlookers make Sign of Distress.

Preservation.
Distress.

17. Fresco of the Brig o' Dred, in Chaldon Church, Surrey.†

Distress.
Preservation.

18. A bas-relief of the Angels Appearing to the Shepherds, now in the Louvre.†

Reverence.
Plucking the Beard.

19. Christ in Majesty, from the Psalter of Westminster Abbey, now in Brit. Museum, shows combined Sign of Blessing and Preservation.

Blessing.
Preservation

20. Font at Eardisley Church, Herefordshire, early 12th century, showing carving of Baptism of Our Lord.

Sign of Water

21. Greek Illuminated Gospels. British Museum.

Reverence.
Preservation

THE STORY OF THE SEVEN DEADLY SINS.

A Tapestry at Hampton Court Palace.

By Gracious Permission of His Majesty The King.

M.13.

AN IVORY PANEL OF THE 9TH CENTURY DEPICTING
THE JUDGMENT OF SOLOMON.

Now in the Louvre.

G.6.

REF. No.	TITLE AND DESCRIPTION.	SIGN CONTAINED THEREIN.
I. 22.	A Series of Miniatures. Scenes from the Life of Christ. Original in British Museum. One of the angels watching the appearance of other angels to the shepherds, makes sign. Also in another scene one of the innocents being slaughtered makes the same sign.	*Preservation.*
23.	West Front of Church of St. Trophime, Arles. Angels on South side make Sign of Distress; several saints place hand on forehead in Sign of Sorrow.	*Distress.* *Sorrow or Sympathy.*
24.	West door as above. Man on the North side makes Sign of Regret. Angels above, Distress, a small figure, combined Preservation and Blessing. Man on the South side, Sign of Destruction with both hands	*Regret.* *Distress.* *Preservation and Blessing combined.* *Destruction.*
25.	South side of the West door of the Cathedral of St. Laurence, Genoa, showing Tree of Jesse, contains one example of Plucking Beard: Three Preservation: Two Secrecy: One Blessing.†	*Plucking Beard.* *Preservation.* *Secrecy.* *Blessing.*
26.	Fresco on South wall of Easby Church, showing The Angel appearing to Shepherds: Angel makes Sign of Preservation. The Three Kings presenting Gifts: Christ makes combined Sign of Preservation and Blessing. Descent from the Cross: Virgin casts hand over shoulder, St. John strikes hand on wrist. Angel by empty tomb: Mary Magdalene makes sign showing He descended.†	*Preservation.* *Combined Preservation and Blessing.* *Sacrifice. (two postions).* *Sign "Heaven and Earth."*
27.	Bas-relief in Cloisters of Church of St. Trophime, Arles, showing the Last Supper. Three Apostles pluck beards.	*Plucking Beard.*
28.	MS. in the Vatican Library. Lat. 4939, "The Chronicle of St. Sophia of Benevento," showing the Proclamation of the Emperor Otto III. by a Bishop who makes the Sign of Preservation combined with the Sign of Horns.†	*Preservation and Horns combined.*
29.	Champlevé enamel on copper gilt, representing the Last Judgment. In Victoria and Albert Museum.	*Preservation.*
30.	Sculpture over the West Door of St. Laurence Cathedral, Genoa, depicting St. Laurence on his grid. Four onlookers make signs and Christ in Vesica Piscis above makes combined Sign of Preservation and Blessing.	*Fidelity.* *Plucking Beard.* *Prayer.* *Regret.* *Combined Blessing and Preservation.*
31.	Capital of the columns separating the Nave and Chancel of Adel Church, near Leeds, depicting scene of Baptism of Christ. Christ makes Sign of Distress and an onlooker, Preservation. See, *Graphic and Historical Illustrator* Published by Bradley, 1834	*Distress.* *Preservation.*

I. 32. Font, Castle, Frome, Herefordshire. — *Fidelity.*

33. Psalter of St. Swithun's Priory, Winchester. Now in British Museum, Miniature depicting our Lord Washing the Feet. St. Peter makes sign. — *Preservation.*

34. The Winchester Bible, Vol. II. Verso of Folio 200. Book of Joel. Illuminated letter "B", showing a prophet addressing a crowd, some of whom make Sign of Preservation. Photo in Victoria and Albert Museum. — *Preservation.*

35. Ditto. Vol. II. Recto of folio 209. Book of Zephaniah. Illuminated "B." A Preacher addressing a crowd, several of whom make sign. Photo in Victoria and Albert Museum. — *Preservation.*

36. Ditto. Vol. III. Verso of folio 131. Illuminated "E." In top scene Mattathias is shown slaying the Renegade Jew and the King of Syria's Messenger. An onlooker makes Sign. — *Sympathy.*

37. Miniature from the Life, Martyrdom and Miracles of St. Edmund, showing him enthroned. Two angels in left and right top panels make sign. Photo in Victoria and Albert Museum. — *"It is Finished."*

38. A Portable Altar in Enamel. North German work, decorated with scene of the Crucifixion. A Saint on the extreme left makes Sign of True till Death with right hand and squares left arm in Sign of Preservation. Saint on extreme right makes Second position of Sign of Sacrifice. Below on front side, are four demi-figures and the two on the left make Sign of Preservation. The one on the extreme left at the same time pointing up with the first finger of the hand lying on the breast. In Victoria and Albert Museum. — *Combined, True till Death and Pres·rva-tion. Preservation.*

39. Twelve Carved Ivory Panels of the 12th—13th centuries, now in the Victoria and Albert Museum. Depict Scenes from the Life of Christ. In Panel in top left hand corner a figure makes the Sign of Destruction with both hands. In the scene of the Raising of Lazarus, an onlooker makes the Sign of Regret. In the scene in the top right hand panel Our Lord makes the Sign of Preservation. Byzantine Work. — *Destruction. Regret. Preservation.*

40. An Ivory Carving from Cologne depicting the Adoration of the Magi. The Virgin makes the Sign of Preservation. Now in the Victoria and Albert Museum. — *Preservation.*

41. An Ivory Carving from the lower Rhine depicting the Crucifixion. St. John makes Sign of Hands Crossed Downward. Now in the Victoria and Albert Museum. — *Hands Crossed Downward.*

Ref. No.	Title and Description.	Sign Contained Therein.

REF. NO.　　　　TITLE AND DESCRIPTION.

I. 42. A Carving in Walrus Ivory, Cologne Work now in the *Preservation.* Victoria and Albert Museum, probably part of a Shrine. Showing the Ascension of Our Lord Who appears in a *Distress.* Vesica Piscis. Two Onlookers make the Sign of Preservation and one that of Distress.

43. On a bronze Font at St. Bartholomew, Liege, is a scene *Preservation.* depicting the Baptism of Cornelius and Graton. See F. Bond, *Fonts and Font Covers*, p. 118*.

44. Another view of the West Door of St. Trophime's, Arles *Distress.* *Sympathy.*

45. A Miniature from the Psalter of St. Swithun's Prory, Win- *Preservation.* chester, showing ţhe Mouth of Hell.

46. The Font at Avebury, Wilts., C. 1101, I. d. p. 140.* *Preservation.*

47. Figures on a capital of a Normal Pillar in the Crypt of York *Distress.* Minster. Illus. in *Old England*, by Ch. Knight. 1844.

48. Figure on an old Cornish Cross on St. Michael's Mount. *Distress.*

49. The Font at Winchester Cathedral, adorned with scenes from *Distress* the life of St. Nicholas of Myra, on the West side shows *Regret* him restoring a drowned person to life. Two onlookers *Preservation* in boat make Signs of Distress and Regret, another on- looker makes that of Preservation. A second scene shows the Saint rescuing three young men about to be slain, one of whom makes the Sign of Preservation.

50. The Bronze Font of St Bartholemew, Liège, contains two *Preservation* scenes—in one, the Baptism of Cornelius, an onlooker makes the Sign of Preservation.

51. The Carved Font at Avebury Church, Wilts., shows a figure *Preservation.* making the Sign of Preservation

52. The Font at Kirburn, Yorks., shows two figures—one mak- *Sign of* ing Sign of Sacrifice, 1st position, and the other the 2nd *Sacrifice* position of the same sign. *(2 positions).*

53. Font at Zedelghem shows St. Nicholas rescuing a boy from *Distress* Drowning. Latter makes Sign.

13th CENTURY.

J. 1. Carved stone Pascal Candlestick in the Church of St. Paul, *Preservation.* Rome, showing the Christ Child, in the Vesica Piscis, making Sign.

2. Mosaic in the Apse of Church of St. Maria Maggiore, Rome. *Preservation.* Coronation of the Virgin. She and St. John the Bap- tist make sign.

3. Mosaic in the Apse of St. John, Lateran, Rome, St. John *Preservation.* Baptist makes sign. Virgin, St. John Baptist, and other Saints adoring the Cross.

J. 4.	Another mosaic in Church of St. John, Lateran. Our Lord enthroned, with emblems of the Four Evangelists and many saints.	*Preservation.* *Fidelity.*
5.	Panel of English Needlework, c.1300, depicting Our Lord and the Apostles. Now in British Museum.	*Preservation.*
6.	A Portable Altar. German work. Sculpture of Crucifixion at top. Virgin makes Sign of Regret. St. John the Evangelist, Preservation. Sculpture below depicting the Virgin and Child. Latter makes Preservation. Onlooker, Sacrifice. Original in British Museum	*Regret.* *Preservation.* *Sacrifice.*
7.	Mosaic in the Baptistery, St. Mark's, Venice. St. John makes Sign.	*Preservation.*
8.	Mosaic in the Baptistery at Florence, depicting Hell.	*Distress.*
9.	Mosaic of the Birth of the Virgin from Orvieto Cathedral. Baby Virgin makes Sign. Now in the Victoria and Albert Museum.	*Distress.*
10.	Another section of the Mosaic in the Baptistery, Florence, showing Hell.	*Distress.* *Sorrow.*
11.	Mosaic at Florence. Illustration showing cupola.	*Preservation.* *Distress.* *Regret.*
12.	Another section of Cupola mentioned above, depicting Jacob being shown Joseph's coat. His wife makes Sign of Distress and Jacob, Regret.†	*Distress.* *Regret.*
13.	Mosaic in St. Mark's, Venice.	
	Scene I Martyrdom of St. Bartholomew, showing Sign of Sacrifice being made by an onlooker.	*Sacrifice.*
	Scene II. Martyrdom of St. Matthew, also his baptism of a King, wherein the King and several onlookers make the Sign.	*Preservation.*
14.	Sculpture behind the High Altar of the Church of the Three St. Maries, shows two people making a grip.	*Grip.*
15.	Capital "B" from a Psalter in the British Museum containing the Tree of Jesse.	*Preservation.* *Blessing.*
16.	A Treatise on Surgery, by Roger of Parma.	
	Above. Three Pictures of Our Lord in two of which onlookers are making the Sign of Preservation.	*Preservation.*
	Below. Three pictures of patients being cured. All making the Sign of Preservation.	*Preservation.*
17.	Mosaics in the Atrium of St. Mark's, Venice. The 13th century mosaics include Joseph sold into Egypt, showing Sign of Distress, and Jacob's Lament, with Sign of Distress. Above, a female saint in a circle makes the Sign of Preservation. (See also L. 43).	*Distress.* *Preservation.*

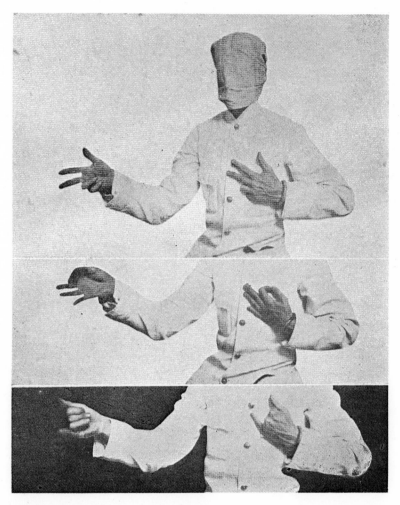

THE THREEFOLD SIGN OF HEAVEN, EARTH AND MAN, USED BY THE HUNG
SOCIETY.

U.34.

THE THREE CHILDREN IN THE FIERY FURNACE,
A 5th Century Coptic Fresco from Wadi Saga.

G.8.

J. 18. St. Paul's Without the Walls, Rome. In a fresco of the *Preservation*
Crucifixion in the unrestored part of the Church, an onlooker makes Sign.*

19. Inlaid mosaic design on pulpit at Ravello near Torento, *Preservation.*
Italy, depicting Jonah and the Whale. Jonah makes
Sign.†

20. The New Testament in Italian, in the Vatican Library, *Combined*
shows Christ in the Vesica Piscis making the combined *Vesica Piscis*
sign of the Vesica Piscis and Blessing. *and Blessing.*

21. Portion of an Orphrey in the Victoria and Albert Museum, *Preservation.*
depicting the Crucifixion. The Virgin makes the Sign *Distress*
of Preservation and St. John Distress.

22. Fragments of a Vestment found in Worcester Cathedral, *Preservation.*
showing three kings making the Sign, probably a Tree of
Jesse. Original in Victoria and Albert Museum.

23. Bible History Moralized. French. Now in the British *Grip.*
Museum. *Sorrow.*

24. Panel of Stained Glass in the 6th window on the South Side *Preservation.*
of Trinity Chapel, Canterbury. Photo in Victoria and
Albert Museum. No. 48501. Depicts a woman making
the Sign of Preservation over a person who is lying sick.

25. Another section of the same Window, shows a woman making *Preservation.*
the Sign of Preservation with her left arm, and thumb
squared. Photo No. 48497 in Victoria and Albert
Museum.

26. Fresco in Splay of Norman Window at Cocking Church, *Reverence.*
Sussex, depicting the Star of Bethlehem, with an Angel
appearing to a Shepherd and his assistant. The Shep- *Preservation.*
herd makes Sign of Reverence, the boy, Preservation.
Photo 52270, Victoria and Albert Museum.†

27. Fresco on the wall of the Apse of St. Mary's Church, Check- *Preservation*
endon, Oxon, depicting Our Lord in Glory, and the
Apostles making Signs. Fresco slightly restored.
Photo 52266 in Victoria and Albert Museum.

28. Panel of Stained Glass in Canterbury Cathedral depicting the *Plucking Beard.*
Magi before Herod. Herod pulls his beard and one of
the Magi makes the Sign of Preservation. Photo 50522 *Preservation.*
in Victoria and Albert Museum.

29. An Illuminated "A" from a French Manuscript showing the *Distress.*
Last Judgment. Souls rising from their graves make *Resignation.*
Signs of Distress and Resignation†

30. A Fresco in the Chapel of the Castle of Chillon, Switzerland, *Exultation.*
at the opposite end to the Reading Desk, the Last Judg- *Preservation.*
ment, shows Our Lord in the Vesica Piscis about to *Distress.*

         Judge the Dead who are rising from their graves.   Three
men make signs.   Fresco rather faded.*

J. 31.   Carved Figures on the Capitals of Pillars in the Sanctuary of   *Distress.*
Coire Cathedral make signs.*

  32.   An Illumination showing Ordeal by Combat.   Royal MS.   *Preservation.*
14 E.iii, in British Museum.   Four onlookers make the
Sign.

  33.   A Miniature from an early 13th Century English Psalter now   *Crooked Finger*
in the British Museum (Royal MS 1D×f4) depicts Our   *Sign.*
Lord Washing the feet of His Disciples, and The Last   *Reverence*
Supper.

  34.   A Fresco on the 2nd Norman Pillar on the North Side of St.   *Resignation.*
Albans Abbey depicts the Crucifixion.   The Virgin make
the Sign.

  35.   A Fresco on the 3rd Pillar as above also depicts the Cruci-   *Regret.*
fixion.   Virgin on left of Cross, makes Sign.

  36.   In the Chapel of the Holy Sepulchre, Winchester Cathedral,   *Preservation.*
a figure in a Medallion on the Ceiling makes the Sign   *Combined   Pre-*
of Preservation.   In a fresco of the Nativity on the   *servation and*
South Wall an onlooker makes the combined signs of   *Crooked Finger*
Preservation and crooked finger.   On the West wall   *Sign.*
appear "The Descent from the Cross" and "The Entomb-   *Crooked   Finger*
ment", the former containing a ritual grip and the latter   *Sign*
the Crooked Finger Sign.

14*th CENTURY.*

K. 1.   "The Marriage Feast of Cana," a miniature from Queen   *Preservation.*
Mary's Psalter.   Now in the British Museum.†   *Fidelity.*

  2.   "The Slaughter of the Innocents and the Marriage Feast of   *Preservation.*
Cana."   Two miniatures from the Arundel MS., now in   *Distress.*
the British Museum.†

  3.   A carved, French, Ivory Casket showing Tristan and Iseult   *Preservation.*
with King Mark in the Tree.   Iseult makes the Sign.
Original in British Museum.

  4.   A Strip of embroidered Velvet showing the Annunciation   *Preservation.*
and the Virgin with St. Elizabeth.   Eng. work now in
the Victoria and Albert Museum.   In the Annunciation
Scene the Virgin makes the Sign of Preservation.

  5.   Another strip of the same embroidery showing the Presenta-   *Preservation.*
tion of the Virgin in the Temple.

  6.   A Page from the Apocalypse, showing our Lord surrounded by   *Preservation.*
Saints, who are making the Sign of Preservation.   *Fidelity.*
Below, the woman, on seeing the seven headed dragon,
makes the Sign of Fidelity.   Original in British Museum.

K. 7. Ivory Diptych, now in the Louvre, Shepherds in Nativity *Preservation.*
scene make the Sign of Preservation, and the Child *Fidelity.*
makes the Sign of Fidelity. In the Epiphany one *Heaven (without*
King makes the Sign of Preservation, another points *earth).*
to Heaven. In the Crucifixion, an onlooker points to
Heaven, St. John makes the Sign of Fidelity. †

8. Illuminated Letters from the Arundel MS., in the British *Preservation*
Museum. *and Blessing*
Combined.

9. A Page from the Psalter of Robert de Lisle containing six
miniatures. East Anglican work.
    Scene II. The Angel appearing to the Shepherds. *Heaven and*
The Angel makes the Sign of Heaven and Earth. Other *Earth.*
Angels reply with the Sign of Preservation. *Preservation.*
    Scene III. The Circumcision. The Child makes the *Preservation.*
Sign of Preservation, as does a woman behind the Virgin. *Heaven and*
    Scene IV. The Epiphany. One King makes the *Preservation*
combined Sign of Heaven and Preservation. Christ *combined.*
makes that of Blessing. *Blessing.*
    Scene V. The Presentation in the Temple. St. *Destruction.*
Joseph makes the Sign of Destruction.
    Scene VI. The Flight into Egypt. St. Joseph and *Destruction.*
an attendant both make the Sign of Destruction as the
statues of the heathen gods fall. †

10. Illustration from the Calendar of Queen Mary's Psalter. *Preservation.*
Now in the British Museum. "The Month of January."
Sign of Preservation.

11. Carved Ivory Coffer, now in the Louvre, showing Scenes from *Preservation.*
a Romance. *Distress.*
Resignation.

12. Medallion in the Top of the Tracery in the East window of *Preservation.*
Whichford Church, depicting the Crucifixion. St. John *True till Death.*
makes the combined Sign of Preservation and True to
Death. The Virgin makes the Sign of Sacrifice. *

13. Part of a Border in the Psalter of the St. Omer family, now *Water.*
in the British Museum. † *Distress.*

14. Ivory Coffer Carved with four scenes from a Romance. † *Preservation.*
Distress.
Heaven and
Earth.

15. Fresco of the Last Judgment in St. James's Church, South- *Distress.*
leigh, nr. Oxford, contains three Signs of Distress, four *Preservation.*
Preservation; one Resignation; the second position of *Resignation.*
the Sign of Sacrifice, also the third position of that Sign. *Sign of Sacrifice*
(2nd and 3rd
positions).

Ref. No.	Title and Description.	Sign contained therein.
K. 16.	Miniature from an Illuminated MS. of Dante's Poem. The Poet on seeing Fraud makes the Sign of Distress Original in the British Museum.	*Distress.*
17.	Miniature from the Apocalypse showing St. John, an Elder and the Angel before our Lord. British Museum. †	*Preservation.*
18.	A Tile in Hitchin Parish Church, showing a stone mason between two pillars.	*Preservation.*
19.	Death and Translation of the Virgin. A sculpture by Orcagna, at Florence.	*Distress (2nd position). Horror.*
20.	A Border from the Arundel MS. showing figures of Saints. Part only reproduced, viz, figures making Signs of Preservation and True till death) British Museum. †	*Distress. True till Death. Preservation.*
21.	An Illumination showing Dante in Paradise. Original in British Museum. †	*Distress. Resignation.*
22.	Gratian's Decretum. Original in British Museum.	*Heaven and Earth.*
23.	An Ivory Diptych. French work, now in British Museum. A Scene of the Crucifixion. The Virgin makes the Sign of Resignation.	*Resignation.*
24.	Miniature of Christ Preaching to His Disciples. From Queen Mary's Psalter.	*Preservation.*
25.	A Wooden Chest Front, carved with the Legend of St. George and the Dragon. Original in the Victoria and Albert Museum. A similar chest is in the Sacristy of York Minster. †	*Preservation.*
26.	A Similar Carved Wooden Chest, showing the Annunciation, Nativity and other subjects. Now in the Victoria and Albert Museum.	*Preservation.*
27.	Sculpture of the Annunciation at Wells Cathedral. The Virgin makes the Sign.	*Distress.*
28.	The Seal of the Convent of Kilburn. Originally illustrated in Mr. Park's *Topography and Natural History of Hampstead*, and reproduced in Brayley, *Graphic and Historical Illustrator*, pub. 1834. Represents St. John the Baptist making the Sign of Preservation.	*Preservation.*
29.	An Ivory Carving, now in the Louvre, depicts the Virgin about to feed the Child while St. Joseph makes the Sign of Preservation.	*Preservation.*
30.	Illuminated MS. of Tristan, c. 1301, sold at Southerbys on Dec. 12th, 1927. An illuminated letter "C" showing a King at a Banquet, the King makes the Sign of Fidelity, an attendant that of Preservation and a guest, the Sign of Destruction, with the left hand.	*Fidelity. Preservation. Destruction.*

D

A 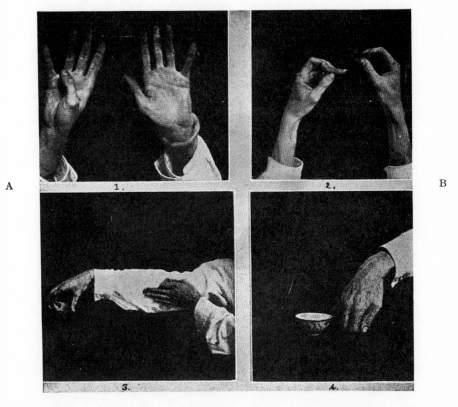 B

"THE NINE FINGER SIGN," "THE VESICA PISCIS," AND OTHER METHODS OF
RECOGNITION USED BY THE HUNG SOCIETY.

U.30.

QUETZALCOATL DESCENDING FROM HEAVEN TO EARTH BY MEANS OF A
LADDER.

REF. No.	TITLE AND DESCRIPTION.	SIGN CONTAINED THEREIN.

K.31. Fresco at the Church at Breage, near Penzance, showing St. Christopher bearing the Christ on his shoulder. The former makes the Sign of Preservation (slightly disguised) as do also a mermaid and someone in a small boat near by. — *Preservation.*

32. Panels from Orphreys, second half of the 14th century, now in the Victoria and Albert Museum. Contains scenes from the life of the Virgin. (1) St. Joachim and St. Ann watching the baby Virgin learning to walk. Both parents make Sign of Heaven and Earth. — *Heaven and Earth.*

(2) An Angel announces to St. Joachim that his wife will bear him a daughter. St. Joachim makes the Sign of Preservation. — *Preservation.*

(3) The Virgin and Child enthroned. A Child makes the Sign of Preservation. — *Preservation.*

(4) The Massacre of the Innocents. A child makes the Sign of Preservation. — *Preservation.*

33. A Portion of a Velvet Band, depicting various scenes. In one an Angel appears to the shepherds, one of whom makes the sign. Early 14th century work, now in the Victoria and Albert Museum. — *Preservation.*

34. Miniature from MS. of *San Graal et Lancelot du lac.* Sold at the Ashburnham sale. Depicts two knights fighting and several onlookers make the Sign of Preservation. — *Preservation.*

35. A Triptych by Bertram of Hamburg, tempera on wood. German work of C. 1390. The central portion shows a scene from the Apocalypse; the Beast appearing to the woman, who is crowned with Stars, has a Sun over her Solar Plexus and beneath her feet the Moon. The woman and her child both make the Sign of Distress. Now in the Victoria and Albert Museum. — *Distress.*

36. The inside, right wing of the same Triptych, showing the Beast and the Woman, who now has wings and stands inside the City. The woman makes the Sign of Preservation. Now in the Victoria and Albert Museum. — *Preservation.*

37. The Brass of Abbot de la Mare. St. Albans Abbey. Foreign work.† — *Hands Crossed Downwards.*

38. Early 14th century Cylindrical Pyx. Gilt Copper, decorated with Champlevé Enamel. French Work. Shows Daniel in the Lions' Den. Photo 45444 in Victoria and Albert Museum. — *Distress'*

39. On the Font at Burford is scupltured a scene of the Crucifixion wherein the Virgin makes the Sign of Regret. F. Bond. *Font and Font Covers*, p. 239. — *Regret.*

Ref. No.	Title and Description.	Sign contained therein.

K. 40. A Miniature in an Illum: MS. in the British Museum (Roy. MS. 14 Eiii) shows a King in bed visited by a Monk. The King makes the Sign with the left elbow squared and the right lying prone on the coverlet. The monk has left arm across his body and right elbow squared.
Preservation.

41. A Painted Wooden Reredos at Romsey Abbey shows Saints and Christ Rising from the tomb. One of the Roman Soldiers makes the Sign
Reverence.

42. The Carved Lid of a Reliquary Chest in Winchester Cathedral shows the Virgin by the Cross making the Sign of Fidelity with her left hand and "It is Finished" with her right.
Combined Sign of Fidelity and "It is Finished."

43. The Font at Burford, Oxon, sculptured with a scene of the Crucifixion shows the Virgin by the Cross making Sign.
Regret.

15th CENTURY,

L. 1. A Miniature from Mandeville's Travels, depicting a King being shown the Hallows and make the Sign. British Museum.
Preservation.

2. A miniature from the Psalter of Humphrey, Duke of Gloucester, showing Christ Rising from the Tomb, Who makes the Sign of Preservation and shows His wounds. An onlooker also makes this Sign and a King the Sign of Prayer.† British Museum.
Preservation.
Prayer.

3. A Chasuble embroidered with scenes from the Life of the Virgin. Scene I. The Presentation of the Vrigin in the Temple. The High Priest and St. Anne both make the Sign.
Scene II. The Brith of the Virgin. An attendant makes the Sign.† In the Victoria and Albert Museum.
Preservation.
Preservation.

4. Fresco of St. Michael weighing a Soul, in St. James's Church, Southleigh, Oxford. St. Michael makes the Sign†
Preservation.

5. An Alabaster Carving of the Incarnation, in the Victoria and Albert Museum.†
Distress.
Blessing.
Preservation.

6. A Wood Block of the Florentine School depicting Christ in Glory, showing His wounds. Christ in the Vesica Piscis makes the Sign,† Now in the British Museum.
Preservation.

7. Fresco of Christ and the Doctors at St. Ambrose Church, Milan.†
Preservation.

8. A Picture at Hampton Court, showing the Baptism of Christ. By Francia.†
Preservation.

Ref. No.	Title and Description.	Sign contained therein.
L. 9.	A Painting by Fra Angelico of the Descent of the Holy Ghost. At Florence.	*Reverence.* *Heaven and Earth.*
10.	A Painting of the Crucifixion by Perugino, at Florenoe	*Resignation.* *"It is Finished."*
11.	A French "Shield of Parade," painted with a picture of a Knight being touched on the shoulder by Death. The Knight makes the Sign of Preservation. British Museum.	*Preservation.*
12.	Miniature from MS. Barberiniano, ref. Lat. 614, by the School of Perugino. Depicting the Crucifixion. St. John makes the Sign. Original in the Vatican Library.	*It is Finished.*
13.	The Raising of Lazarus, by Nicholas Froment. Late 15th century. In Louvre.†	*It is Finished.* *Heaven and Earth.* *Horror.* *Prayer.*
14.	A double Portrait of St. Mary Magdalene and the Donor. Late 15th century. Now in the Louvre.	*Preservation.*
15.	A Wood Block of the Florentine School, now in the British Museum, depicting the Virgin and Child with St. Helen and St. Michael. The Child makes the Sign.	*Preservation.*
16.	A Miniature from a Book of Hours showing the Last Judgment. Formerly in the possession of Messrs. Southeran, Piccadilly.	*Preservation.*
17.	An Alabaster Carving of St. Christopher, now in Victoria and Albert Museum. The Child makes the Sign.	*Preservation.*
18.	A Fresco of the Last Judgment, at St. Thomas's Church, Salisbury.†	*Preservation.* *Distress (2nd position).*
19.	"The Final Judgment," by Giovanni di Paola, in the Gallery of Fine Arts, Vienna.	*Preservation.* *Horror.* *Grip.*
20.	"The Last Judgment," by Fra Angelico, lower section. In St. Mark's Monastery, Florence.	*Preservation.* *Distress.*
21.	The Frontis. to a Choir Book, by George Beck. German work, 1491-95.	*Preservation.* *Heaven (no earth.)*
22.	St. Barbara. A Miniature from a Flemish Book of Hours. C. 1500. Original in the British Museum.	*Preservation.*
23.	A Miniature from a Book of Hours, depicting St. Christopher and the Christ Child. The latter makes the Sign. Photo 23953, Victoria and Albert Museum.	*Preservation.*

REF. No.	TITLE AND DESCRIPTION.	SIGN CONTAINED THEREIN.
L. 24.	Statue of St. Roche, in the Museum at Avignon. St. Roche squares his left arm and with the right pulls up the robe from his left leg. This variation of the sign is used among the Yaos.	*Preservation.*
25.	A Miniature from a Flemish Book of Hours. The Angel appearing to the Shepherds. One of the latter makes the Sign. Original in British Museum.	*Reverence.*
26.	Fresco of the Transfiguration by Fra Angelico in St. Mark's Monastery, Florence.†	*Distress.* *Reverence.* *Resignation.* *Prayer.*
27.	Painting of the Last Judgment, by the Flemish School. Formerly in the Town Hall at Dieste and loaned to the Exhibition of Flemish Art at the Royal Academy, 1926.†	*Distress.* *Preservation* *Fidelity.* *Regret.* *Reverence.* *Hand on Head.* *Sympathy.*
28.	"The Virgin and Donor," by Jan Van Eyck, now in the Louvre. The Child makes the Sign of Preservation in answer to the Donor's Sign of Prayer.	*Preservation.* *Prayer.*
29.	An Alabaster Altar piece showing the Annunciation. The Virgin makes the Sign. Now in the Victoria and Albert Museum.	*Distress* *(3rd position)*
30.	"The Last Judgment." A Stained Glass window in Fairford Church, Gloucester. A Devil carries off a woman, who makes the Sign of Distress.†	*Distress.*
31.	Another section of the above. One of the lost in a Hooper, makes the Sign of Distress.	*Distress.*
32.	Fresco of Hell by Giovanni di Paola. At Sienna.	*Distress.*
33.	A Miniature from a Book of Hours showing the Last Judgment. Add. MS. 35313 British Museum.†	*Royal.* *Distress.* *Hand on Head.* *Regret.*
34.	A Miniature from a Book of Hours of the early 15th century, depicting Hell. Add. MS. 29433 F.89 British Museum.	*Distress.*
35.	An Italian Ivory Coffer, carved with the representation of the Triumph of Renown. Judith, carrying the head, makes Sign of Destruction with left hand. Joshua with the Sun makes the Sign of Preservation. Homer makes that of Destruction with his right hand. Original in Louvre.†	*Destruction.* *Preservation.*
36.	A Miniature of the Last Judgment from a Flemish Book of Hours, now in Bodleian Library, Oxford,†	*Distress.* *Royal.* *Preservation.*

THE STONING OF ST. STEPHEN.
In the Cloisters of St. Trophime's, Arles.

H.5.

THE LAST JUDGMENT.

A Fresco at St. Thomas's Church, Salisbury.

L.18.

L. 37   Two Miniatures from a Book of Hours, in private possession.   *Distress.*
     Scene I. The Annunication. The Virgin makes the
     Sign of Distress. *Scene II.* Gethsemane. An Apostle   *Regret.*
     makes the Sign of Regret and two of the people looking   *Preservation.*
     over the fence make the Sign of Preservation.

38.   The Martelli Mirror. Relief in Bronze encrusted in gold   *Horns.*
     and silver, ascribed to Donatello. In Victoria and
     Albert Museum.†

39.   A Wood Block of the Florentine School showing the Resurrec-   *True till Death*
     tion of Christ. Original in British Museum.   *(Left hand).*
     Reverence.
     Resignation.

40.   An Alabaster Carving of the Resurrection. In Victoria and   *Reverence.*
     Albert Museum.

41.   The Breviary of Isabella of Castile. Flemish work. Now in   *Reverence.*
     British Museum.   *Prayer.*

42.   An Alabaster Carving of the Entombment. Now in the   *Hands crossed*
     Victoria and Albert Museum. Christ's hands are   *down.*
     crossed downward and an Apostle makes the Sign of   *Regret.*
     Regret ; Mary Magdelene makes the Sign of Preservation.   *Preservation.*

43.   A 15th century fresco of St. Christopher and Child, on the   *Preservation.*
     North side of Atrium of St. Mark's, Venice. The latter
     makes the Sign.

44.   "The Deposition from the Cross" by the French School of   *Sacrifice*
     the 15th century. Now in the Louvre.†   *(Striking off*
     hand).

45.   A Sculptured Medallion in the National Museum, Florence,   *Reverence.*
     showing the Madonna adoring the Infant Christ. An
     angel makes the Sign of Reverence.

46.   A Miniature from a Book of Hours, C. 1470, now in Victoria   *Reverence.*
     and Albert Museum, showing the Angel appearing to
     Shepherds. Photo. 37696.

47.   An Illum. French MS. now in Victoria and Albert Museum   *Fidelity.*
     from the Salting Bequest, made for the Duchess of   *Preservation.*
     Britanny. C. 1480. Above, a scene of the Nativity,   *Resignation.*
     containing the Signs of Preservation and Resignation.   *Sacrifice.*
     Below, the Flight into Egypt.†   *Preservation.*
     Fidelity.

48.   "The Assumption of the Virgin," by Perugino. Now in the   *Resignation.*
     Uffizi Gallery, Florence.

49.   "The Deposition from the Cross," by Fra. Angelico: at   *Preservation.*
     Florence. The Angles make the Sign of Preservation ;   *Resignation.*
     one onlooker that of Resignation and a kneeling disciple,   *It is Finished.*
     "It is Finished."

L. 50.	"The Last Judgment," by Fra Angelico. At St. Mark's Monastery, Florence. In the upper part, showing Our Lord surrounded by Saints and Angels, the Virgin is in the Vesica Piscis. †	*Prayer.* *Resignation.* *Heaven and Earth.*
51.	"The Resurrection," by Fra Angelico. In St. Mark's Monastery, Florence. Christ shown in the Vesica Piscis, above the empty tomb. †	*Heaven and Earth.* *Reverence.* *Sacrifice.*
52.	Wood Block of the Florentine School. In British Museum. Nativity. The Child Christ makes the Sign of Preservation.	*Preservation.*
53.	A Fresco of the Circumcision, by Fra Angelico. At Florence, as 51. †	*Distress* *(2 positions).*
54.	An Initial "D," from a French MS., Circa 1450, in a private collection. The Virgin makes the Sign of Prayer ; an Angel, Resignation ; the Christ child, Preservation.	*Prayer.* *Resignation.* *Preservation.*
55.	A MS. of Valerius Maximus, in French. In British Museum, c. 1475. *Scene II.* The Execution of captives. An onlooker makes the Sign of Horror. *Scene III.* The Sign of Preservation, made by two people viewing the bodies of slain.	*Horror.* *Preservation.*
56.	The Covenant of Cristoforo Mauro, Doge of Venice. A Miniature shows the Doge worshipping the Virgin and Child and the latter makes the Sign.	*Sacrifice.*
57.	A Bracket in Gloucester Cathedral, called, "The Mason's Square" because it is shaped like a square and supported by a figure of a mason, who [is making the Sign of Preservation.	*Preservation.*
58.	Frescoes on the South Wall of the Chapter House of Westminster Abbey, near the entrance. Three men make Signs. *	*Preservation.* *Alas.* *Plucking beard.*
59.	Back of a Chasuble. Italian work, now in the Victoria and Albert Museum. Depicts St. Lawrence with his gridiron in his right hand, and with his left arm squared, as he speaks to an abbess, probably St. Etheldreda.	*Preservation.*
60.	A Miniature in an illuminated French MS., c. 1465, now in British Museum, depicting David's Penitence. David makes the Sign.	*Distress.*
61.	A Rhenish Ill. MS., now in the Victoria and Albert Museum, showing Tree of Jesse, wherein are figures making signs.	*Preservation.* *Distress.* *Heaven and Earth.*

L.62. The Monumental Brass of B. Roucliffe, a judge, and his wife.   *Preservation.*
1494. At Cowthorpe, Yorks. The figures are holding between them a model of the Church which they built. The Judge makes the Sign with his right arm and his wife with the left, implying that they hope for preservation because they have made this offering to God. †

63. A Miniature from a Book of Hours. Now in the British Museum. In the Meditation on Death is depicted the figure of a naked man lying on his tomb, with his hands crossed downwards.   *Hands crossed Down.*

64. The Coventry Ring, engraved with the five wounds and a picture of Christ standing in the tomb with His hands crossed downwards.   *Hands crossed Down.*

65. Four leaves from a Book of Hours. French work of 1480. Part of the Salting Bequest, now in the Victoria and Albert Museum. Shows a woman seated with her hands crossed downward, probably dead.   *Hands crossed downward.*

66. A Woodcut of the Temptation and Expulsion of Adam and Eve. Foresti, Venice. C. 1490. Photo. 58240 in the Victoria and Albert Museum. As Eve takes the apple Adam makes the Sign of Death with his left hand. During the Expulsion, Eve makes the Sign of Preservation. †   *True till Death.*
Preservation

67. A Roundel of Stained Glass. English work. Photo. 52096 in Victoria and Albert Museum, depicting the Angel Appearing to the Shepherds. The Angel makes the Sign of Heaven and Earth, a Shepherd that of Reverence. †   *Heaven and Earth.*
Reverence.

68. "The Birth of St. Nicholas," depicted in a Panel of Flemish stained glass. First half of the 15th century. Photo. 51475 in the Victoria and Albert Museum. Mother in bed, and Nurse, bathing child, both make the Sign of Preservation.   *Preservation*

69. A Byzantine Embroidered Silk Shroud of Epitaphios Sindon. A.D. 1407. The Dead man is represented lying in the shroud with his hands crossed downwards. Original in Victoria and Albert Museum.   *Hands crossed Downwards.*

70. The Monumental Brass of the Rev. John Sleford, Balsham, Cambs., who is represented vested in Cope, and making the Sign of Prayer. †   *Prayer.*

71. A Sketch in Terracotta of the Crucifixion by Donatello. Italian work of the early 15th century. Three onlookers make the Sign of Distress; one that of Reverence and one Sympathy. Orignal in the Victoria and Albert Museum.   *Distress.*
Reverence.
Sympathy.

Ref. No.	Title and Description.	Sign contained therein.
L. 72.	A Limoges Enamel of the Last Judgment now in the Victoria and Albert Museum. Date 1500. The Virgin makes the sign of Resignation and various souls the Sign of Distress, (first and third positions) also Prayer.	*Resignation.* *Distress.* *Prayer.*
73.	A Stained Glass Panel depicting St. Catherine Disputing with the Philosphers. St. Catherine makes the Sign. Original at Tabarn Church, Essex. Photo. in the Victoria and Albert Museum, No. 55221.	*Preservation.*
74.	Picture entitled, "The Coronation of the Virgin," with Saints Bernardino and Antonio, by Niccolo Alunno. The Virgin makes the Sign of Resignation, the Angels those of Resignation, Adoration and Prayer, and one of the Saints in the foreground, Reverence.	*Resignation.* *Adoration.* *Prayer.* *Reverence.*
75.	On the Font at Stalham, in a carving of the Baptism of Christ, is shown the Sign of Preservation.	*Preservation.*
76	A Scene of the Crucifixion sculptured on the Font of St. James, Taunton, Somerset, shows an onlooker making the Sign of Resignation.	*Resignation.*
77.	"Dante in Purgatory." A woodcut by De Plasiis. 1491. Now in the Victoria and Albert Museum.	*Regret.*
78.	"Dante in Hell"; as above.	*Preservation.*
79.	A bas-relief in the Church at Mont Saint Michel.	*Sacrifice.* *Destruction.*
80.	Fresco formerly at St. John's Church, Winchester, depicting the Resurrection and Last Judgment.	*Preservation.*
81.	A Miniature of the Angel Appearing to the Shepherds, from a Flemish Book of Hours, C. 1475. Original in Author's possession.	*Reverence.*
82.	A Woodcut by De Plasiis, 1491, illustrating the 33rd Canto of Paradiso. Now in the Victoria and Albert Museum.	*Resignation.* *Fidelity.*
83.	A Carved Wooden Triptych behind the High Altar at Coire Cathedral, Switzerland. On carved reverse panel is a scene of Christ bearing the Cross. Three onlookers make signs.*	*Preservation* *Distress.* *Resignation.*
84.	A Miniature depicting a Bishop and five of the laity at dinner shows the Bishop saying Grace. Three of the laity make the Sign of Preservation and two, fidelity. Original in British Museum. Roy. MS. 14. E iii.	*Preservation.* *Fidelity.*
85.	A Miniature of the Annunciation from a Book of Hours in the British Museum (Harley MS. 2952. f. 126).	*Sacrifice.* *Fidelity.*
86.	A Fresco by Fra Angelico, C1453, at St. Mark's Monastery, Florence, depicting the Annunciation. The Angel makes the Sign with right arm uppermost; the Virgin answers with the same sign but with left arm uppermost.	*Resignation.*

218

CARVED YORUBA GATES FROM OYO NIGERIA.

S.I.

AN ALABASTER STATUE OF HANUMAN.

REF. No.	TITLE AND DESCRIPTION.	SIGN CONTAINED THEREIN.
L. 87.	A Picture of the Last Supper by Ghirlandaio, at Florence. C. 1480.	*Resignation.* *Crooked Finger.* *Tearing out Heart. (both hands used).*
88.	A Picture of the Adoration of the Shepherds, by Ghirlandaio at Florence. C. 1480.	*Reverence.* *Fidelity com-bined with the Sign of Earth.* *Prayer.*
89.	A bas-relief of the Epiphany, in the Via Orefici, Genoa.	*Resignation.*
90.	A Miniature of the Visit of the Shepherds, one of whom makes Sign. Original in the Victoria and Albert Museum. From a Book of Hours of Margaret of Foix.	*Reverence.*
91.	The Font at Gresham, Norfolk, carved with the Baptism of Christ, shows St. John making the Sign of Preservation.	*Preservation.*
92.	The Emblem of St. Matthew in Stained Glass, at Headbourne Worthy Church, nr. Winchester.	*Preservation.*

16th CENTURY.

M. 1.	A Miniature of the Nativity from a French MS. of the early 16th century. Add. MS. 25693. F. 10. Depicts the shepherds adoring the Infant Christ. One shepherd takes off his hat and with it makes the Sign of Preserva-tion; the Christ answers with His left arm squared only.	*Preservation (2 forms).* *Prayer.*
2.	A Spanish woodcarving of Christ indicating His Wounds and making the sign.†	*Preservation.*
3.	A Printed Book of Hours, C. 1527, in the Victoria and Albert Museum. A Miniature depicting the Nativity.†	*Preservation.* *Resignation.* *Distress.*
4.	A Sculpture of the Nativity in St. Maria Maggiore, Rome. St. Joseph makes the Sign of Sacrifice and the Virgin, Prayer.	*Sacrifice.* *Prayer.*
5.	"The Sacrifice of Iphigenia" by Giov. Batt. Tiepolo, in the Uffizi, Florence. A Priest makes the Sign.	*Preservation.*
6.	An Angel Appearing to the Shepherds. A Miniature in an Ill. M.S. from Heures à l'Usage de Rome, Paris. Now in Victoria and Albert Museum.	*Preservation.*
7.	A Flemish Tapestry, showing the Three Fates. Now in the Victoria and Albert Museum.†	*Preservation.* *It is Finished.* *Left Foot First.*

Ref. No.	Title and Description.	therein.
M. 8.	The Sforza Book of Hours. A Flemish Miniature of the Angels appearing to the Shepherds, C. 1519. Now in British Museum. *Note* this book was started at the end of the 15th century in Italy, but finished, C. 1519, by Flemish artists.	*Reverence.*
9.	A Fresco in the Town Hall, Basle, by Hans Dyg. 1519. Depicting the Last Judgment.†	*Resignation.* *Regret.* *Distress.* *Preservation.* *Sacrifice.*
10.	A Picture of the Damned, by Bosch, now in the Louvre.	*Distress.* *Both hands on Head.*
11.	A Picture by the Master of *The Death of Mary*, showing the Descent from the Cross. Flemish work, now in the Louvre. The Sign of Heaven and Earth is made by a man holding a lily; Distress, by St. Mary Magdalene.	*Distress.* *Heaven and Earth.*
12.	Martyrdom of St. Catherine. A Picture by Luini, in the Monastery of St. Maurice, Milan.	*Distress.* *Prayer.*
13.	A Tapestry of the Seven Deadly Sins, Hampton Court. Justice attacks a man, an onlooker makes the Sign of Distress.†	*Distress.*
14.	An Italian Printed Book of Hours. Printed by Ferrari. A Miniature of the Crucifixion. St. John makes the Sign "It is Finished" and the Virgin interlocks her fingers and places her hands over her heart. Now in the Victoria and Albert Museum.	*It is Finished.* *Hands over Heart.*
15.	The Raising of Lazarus, C. 1517. A Picture by Piombo, Now in the National Gallery.†	*Horror.* *Distress.* *Prayer.* *Preservation.*
16.	A Printed Book of Hours of 1527. Photo. 23939 in the Victoria and Albert Museum. An Angel appearing to Shepherds makes the Sign of Preservation, the Shepherds, that of Distress.	*Distress.* *Preservation*
17.	Another panel of the Tapestry of the Seven Deadly Sins, at Hampton Court.	*Distress.* *Reverence.* *Horror.* *Sacrifice.* *Prayer.* *Heaven and Earth.*
18.	"Diana Surprised by Actæon," A Picture by Bonifazio di Pitati, now in Hampton Court Palace. As he is turned into a stag, Actæon makes the Sign.†	*Horror.*

Ref. No.	Title and Description.	Sign contained therein.
M. 19.	Sforza Book of Hours. A Miniature of St. Albert of Trapani. Now in the Biritish Museum. †	*Reverence.* *Prayer.* *Fidelity* *Resignation.*
20.	Sforza Book of Hours. A Miniature of Henry, the Bishop. Now in the British Museum.	*Prayer.* *Reverence.*
21.	"The Departure of Æneas." A Painting at Hampton Court.	*Regret.*
22.	"The Deposition from the Cross." A Picture by Del Sarto, at Florence.	*Grip.* *Resignation.*
23.	The Sforza Book of Hours. A Miniature of the Virgin and Angels adoring Christ.	*Prayer.* *Resingation.*
24.	The Sforza Book of Hours. A Miniature showing St. James baptising Josias. St. James has a halter round his neck. Two onlookers make Signs of Preservation.	*Prayer.* *Preservation.*
25	A Triptych by the Dutch painter, Bles, now in the Wolsey Rooms at Hampton Court. The Central panel contains a scene of the Crucifixion, with Mary Magdalene making the Sign. *	*Preservation.*
26.	The Tomb of Spinetta Malaspina, erected 1536, at Verona, now in the Victoria and Albert Museum, contains a statute of the Virgin and Child, underneath an equestrian figure. The Child makes the Sign.	*Preservation*
27.	A wax portrait from Nuremberg, Germany, 1596. Now in the British Museum. A Man makes the Sign.	*Fidelity.*
28.	A figure of St. Christopher, from the tomb of Henry *VII.*, Westminster. The Child makes the Sign of Preservation. C. 1505.	*Preservation*
29.	A Painting of Death and the Last Judgment, by Marten Heemskerk. No. 528 in the Public Dining Room, Hampton Court. *	*Distress.*
30.	The Back of a Chasuble, showing rebus and monogram of Robert Thornton, Abbot of Jerveaulx. Early 16th century. Figures make the Sign. Now in the Victoria and Albert Museum.	*Resignation.*
31.	The Back of a Chasuble, adorned with an embroidered cross. In the compartment below a scene of the Crucifixion is a figure of the Virgin, making the Sign of Sacrifice. Original in the Victoria and Albert Museum.	*Sacrifice.*
32.	The Sforza Book of Hours. A Miniature showing St. Francis receiving the Stigmata. Onlooker makes the Sign.	*Reverence.*
33.	Above book, another Miniature showing the **Raising of Lazarus.** An onlooker makes the Sign of **Horror.**	*Horror,*

M. 34. Above Book. Another Miniature showing the death of St. Peter Martyr, who, as he is stricken down, makes the Sign. † — *Heaven and Earth.*

35. Above Book. A Miniature showing St. Clare repelling the Saracens. One of the nuns makes the Sign of Resignation, another, the Sign of True Till Death, with her left hand. In the sculpture behind, the figures of the Virgin and Child are depicted and the latter makes the Sign of Preservation. † — *Resignation. True till Death. Preservation.*

36. Above Book. A Miniature showing the Assumption of Mary Magdalene, the Sign of Reverence is made by a helmsman who witnesses the event. An onlooker makes the Sign of Adoration. — *Reverence. Adoration.*

37. Above book. A Miniature showing the Martyrdom of St. Catherine. An onlooker makes the Sign of Reverence on seeing the miracle. [1] — *Reverence.*

38. A Book of Hours, c. 1520. B.P.G. 10 Ill. MS. given by Mr. G. Reid. No. 73. now in the Victoria and Albert Museum. The Angels appear to the Shepherds watching their sheep. — *Reverence. Distress.*

39. Stained Glass. Flemish panels C. 1510-30 in the same room as the Ill. MS. above (No. 38) representing Susannah led to Judgment. In panel 3 a man makes the Sign of Distress while Susannah replies with the Sign of Resig-tion. Original in the Victoria and Albert Museum. — *Distress. Resignation.*

40. Stained Glass. Flemish or German work. C. 1550. A Roundel of stained and painted glass depicting "Death on the Pale Horse." Among the crowd a woman makes the Sign of Distress: a boy puts his right hand on top of his head and squares his left arm, with his thumb squared also. Another boy strikes his right temple with his right hand; the Sign of Sympathy, or Sorrow. Photo. No. 53222 in Victoria and Albert Museum. — *Distress. Hand on Head & Preservation Combined. Sympathy or Sorrow.*

41. A Medallion of French Stained Glass, C. 1530, now in Victoria and Albert Museum. It shows St. John's Head being brought in during a banquet and a man makes the Sign of Preservation. — *Preservation.*

42. A Stained Glass window depicting the Crucifixion. German work, probably from the Abbey of Attenberg, near Cologne. Early 16th century. An Angel holding the chalice to catch the blood from Christ's right hand makes the Sign of Sympathy; a Second Angel makes the Sign of Fidelity. Photo. 48594 in Victoria and Albert Museum. — *Sympathy. Fidelity.*

---

[1] Nos. 32-37 are all in the British Museum.

A XIITH CENTURY BRONZE BOWL ENGRAVED WITH
SCENES FROM THE LEGEND OF ST. THOMAS.

I.7.

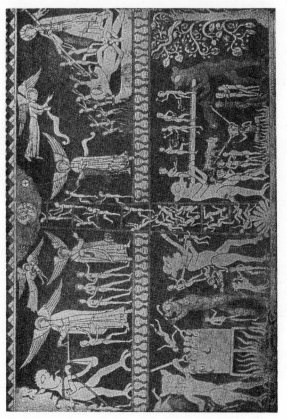

FRESCO OF THE BRIG O' DRED.

From Chaldon Church, Surrey.

I.17.

M. 43.   A Tapestry from Rheims Cathedral.
          Main Scene. "St. Joachim Before the High Priest."   *Adoration.*
          The High Priest makes the Sign of Adoration. St.   *Resignation.*
          Anne, Resignation; an onlooker, Fidelity; a man at the *Fidelity.*
          right hand corner as we face the picture, Preservation. *Preservation.*
          Subsidiary Scene in the left hand top corner. "The expul- *Preservation.*
          sion of Adam and Eve." Adam makes the Sign of   *Sacrifice.*
          Preservation, and Eve touches her left ear with her
          right hand, a variation of the Sign of Sacrifice.

44.   A Tapestry from Rheims Cathedral.
          Main Scene. "Mary in the Temple, Her Perfections."   *Preservation.*
          Mary seated between two pillars. Man in right hand   *Fidelity.*
          corner, Sign of Preservation. Man on left hand side,
          fidelity.

45.   A Tapestry from Rheims Cathedral.
          Main Scene. "The Annunciation." The Virgin makes   *Horror.*
          Sign of Horror, and an angel, Resignation. The Angel   *Resignation.*
          announcing the message makes the Sign of Sacrifice.   *Sacrifice.*
          A Group of soldiers are at the right side, one of whom *Fidelity.*
          makes the Sign of Heaven. A Man in the left hand
          corner makes the Sign of Fidelity.
          Subsidiary Scene in the left hand top corner. "Eve, the   *Preservation.*
          Apple, and the Serpent." Above, Our Lord makes
          the Sign of Preservation.

46.   A Fragment of a Tapestry from Rheims Cathedral.
          Main Scene. "St. Elizabeth Visiting the Virgin."   *Distress.*
          Subsidiary Scene in the left hand top corner. "Daniel
          in the Lions' Den." Daniel makes the Sign.

47.   A Tapestry from Rheims Cathedral.
          Main Scene. "The Nativity." The Child makes the   *Preservation.*
          Sign of Preservation as do also several onlookers. St. *Prayer.*
          Joseph makes the Sign of Prayer.
          Subsidiary Scene, in centre, immediately above main   *Preservation.*
          picture. An Angel appears to the Shepherd, who
          makes the Sign of Preservation.
          Subsidiary Scene in the Centre Top. An Angel makes   *Resignation.*
          the Sign of Resignation.
          Subsidiary Scene in the right hand top corner. Aaron   *Heaven and*
          makes the Sign of Heaven and Earth.   *Earth.*

48.   A Tapestry from Rheims Cathedral.
          Main Scene. "The Adoration of the Magi." An   *Preservation.*
          onlooker makes the Sign of Sacrifice, and another,
          Preservation. A man looking through a window at   *Heaven and*
          the back makes the Sign of Heaven and Earth, and one   *Earth.*
          in the front, right hand corner, the Sign of Heaven.

Higher up, on the same side, an attendant of the Magi makes the Sign of Preservation.

At the centre top, an Angel on the left hand makes the Sign of Resignation, and one on the right, Distress. The latter Angel represents the Angel of the Old Covenant and is in front of a ruined building.

Sacrifice.
Resignation.
Distress.

M. 49. A Tapestry from Rheims Cathedral.

Main Scene. "The Presentation in the Temple." Onlookers make Signs of Heaven and Earth, and Adoration. The Virgin also makes the Sign of Heaven and Earth. *Subsidiary Scenes.* Left hand, top corner. "The Presentation of the Firstborn." Right hand, top corner, "The Presentation of Samuel." A Priest makes the Sign of Heaven and Earth and two women onlookers, Sacrifice and Preservation.

Heaven and Earth.
Adoration.
Sacrifice.
Preservation.
Heaven and Earth.
Sacrifice.

50. A Tapestry from Rheims Cathedral.

Main Scene. "The Flight into Egypt." An Angel accompanying the Holy Child makes the Sign of Resignation, another that of Sacrifice. A baby whom the Holy Child has passed, makes the Sign of Preservation. *Subsidiary Scene on the left of the picture.* "The Slaughter of the Innocents." A boy makes the Sign of Horror. *Subsidiary Scene in right hand top corner.* "The Escape of David," who makes the Sign of Preservation.

Resignation.
Sacrifice.
Preservation.

Horror.

Preservation.

51. A Tapestry from Rheims Cathedral.

Main Scene. "The Holy Family and the Three Maries." The Christ Child makes the Sign of Preservation, as does also a woman in the foreground and a man standing at the right side. Two angels behind make the Signs of Resignation and Adoration respectively.

Preservation.
Resignation.
Adoration.

52. A Tapestry from Rheims Cathedral.

Main Scene. "The Death of the Virgin." The Virgin has her hands crossed downwards. Two onlookers make Signs of Resignation; Three, the Sign of Prayer; two, that of Heaven and Earth. *Subsidiary Scene in the Sky Above.* Two Angels make the Sign of Distress and one that of Prayer. *Subsidiary Scene in left hand, top corner.* "The Death of Sarah." Sarah lies with her hands crossed down; a woman makes the Sign of Resignation and two other onlookers that of Prayer. *Subsidiary Scene in the top, right hand, corner.* "The Death of Miriam, Sister of Moses." Miriam lies with her hands crossed down. One onlooker makes the Sign of Resignation and another that of Heaven and Earth.†

Hands crossed Down.
Resignation.
Prayer.
Heaven and Earth.
Prayer. Adoration, Preservation. Distress.
Resignation.
Hands crossed Prayer.
Hands Crossed Down.
Resignation.
Heaven and Earth.

M. 53.   A Tapestry from Rheims Cathedral.

Main Scene. "The Assumption." The Virgin makes the   *Prayer.*
Sign of Prayer as she goes up in the Vesica Piscis.   *Resignation.*
Attendant Angels makes Signs of Adoration, Prayer,   *Adoration.*
Resignation, Preservation.   Two men are shown in the   *Preservation.*
foreground; one makes the Sign of Preservation; one the   *Sacrifice.*
Sign of Sacrifice.

54.   A Triptych in coloured Limoges enamel.   Early 16th century.

In the Centre. "Our Lord in Majesty." On His right,   *Prayer.*
the Virgin is shown making the Sign of Prayer. On His   *Resignation.*
left St. John the Evangelist is making the Sign of   *Distress.*
Resignation. Beneath, the dead are rising from their   *Resignation.*
graves, some of whom are making Signs of Resignation,
Distress and Preservation.

Panel on the left of Christ shows the demons taking the   *Distress.*
Damned to Hell, and two of the latter make the Sign of   *Resignation.*
Distress, two, that of Resignation and two, that of   *Preservation.*
Preservation.

Original owned by J. Pierpont Morgan and on loan at
the Victoria and Albert Museum.   Photo 23609. †

55.   A Portion of a Votive Picture in Limoges Enamel, by Leonard   *Horror.*
Limosin, showing the Descent from the Cross. One of
the Apostles makes the Sign of Horror.

56.   A Plaque of Limoges Enamel. 1530. In the Centre is de-   *Distress.*
picted the "Ascension" and an apostle is making the   *It is Finished.*
Sign of Distress. In the left, lowest corner, is a scene
of the Crucifixion, and St. John makes the sign "It is
Finished." In the centre, at the bottom, is shown the
Descent from the Cross, in which a woman makes the
Sign of Distress. Original in the Victoria and Albert
Museum.

57.   A Plaque of Limoges Enamel. 1520. Depicting the Cruci-   *Destruction.*
fixion and showing Mary Magdalene making the Sign
of Destruction with her left hand. Original in the
Victoria and Albert Museum. Photo. thereof, No.
33847.

58.   A Plaque of Limoges Enamel. Early 16th century. Depict-   *Destruction.*
ing the Crucifixion, but differing from M. 57. Mary
Magdalene makes the Sign of Destruction, this time
with her right hand.

59.   A Portion of a Retable in Oak, painted with a scene of the   *Reverence.*
Crucifixion. French work. Original in the Peyre Col-
lection in the Victoria and Albert Museum. Early
16th century. St. John makes the Sign.

M.60. A Limoges Plaque "en grisaille" showing the Crucifixion. *Resignation.*
The Virgin makes the Sign of Resignation and St. *Heaven and*
Joseph of Arimathæa makes the Sign of Heaven and *Earth.*
Earth. Original in the Victoria and Albert Museum.

61. A Limoges Plaque of the middle of the 16th century, showing *Sacrifice.*
the Crucifixion. The Virgin makes the Sign of Sacrifice,
2nd position, and St. John that of Tearing out the *Tearing out*
Heart. Below is a picture of the Resurrection of Christ, *Heart.*
and a soldier makes the Sign of Reverence. Original *Reverence.*
in the Victoria and Albert Museum.

62. A Limoges Plaque showing the Crucifixion. Late 16th or *It is Finished.*
early 17th century. The Virgin makes the Sign "It is
Finished." Photo. No. 16975 in the Victoria and Albert
Museum.

63. "The Holy Family." A Picture by Fra Bartolommeo. C.1510. *Resignation.*
In the Mond Collection. Virgin makes Sign of Resigna-
tion.

17th CENTURY.

N. 1. A Carved, Panelled, Room. Now in the Engandine Museum, *Sacrifice.*
St. Moritz, having been removed there from an ancient *Resignation.*
Chateau in the district. Contains caryatides, all of *Heaven and*
whom are making signs. *Earth.*
Secrecy.
Fidelity.
Hand on Head.

2. A Canvas Panel embroidered with Silk and Wools, depicting *Preservation.*
Abraham and the Angels and the Sacrifice of Isaac. *Sacrifice.*
Now in the Victoria and Albert Museum. † *Resignation.*
Fidelity.

3. Another portion of the panelled Room described above. *Resignation.*
(See N.1)† *Heaven and*
Earth.

4. A Mosaic on the West Front of St. Mark's, Venice, showing *Horror.*
the Embarkation of the Body of St. Mark. †

5. A Mosaic on the West Front of St. Mark's, Venice, showing *Preservation.*
the Arrival of the Body of St. Mark at Venice. † *Distress.*
Resignation.
Prayer.

6. A Painting on the Ceiling of the Bedroom of William III., *Preservation.*
Hampton Court. *Right Finger to*
side of Nose.

7. A Woodcut of the 17th century. Dutch work, representing *Preservation.*
an old Morality Play of the Prodigal Son. As the

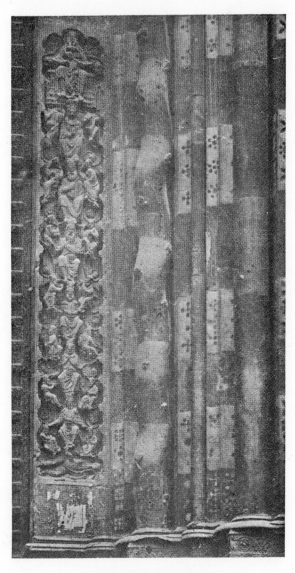

THE TREE OF JESSE.
*From the South Side of the West Door of the
Cathedral of St. Laurence, Genoa.*

I.25.

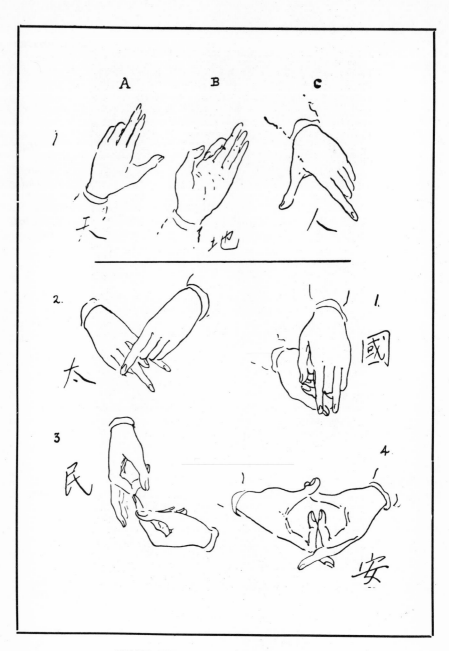

DEAF AND DUMB ALPHABET SIGNS.

Father embraces and raises his Son, an onlooker makes the Sign. See also the fool. Reproduced in Bradley, *The Graphic and Historical Illustrator.* 1834.†

N. 8. A Painting by Geurcino. Original in possession of the Supreme Grand R. A. Chapter of Scot., Edinburgh. Entitled, "The Raising of the Master."† — *Distress.*

9. Painting by Geurcino, entitled, "Driving out the Money Changers." Original in Palazzo Rosso, Genoa.† — *Hand on Head. Distress (Two forms. The second being hand across forehead).*

10. Plate from Azoth Pilosophorum, entitled, "Rebis."† — *Left Foot First.*

11. Three Circular Medallions of Painted Glass, German or Swiss work.
   (a) "Moses and the Brazen Serpent." A woman on seeing the dead makes the Sign of Distress. — *Distress.*
   (b) "The Israelites Picking up Manna." God the Father in the sky makes the Sign of Preservation. — *Preservation.*
   (c) "Jacob's Ladder." God seated at the top makes the Sign of Preservation. Photo. 57796, Victoria and Albert Museum.† — *Preservation.*

12. Panel of Swiss Stained Glass showing the Call of St. Peter and St. Andrew by Christ. One of the attendant disciples makes the Sign. Photo. 48,325 in Victoria and Albert Museum. — *Preservation.*

13. A Picture by Gherardo delle Notti of the Adoration of the Shepherds, at Florence. C. 1610, contains two signs of Reverence, one made with the right hand and the other with the left, also Sign of Surprise, which is shown by raising one hand higher than the other. — *Reverence* / *Surprise.*

18th CENTURY.

O. 1. A Four Poster Bed with a Wooden Canopy. Early 18th century work. Now in the Museum at Zurich, Switzerland. On the canopy is painted Jacob's Ladder. Some of the Angels, and Our Lord at the top, make the Sign.* — *Preservation.*

2. A Drawing by H. Fuseli, R. A. Drawn at Rome in 1777 and depicting Dante listening to the story of Ugolino. Now in the British Museum. — *Distress.*

3. The Private Chapel of the Bishop of Coire, in his Palace in that City. Two Cherubs in opposite corners of the room just beneath the ceiling make the Sign of Preservation and that of Heaven and Earth respectively.* — *Preservation. Heaven and Earth.*

O. 4.   Pen and Ink Drawings made in 1793 by John Flaxman, R.A., for Dante's Paradise. Now in the British Museum.

     First Illustration.   Dante and Beatrice in Paradise see a Vision of the Crowned Virgin, surrounded by Angels. The Virgin makes the Sign of Resignation and several angels, the Sign of True till Death.   *Resignation.*   *True till Death.*

     Lower Picture.   The Virgin is shown surrounded by Saints and more distant souls. The Saints make the Signs of Resignation, Prayer and Preservation. The more distant souls make those of Resignation, Distress (3rd pos.), and True till Death (with the left hand).   *Resignation.*   *True till Death.*   *Preservation.*

19*th* CENTURY.

P. 1.   The Tomb of Cardinal Lavigerie in the Cathedral, Carthage. On either side stand two slaves. The man has broken his chains, holds the Crucifix to his heart with his right hand and completes the Sign with his left. On the other side stands a woman with a child on her shoulder and the latter makes the Sign. Note, the Cardinal secured the freeing of all slaves in Tunis.†   *Preservation.*

2.   A Mosaic on the West Front of St. Mark's, Venice, showing Our Lord in Glory. Made 1836.†   *Resignation.*   *Royal.*   *Touching the Head.*

3.   A Mosaic of St. Peter Raising the Beggar at the Gate, over a side altar in St. Peter's, Rome. St. Peter presses the first knuckle joint of the beggar's right hand while raising him. St. John makes the Sign of Fidelity and a woman the Sign of Distress (3rd position). 19th century work, but possibly copied from an older picture.*   *Grip.*   *Fidelity.*   *Distress.*

20*th* CENTURY.

R. 1.   The Illumination of a Pastoral letter of Cardinal Mercier by the Nuns of Maredret, Belgium. Done about 1915 and presented to the British Museum by the Abbess in 1921. It depicts Daniel in the Lions' Den, representing Belgium, being fed by Habakuk. Below is shown a battle between the Germans and the English and French.†   *Preservation.*   *Distress.*

2.   An American Dollar Note showing the Pilgrim Fathers Sighting Land.   *Distress.*   *Fidelity.*   *Tearing out Heart.*

3.   Buckfast Abbey. Altar of the Holy Souls. The Reredos shows the Dead rising from the Sea making various signs.†   *Preservation.*   *Distress.*   *Sacrifice.*

Ref. No.	Title and Description.	Sign contained therein.

R. 4. Buckfast Abbey. Chapel of St. Joseph. Reredos depicting the Marriage of the Virgin. The Priest performing the ceremony makes the Sign. — *Preservation.*

5. Buckfast Abbey. Chapel of St. Benedict. Reredos showing the Crucifixion. St. John makes the Sign of Preservation and the Virgin, Regret.† — *Preservation.* *Regret.*

6. At the beginning of the Cannon of the Mass a Roman Catholic Priest makes the sign. * — *Exultation.*

AFRICA.

S. 1. Carved Yoruba Gates from Oyo, Nigeria.† — *Distress. Preservation. Resignation*

2. A Design Drawn in Sand for use during the Yao Initiation Rites, Nyasaland, entitled "The Great Mother."† — *Distress*

3. Ditto Round a Grave, cut to form a Man making the Sign.† — *Distress*

4. During the Setting up of the Pole at the beginning of the Rites, the men erecting it make the Sign. * — *Preservation*

5. Initiation Rites in British East Africa. A boy of the Chuke Tribe of Kenya makes the Sign for the men to start cutting. See Article No. 39, Plate F. "Man," 1915.† — *Distress*

6. Gilt Bronze Cross from Abyssinia, now in the British Museum.† — *True till Death Distress. Preservation. Resignation. Prayer.*

7. Initiation Rites in British East Africa. A Boy makes the Sign of Sacrifice after the operation has been completed. See Article No. 39, Plate F. "Man," 1915. — *Sacrifice.*

8. A Native Dance in Nyasaland, Two examples.† — *Touching Head.*

9. A Zulu Chief, saluting. — *Reverence.*

10. A Benin Bronze of the 16th Century, representing one of the Amazon Guards of the King of Dahomy. Original in the private collection of the author. — *Preservation.*

11. A Konde Dance. North Coast of Lake Nyasa. — *Resignation. Sacrifice.*

12. Congo, Central Africa. On a Roadside Fetish Shrine painted with Six Figures, on the Zombo Plateau. Illustration on p. 638, Vol. II. of "George Grenfell and the Congo," by Sir H. Johnston, published Hutchinson, 1908. Three figures make the Sign of Distress; one the Sign of Water. — *Distress. Water.*

S. 13.	The Sudanese Negroes along the Nile use this Sign to confirm an Oath.*	*True till death.*
14.	The Manner of Swearing an Oath in Nyasaland is by making this Sign and placing the other hand on the grave of one's Father.*	*True till Death.*
15.	A Processional Gilt Cross from Abyssinia, now in the British Museum. *Scene I.* "The Crucifixion." The Virgin makes the Sign of Regret. *Scene II.* "Daniel in the Lions' Den." Daniel makes the Sign of Distress.*	*Regret.* *Distress.*
16.	A Woven Altar Cloth from Abyssinia contains figures making the Sign of Distress. Now in British Museum.*	*Distress.*
17.	A Fresco from a Church at Adoua, Abyssinia, now in British Museum, depicts incidents of the Passion. During the Triumphal entry the onlookers make the Sign.*	*Preservation.*
18.	A Coptic Bronze Reliquary Cross, No. 559, in British Museum, has on it a human figure making the Sign.	*Distress.*
19.	A Cedar Panel from a Coptic Church in Cairo. 13th century work, the original being in the British Museum, represents the Ascension. One apostle makes the Sign of Sacrifice and another that of True till Death.	*Sacrifice.* *True till Death.*
20.	A Large, Carved, Wooden Bead, part of a regalia worn by a Sudanese Chief, carved with two human figures making Signs. Original in the private collection of the Author.	*Distress.*
21.	A Kabyle Hanging, at the Grand Hotel, Setif, Algeria, contains figures making Signs of Distress and Preservation.*	*Distress.* *Preservation.*
22.	A Processional Brass Cross from Abyssinia. 17th or 18th century work, with the Passion and the Triumph of St. George engraved therein. Original in British Museum.*	*Distress.* *Resignation.* *Preservation.*
23.	A Photograph of the wall of a native house in a Bakuma Village, Congo, shows it adorned with charcoal drawings of a magical significance. One scene is of a man struggling with a gorilla, while another man looking on makes the Sign of Water. See p. 335 "Wide World Magazine." Jan. 1928.	*Water.*

AMERICA.

T. 1.	A Totem Pole of the Red Indians. Originally in Haida, Queen Charlotte Isle: now in the British Museum. Illus. *Handbook of Ethnology,* p. 269.	*Sign of Destruction with both Hands.*
2.	A Basket with Interwoven Patterns, made by the Umqua Indians. California. Illus. id. p. 287.	*Distress.*
3.	A Pre-Spanish Conquest Carving from Jamaica.†	*Distress.*

THE BRASS OF B. ROUCLIFFE AND WIFE.

At Cowthorpe, Yorks, 1494.

L. 62.

PICTOGRAPHIC WRITING FROM EASTER ISLAND.

T.13.

T. 4.	A Stone Vesica Piscis, or Yoke, with a skeleton severed in twain sculptured thereon. †	*Distress.*
5.	Quetzalcoatl, with Corn in His Hair, is Wounded in the Foot and makes the Sign. From Mexico Codices reproduced in "The Bulletin of the Smithsonian Institute."†	*Preservation.*
6.	Quetzalcoatl without Corn in hair makes the Sign. Ref. as above.	*Preservation*
7.	Quetzalcoatl as Regent of the Planet Venus makes the Sign. Ref. as above. †	*Distress.*
8.	A Pre-Spanish Conquest Stone Charm, from Jamaica. †	*Distress.*
9.	A Sculpture over a Doorway in the Temple at Uxmal, Mexico. Depicts a Skeleton sculptured as far as the waist making the Sign of Distress while near by are two crossed bones. *	*Distress.*
10.	A Vase from Chama, Mexico, with an Initiation Scene shown thereon, wherein the candidate is being taught to make a Sign.	*True till Death.*
11.	Quetzalcoatl Dancing Before some Higher God, who makes the Sign of Preservation with his right hand on his heart and his left elbow squared, but with hand thereof pointing down. Quetzalcoatl tears out his heart. †	*Preservation.* *Tearing out Heart.*
12.	A Corner of the Relief Covering the Interior Wall of the Chamber of Commerce at Chichen, Itza, Yucatan. A Man Kneeling makes the Sign of Preservation. Ancient Mexican. Illustrated in "Man."*	*Preservation.*
13.	Pictographic Writing on Wood from Easter Island. "Journal of the Anthropological Society," and in British Museum. †	*Distress.* *Preservation.*
14.	A Funerary Vase from an Inca Grave, Peru. Now in the Museum of the Quatuor Coronati. Great Queen Street. *	*Distress.*
15.	Quetzalcoatl is Challenged by the God of Death, who points upwards. Quetzalcoatl replies by pointing his right hand up and his left down. Both figures stand on a boat. †	*Heaven and Earth.*
16.	Teaching a Candidate a Sign. The Candidate places his finger on his lips while the Hierophant makes the Sign of Heaven and Earth. *Mexican Codices*, as above. †	*Secrecy.*
17.	Another picture, as above. A Candidate being taught a Grip and pointing down at same time. †	*Grip.* *Earth.*
18.	Quetzalcoatl descending to Earth by a Ladder.	*Sacrifice combined with Earth.*

REF. No.	TITLE AND DESCRIPTION.	SIGN CONTAINED THEREIN.

T. 19. The Navaho Indians. An Illustration of two Medicine Men making a Ceremonial Sand Picture entitled, "The Grinding Snakes." Made on the last day of the Nine Days' Ceremonial and used only on important occasions. Eight Figures are drawn in the Original, but only five can be seen in the illustration, all of whom make the Sign of Distress and wear triangular aprons. Illustrated in *American Indians*, by J. F. Huckle. Pub. by F. Harvey. Kansas City, U.S.A.* — *Distress.*

20. A Hopi Kiva, or Underground Room, used by the Hopi Indian Secret Societies for their Rites. The Altar of the Powamee Society is flanked by painted boards whereon are Gods making the Sign of Distress, i.e., one on each side, while on the left side as we face the altar, beyond the board, is another crude figure of a god who makes the same sign. Illus. as T. 18.* — *Distress.*

21. One way to greet a Friend among the North American Indians is by drawing the Hand across the Throat.* — *True till Death.*

ASIA.

U. 1. A Turkish Miniature of the 17th century, showing the Dancing Dervishes, at Constantinople.† — *Distress (3 positions). Preservation. Destruction. (With both hands).*

2. A Relief in Black Stone, "The Teacher Group." From Konarak, Orissan School. 15th Century. Now in Victoria and Albert Museum. — *Preservation. Sacrifice.*

3. A Persian Miniature depicting Joseph being drawn up from the Pit. Now in the British Museum. — *Secrecy. Regret and Secrecy combined. Preservation.*

4. A Persian Miniature, now in British Museum, showing a Dispute between Two Learned Men. The first disputant pretends to strike off his hand: the Second places his hand on his shoulder. An Onlooker makes the Sign of Fidelity. — *Fidelity. Sacrifice.*

5. A Persian Miniature now in British Museum. "Alexander Defeats Raja Fur of Kanauj." — *Preservation. Distress.*

6. A Persian MS. C. 1486, with scene from the Epic of Shah Namah of Firdausi. A man in a pit, about to be drawn up, on seeing rope lowered makes the Sign of Preservation. British Museum. Add. 18188.* — *Preservation.*

232

U. 7.	An Illum. MS. of the Northern School. A.D. 1567. Painted at Bokhara. "The Gulisan of Sadi." Two men are shown making the Sign of Preservation and a woman placing her thumb under her chin. Original in the British Museum.*	*Preservation.* *Secrecy.*
8.	An Indian MS. Miniature of the Mogul School, depicting a Battle Scene, illustrating the Emperor Barbar's Memoirs. C. 1600. The Emperor on horseback makes the Sign. British Museum.*	*Preservation.*
9.	An Alabaster Statue of Shiva making the Sign of the Horns over his Solar Plexus and holding in that hand the lariat of death. Original in the author's private collection.†	*Destruction and Horns combined.*
10.	A Bas-relief at Borabudur, Java. Illus. in *Indian Sculpture and Painting*, by E. V. Havell. It shows a Prince on his Throne, making the Sign with his right hand.	*Destruction.*
11.	A Buddhist Sculpture in India, illustrating the Worship of the Sacred Tree.	*Preservation.* *Resignation.*
12.	A Chinese Bronze Statue of Kwan Yin.†	*Horns.* *Vesica Piscis.*
13.	An Alabaster Statue of Hanuman bearing the Fruit of the Tree of Life. In the Author's Private Collection.†	*Preservation.*
14.	A Persian Miniature, C. 1539, showing the Assumption of Mahomet. Original in the British Museum.	*Preservation.*
15.	A Persian Miniature of the 17th century, showing the Descent from the Cross. Original in the Sarre Collection, Berlin.†	*Distress.* *Resignation.* *Reverence (with hands flat over eyes).*
16.	A 17th century Persian Miniature, now in the British Museum depicting "The Death of the Savant."	*Resignation.* *Preservation.* *Finger on side of Nose.*
17.	An Indian Miniature, late 16th century, by Mihr Tchand, now in the State Museum, Berlin, entitled, "The Visit of the Prince."†	*Preservation.* *It is Finished.* *Distress.*
18.	An Indian Miniature of the end of the 16th century, depicting a Fantastic Camel. The camel is composed of drawings of men and animals, symbolising this world. One man in its body makes the Sign of Preservation. Now in the State Museum, Berlin.	*Preservation.*

REF. No.	TITLE AND DESCRIPTION.	SIGN CONTAINED THEREIN.
U. 19.	An Indian Miniature of the 16th century, now in the Museum at Leipzig, depicting the Deposition of Dubun-i-Nayan.	*Distress.* *Touching Head (with both hands and with one only).*
20.	An Indian Miniature of the 17th century, depicting the Virgin Adoring the Christ Child. In the Sarre Collection, Berlin.	*Resignation.*
21.	An Indian Miniature depicting Krishna Driving Cattle. 18th century work now in Coomarasvamy College, Boston.	*Hand touching top of Head.*
22.	A Miniature from a Persian Ill. M.S. now in the British Museum. Painted by Shahm. It depicts a Wrestling Match in ancient Persia.	*Preservation.* *Fidelity.* *Tearing out Heart.* *Secrecy.*
23.	A Persian Miniature from Hafiz-Diwan. 16th century work. A man on horseback makes the Sign.	*Obligation.*
24.	A Miniature from Firdusi's Shah-Nameh. 1622. Persian. Two men behind the Shah make the Sign.	*Preservation.*
25.	A Persian Miniature of "The King and Council." Three courtiers make the Sign.	*Hands Crossed Downwards.*
26.	A Portrait of Bahadur, Emperor of Delhi, surrounded by his sons. Three courtiers make the Sign.	*Hands Crossed Downwards.*
27.	A Persian Lacquered Bookcover of the 18th century, with scene entitled, "A Battle in Progress."	*Touching top of head.* *Tearing heart with both hands.*
28.	A Chinese Bronze Statue of the Child Buddha wearing an apron. †	*Heaven & Earth.*
29.	A Similar Figure standing on a Lotus but wearing no apron.	*Heaven & Earth.*
30.	Signs of the Hung Society. The Nine Finger Sign. †	*9 Finger Sign.*
31.	Two Signs of the Hung Society for use when a Fight is in Progress. †	*Combined Pres. and Vesica Piscis.*
32.	The Signs of the Five Elements of the Hung Society. †	*Exultation.* *Hands Crossed down-wards.* *Destruction (with both hands).* *Distress.* *Water.*

234

THE LAST JUDGMENT.
From a Book of Hours now in the Brit. Mus.

L.33.

A 15TH CENTURY STAINED GLASS PANEL,
Showing the Emblem of St. Matthew,
At the Parish Church, Headbourne Worthy,
near Winchester.

U. 33. Two Signs of the Hung Society (a) Sign for use if attacked,   *Reverence.*
       (b) Sign of Vesica Piscis. †   *Vesica Piscis*

34. The Threefold Sign of Heaven, Earth and Man, used in the   *Horns.*
       Hung Society. †   *Vesica Piscis.*

35. Deaf and Dumb Alphabet Signs of the Hung Society. †   *Deaf & Dumb*
                                                                      Alphabet.

36. A Bronze Statue of Vishnu standing within the Vesica Piscis.   *Heaven and*
       An attendant makes the Sign.   *Earth.*

37. A Malay Brass Drum purchased in Borneo.   Four figures   *Distress.*
       making the Sign.   Illus. in "Man." February, 1918. †

38. An Old Chinese Painting depicting the Five Buddhas.   *Vesica Piscis.*
       Original in author's possession. †   *Hands Crossed*
                                                                      Downwards.
                                                                      Heaven & Earth.
                                                                      Prayer.
                                                                      Obligation.

39. A Sculpture on a pillar in a Hindu Temple depicting the   *Destruction.*
       Lion Incarnation of Vishnu.   The God who is shown   *Heaven &*
       emerging from the Vesica Piscis makes the Sign of   *Earth.*
       Destruction with both hands, and an attendant that of
       Heaven and Earth. †

40. A Bas-relief showing Vishnu asleep under a Cobra.   Both   *Preservation.*
       Gods and human beings make the various signs. †   *Heaven &*
                                                                      Earth.
                                                                      Resignation.
                                                                      Sacrifice.

41. The Veddas Birth Ceremony, Ceylon.   "The Invocation of   *Reverence.*
       the Ancestors."

42. A Persian Miniature of the 16th century in the Sarre Collec-   *Preservation.*
       tion, Berlin, representing Travellers on a journey,
       several of whom are making the sign.

43. An Indian Miniature of the 18th century representing   *Sacrifice*
       "Krishna Playing the Flute."   A woman makes the   *(First*
       Sign of Sacrifice and another that of Secrecy.   In the   *position.)*
       State Museum. Berlin.   *Secrecy.*

44. An Indian Miniature of the 16th century.   "Travellers   *Secrecy.*
       Embarking on a Ship."   Original in Museum of   *Distress*
       Industrial Art, Vienna.   Travellers in the boat make   *(3rd position.)*
       Signs of Secrecy and Distress, the people on the shore,   *Preservation.*
       Secrecy and Preservation.

45. A Persian Miniature of the 14th century, "The Mirror of the   *Preservation.*
       World."   In the Sultan's Library at Constantinople.
       Two men make the Sign.

		SIGN CONTAINED
REF. No.	TITLE AND DESCRIPTION.	THEREIN.

U. 46. A Miniature from Mesopotamia. 1222 A.D. In Sarre *Heaven &*
Collection, Berlin.† *Earth.*
Secrecy.

47. A 15th century Persian Miniature in the Museum of Decora- *Resignation*
tive Arts, Paris, entitled, "Humay and Humayun." A
scene in a garden.

48.. A Persian Miniature of the 15th century, in the Museum of *Secrecy*
Fine Arts, Boston. "Khosran and Chirin."

49. An Indian Portrait of Shir Muhammad Kabbal. 17th *Vesica Piscis*
century work, now in British Museum.

50. "La Visite du Malade." A Miniature from Mesopotamia. *Preservation.*
1333 A.D. Now in State Library, Vienna.

51. "The Acrobats." An Indian Miniature of the 16th century, *It is Finished.*
in the Stchoukin Collection, Moscow. A wrestler has
thrown his opponent and the umpire makes the sign.

52. An Indian Miniature of 1600 A.D. in the State Museum, *Hands Crossed*
Berlin, entitled, "A Visit to a Hermit." An attendant *Downwards.*
makes the Sign.

53. Rev. W. A. Wigram, D.D., informs me that in Turkey the *Reverence*
Howling Dervishes, on changing their invocation from
Allah to Yahuah (Jehovah), make the Sign of Reverence*

54. A Japanese Statue of Buddha in the Author's possession *Vesica Piscis*
shows him making the Sign of the Vesica Piscis.

55. Statues of Burmese Buddhas which adorn their Temples *Vesica Piscis*
make the Sign of the Vesica Piscis.*

56. A Bronze Statue of Krishna shows him stepping on Kaliya, *Left Foot First.*
the Serpent of Evil, with his Left Foot.

57. An Indian Miniature of the 18th century in the Coomaras- *Sympathy.*
vamy Collection, Boston. "The Legend of Kaliya," *Left Foot First.*
Krishna is Slaying the serpent. An onlooker makes
the Sign of Sympathy and Krishna places his left
foot on the monster.

58. A Persian Book Cover in Lacquered Papier Mache, 17th *Regret.*
century work, now in the Victoria and Albert Museum.
Depicts a dead man; some of the onlookers make the
Sign of Regret.

59. Another Persian Book cover, as above. A man standing *Heaven & Earth*
over a dead man makes the Sign of Heaven and Earth, *& Secrecy com-*
and Secrecy. In the Victoria and Albert Museum. *bined.*
Secrecy.

60. A Cloisonné Enamel Figure of Maitrêya, the Coming Buddha. *Heaven & Earth*
17th century Chinese work. *combined with*
Vesica Piscis.

236

Ref. No.	Title and Description.	Sign containde therein.

U.61. The Signs of Sacrifice and Resignation are made by members of the Hung Society. This information was given to me by an actual member of the Society in 1928, that is, subsequent to my book on the Hung Society. — *Sacrifice. Resignation.*

62. An Indian MS., Mogul Work, late 16th century, signed Hasan' Ali, depicts the Last Hours of Bhishma. Two onlookers are making the Sign of Preservation and one that of Fidelity.† — *Preservation. Fidelity.*

AUSTRALASIA.

W. 1. A Bark Book with Charms from Batak, Sumatra. The Devil makes the Sign. Illustrated p. 104 "Handbook of Ethnology," British Museum. — *Distress.*

2. Shell Carvings from Rubiana in the Solomon Islands. Ref. as above, p. 128. — *Water.*

3. A Door Lintel, Maori Work. New Zealand. Now in the British Museum. Illus. p. 182. Three figures make the Sign of Distress. — *Distress.*

4. A Dancing Belt of a Fully Initiated Man from New Guinea.† — *Distress*

5. A Tipperu, or Bull-roarer, used in the Initiation Rites in New Guinea.† — *Distress.*

6. House Boards of the Kenya-Kayan Tribes, Borneo. Carved and Painted. One man makes the Sign of Distress and another that of Preservation. Illus. op. p. 94 "Handbook of Ethnology," British Museum. — *Distress. Preservation*

7. Two Paintings of Gods on Bark. From New Guinea. — *Distress.*

8. A Photograph of the Bushmen of Sunday Island shows them making the Sign near a pile of their weapons. "National Geographical Magazine of U.S.A." Vol. 51, No. 1, p. 90. — *Preservation*

9. The Sitting Dance of the Taupou or Official Hostess, Samoa. See, "Customs of the World" Vol. I., op. p. 122. — *Preservation.*

10. A Rock Painting from the Central District, Papua. Illustrated Fig. 4, Plate N. Article 119, Dec., 1923, *Man*.† — *Distress.*

11. The Engura Ceremony and the Burning Bush. Illustrated in *Northern Tribes of Australia* by Spencer and Gillan. — *Reverence.*

12. Photograph of a Bushman who has been *Boned*, or stricken by magic means, namely, by pointing a bone at him. See Photo in Basedow, *The Australian Aboriginal*, op. p. 192. — *Distress*

13. The Sign Language of the Arunndta Tribe, Australia. Id. p. 391. — *Deaf & Dumb Alphabet.*

14. At the Ceremony of Sub-incision the men make the Sign of Distress, See, Basedow, id. p. 246 and compare with the attitude adopted by the Kenya Boy. — *Distress.*

INDEX.

INDEX.

INDEX.

INDEX.

INDEX.

INDEX.

INDEX.

INDEX.